British Women Writers and the Reception of Ancient Egypt, 1840–1910

Also by Molly Youngkin

Feminist Realism at the *Fin de Siècle*: The Influence of the
Late-Victorian Woman's Press on the Development of the Novel
Annotated edition of Sarah Grand's *Ideala* (1888)

British Women Writers and the Reception of Ancient Egypt, 1840–1910

Imperialist Representations of Egyptian Women

Molly Youngkin

palgrave
macmillan

First published 2016 by
PALGRAVE MACMILLAN

The author has asserted her right to be identified as the author of this work in accordance with the Copyright, Designs and Patents Act 1988.

Palgrave Macmillan in the UK is an imprint of Macmillan Publishers Limited, registered in England, company number 785998, of Houndmills, Basingstoke, Hampshire, RG21 6XS.

Palgrave Macmillan in the US is a division of Nature America, Inc., One New York Plaza, Suite 4500, New York, NY 10004-1562.

Palgrave Macmillan is the global academic imprint of the above companies and has companies and representatives throughout the world.

Hardback ISBN: 978-1-137-57076-5
E-PUB ISBN: 978-1-137-56609-6
E-PDF ISBN: 978-1-137-56614-0
DOI: 10.1057/9781137566140

Distribution in the UK, Europe and the rest of the world is by Palgrave Macmillan®, a division of Macmillan Publishers Limited, registered in England, company number 785998, of Houndmills, Basingstoke, Hampshire RG21 6XS.

Library of Congress Cataloging-in-Publication Data

Names: Youngkin, Molly, 1970–
Title: British women writers and the reception of ancient Egypt, 1840–1910: imperialist representations of Egyptian women / Molly Youngkin.
Description: New York : Palgrave Macmillan, 2016. | Includes bibliographical references and index.
Identifiers: LCCN 2015023508 | ISBN 9781137570765 (hardback)
Subjects: LCSH: English literature—19th century—History and criticism. | English literature—Women authors—History and criticism. | English literature—Egyptian influences. | Women in literature. | Egyptians in literature. | BISAC: LITERARY CRITICISM / European / English, Irish, Scottish, Welsh. | LITERARY CRITICISM / Women Authors.
Classification: LCC PR115 .Y68 2016 | DDC 820.9/35832—dc23 LC record available at http://lccn.loc.gov/2015023508

A catalogue record of the book is available from the British Library.

For my father, Bill Youngkin (1937–2014), and mentor and friend, Marlene Longenecker (1945–2014).

Contents

List of Illustrations

Acknowledgments

Institutional support was key to the completion of this book. Loyola Marymount University Los Angeles provided funds for a sabbatical in spring 2010 and a college fellowship in spring 2011, which enabled me to do preliminary research for this book. It also provided funds for a summer research expense grant in summer 2011, which helped to fund a research trip to the United Kingdom to work on Chapters 3 and 5; funds for three of the images included inside this book; and funds for my Rains research assistants, Megan Brown, Leila Grace Pandy, and Michael Robinson, to work on specific research questions related to this book. My thanks to Michael Engh, Paul Tiyambe Zeleza, Mike O'Sullivan, and Robbin Crabtree for their support as Deans of the Bellarmine College of the Liberal Arts; and to David Killoran, Paul Harris, and Barbara Rico as Chairs of the Department of English during the period in which I was working on this book.

I respectfully acknowledge other institutions that and individuals who supported my work in various forms. Thank you to the librarians who assisted my research at the British Library, Dr Williams's Library, Loyola Marymount University Library, University of California Los Angeles Library, and University of Reading Special Collections.

Thanks also to organizers of the British Women Writers Conference 2011 and 2012, for providing a venue for me to present early arguments about Chapters 2 and 3, and to Clare Simmons, editor of *Prose Studies*, who facilitated the publication of portions of Chapter 2. This chapter is derived in part from an article published in *Prose Studies* 33.2 (2011), available online: http://www.tandfonline.com/.

Portions of Michael Field's unpublished journals, discussed in Chapter 4, are quoted with kind permission from Leonie Sturge-Moore and Charmian O'Neil. © The British Library, London, Add. Mss. 46777–46784, 46799, 45853.

Thank you to editors Brigitte Shull, Ryan Jenkins, Leighton Lustig, and Jennifer Crane, for facilitating the process of publication; and to the anonymous reviewer for Palgrave, who understood what I wanted to achieve with this book and provided thoughtful comments about how to achieve this goal.

Thanks to Megan Brown, Paul Harris, Neil Hultgren, Bruce Mackay, Robin Miskolcze, Leila Grace Pandy, Barbara Rico, Michael Robinson, Dermot Ryan, Casey Shoop, Lucy Wilson, Amy Woodson-Boulton, and Bill Youngkin, who read and responded to portions of the manuscript with helpful suggestions for improvement. Thanks also to Sharon Bickle, Felicia Bonaparte, Elspeth Chowdharay-Best, Eduardo Lerro, Kirstin Noreen, Talia Schaffer, and Marion Thain, for their responses to research questions I posed while working on this book.

Finally, a special thank you to Rodney Gordy and Betty Youngkin, for their personal support during both easy and difficult times; your love and care are much appreciated.

Introduction

On November 17, 1849, Florence Nightingale traveled to Egypt with Charles and Selina Bracebridge, family friends eager to give Nightingale a respite from familial pressure exerted on her to marry and become the ideal Victorian woman, the "Angel in the House." As Nightingale approached Alexandria by sea, she wrote back to her family,

> My dearest people, I meant to have finished my last letter ages ago, but seagoing is not favourable to literary pursuits. We did not come in sight of Sicily on Monday, as we expected, but passed Marettimo in the night . . . and in the morning we coasted the whole southwest of Sicily from Marsala and Mazzara. We could see the temple of Girgenti quite plain on their heighth . . . Venus and Isis [with] Agrigentum below. (Vallée, *Florence Nightingale on Mysticism* 137–38)

After noting the presence of both Venus and Isis at the temples on the southern coast of Sicily, Nightingale continued, detailing the highlights of her voyage to Malta, during which she conversed with another traveler, Lord Nugent, about the similarities between Greek and Egyptian architecture: "He says that the two architectures of Greece and Egypt originate from the tent and pine forest. All the lines of the Egyptian temple tend inwards towards the top showing the nation that has lived in tents. Take the Greek temple and you see first fluted columns; those were the faggots [tree branches] bound together, bowing out a little at the top for better support to the roof" (141). Nightingale's arrival at Malta was a significant experience, since she felt she was "stepping from the West to the East at a stride" (138). She contrasted the landscape and atmosphere of Valetta, the capital of Malta, to that of Sicily, writing that Valetta was her "first initiation into Arab life": "Valetta, busily piled up on her barren mound, is as great a contrast to the cities of Sicily, lazily stretched out along the shore. . . . The one island with its beautiful soft blue heights . . . the other bare and flat and yellow as a gravel walk, . . . yet busy, gay and clean, . . . as clean as a Mussulman [Muslim]" (138).

In contrasting Malta to Sicily, Nightingale's letter clearly expresses the British imperialist attitude that as one traveled east, there was a clear boundary separating East from West, with cultures beyond Malta (such as Egypt) clearly in the Eastern realm. Yet, her letter also indicates she recognized the intermingling of cultures as one coasted through the Mediterranean, signified by the temple at Girgenti, which brought together Greek and Egyptian culture with statues of *both* Venus and Isis. Once in Egypt, Nightingale again noted the separation between West and East, describing the landscape as different from anything she had experienced in the West—"beautiful" but "unnatural . . . as if a child had painted it and did not know how, and had made it unlike nature" (181–82). Still, she also recognized the intermingling of cultures, as she viewed images of ancient Egyptian women in the temples and compared these women to contemporary Christian women: Nefertari, wife of Ramesses II, for example, "occupies the place which the most advanced Christian civilization gives to woman" (269). Even as Nightingale reacted to Egypt through an imperialist perspective, seeing the parallels between women's roles in ancient Egyptian religion and contemporary Christianity helped Nightingale understand her own spiritual development more fully, and this experience later served as an important catalyst for her "emancipation" from her family, marriage, and other repressive aspects of Victorian culture when she chose to embrace the profession of nursing instead of marrying.

This book examines encounters such as Nightingale's as part of a larger argument about how white, British women writers encountered and responded to representations of ancient Egyptian women from 1840 to 1910, the period in which British imperialist interest in Egypt developed most significantly and during which British women writers of a particular class had access to Egyptian culture, either directly through travel to the East or indirectly by reading about ancient cultures in books, newspaper articles, and other media produced as a result of increased travel to Egypt.[1] British women writers' encounters with representations of ancient Egyptian women serve as examples of the ways in which British imperialism influenced women's visions for their own emancipation—broadly defined as the ability to think, speak, and act for oneself.[2] Expanding Deidre David's assertion in *Rule Britannia: Women, Empire, and Victorian Writing* (1995) that "Victorian culture placed women in imperial spaces and authorized their function with those spaces" (6–7), I show how British women's ideas about their own emancipation were contingent on denying emancipation to Eastern women, who were subject to the imperialist views and practices of British women.[3] As Antoinette Burton explains, in *Burdens of History: British Feminists, Indian Women, and Imperial Culture, 1865–1915* (1994),

Organized feminism in Britain emerged in the context of Victorian and Edwardian imperialism. Historically speaking, arguments for British women's emancipation were produced, made public, and contested during a period in which Britain experienced the confidence born of apparent geopolitical supremacy as well as the anxieties brought on by challenges to imperial permanence and stability. (1)

Critics such as Burton, as well as Gayatri Spivak and Sara Suleri (whose work I discuss in Chapter 1), have effectively shown how British feminists took an imperialist view of Indian women, but few critics have shown how British feminists' imperialist views influenced their encounters with representations of ancient Egyptian women. I argue that British women writers' encounters with representations of these women (who clearly belonged to Eastern culture in the minds of the British) influenced how British women represented their own emancipation in novels, poetry, drama, romances, and fictional treatises.

Although British women's encounters with representations of women from other ancient cultures (such as Greek and Roman cultures) were important, their encounters with ancient Egyptian women were particularly significant, since Egypt was a key location in British imperialist development and a site for British women to negotiate their relationship with "women of color."[4] In fact, Egyptian encounters defined the limits of British women writers' willingness to incorporate women from other cultures into their visions for emancipation, marking the overwhelming influence of imperialism, even in the more progressive British minds of the nineteenth century. Canonical women writers such as Nightingale and George Eliot—and less canonical figures such as Katharine Bradley and Edith Cooper (an aunt and niece who wrote poetry and drama together under the name "Michael Field") and Elinor Glyn (best known for turning her controversial cross-cultural romances into successful films in 1920s' Hollywood)—incorporated their knowledge of ancient Egyptian women's cultural power in only a limited fashion when presenting their visions for emancipation. Often, they represented ancient Greek women or Italian Renaissance women (who possessed many of the qualities of ancient Greek women) rather than ancient Egyptian women, since Greek and Italian cultures were more familiar and less threatening to a British audience.

While Churnjeet Mahn has effectively argued in *British Women's Travel to Greece 1840–1914: Travels in the Palimpsest* (2012) that British women were "enfranchise[d]" by their writing about Greece, precisely because "disenfranchising the modern inhabitants" of Greece created room for their own emancipation, she also acknowledges that British women drew on ancient Greece to articulate their own emancipation: they became "the more legitimate heirs xvi • Introduction

to the Ancients, the authentic Greeks" (8–9). Further, as T. D. Olverson
has argued, in *Women Writers and the Dark Side of Late-Victorian Hellenism*
(2010), British women preferred ancient Greek imagery to that of ancient
Egyptian imagery because they were inculturated into believing Greek
women were more similar to themselves because Greek women were "white"
(9). Still, as will be evident in this study, British women writers, in thinking
through their visions for emancipation, reflected upon the powerful status
of Egyptian women such as Isis, Hathor, and Cleopatra (who presented herself as possessing the power of ancient Egyptian women even if her cultural
heritage cannot be definitively determined). Still, despite their knowledge
of ancient Egyptian women, British women writers often did not incorporate representations of ancient Egyptian women into their literary works or
revise negative stereotypes about Egyptian women as fully as they might have,
following instead the boundaries of imperialist discourse, which focused on
contemporary Egyptian women (and presented them as oppressed because
of the influence of Arab/Muslim culture) rather than emphasizing the power of
ancient Egyptian women.[5]

George Eliot, for example, was well versed in typical representations
of Eastern women in nineteenth-century British feminist texts, such as
Mary Wollstonecraft's *A Vindication of the Rights of Woman* (1796), Sarah
Lewis's *Woman's Mission* (1839), and John Stuart Mill's *The Subjection of
Women* (1869) (Wiesenfarth, *A Writer's Notebook* 145; Eliot, *George Eliot
Letters* 1:66, 8:458). These texts, as I will show in my chapter about Eliot,
presented Eastern women (particularly those who were Arab/Muslim) as
"enslaved," incapable of asserting agency, and argued that British women
should not be subject to the same type of oppression by their husbands. Eliot
was familiar with these arguments, yet she also read contemporary accounts
of ancient Egypt, such as John Gardner Wilkinson's *Manners and Customs of
the Ancient Egyptians* (1836), which characterized ancient Egyptian women
as holding more privileges, including control over their husbands, than
women from other ancient cultures. Wilkinson drew on Heredotus's account
of the differences between Egyptian and Greek women, which emphasized
the idea that Greek women had "no independent political or social rights,"
while Egyptian women "were free to live alone, and to own, inherit, buy and
sell property: they could choose their own husbands, initiate a divorce and
raise children without male interference" (Tyldesley 17). Although twenty-
first-century historian Joyce Tyldesley does not trust Heredotus's account on
all matters, she does trust his account of ancient Egyptian women's lives and
affirms that the rights Egyptian women held were "unusual when compared
to the women in Heredotus's own family" (17). Still, according to Wilkinson, ancient Egyptian women also were threatening, since they adopted

transgressive sexual practices that had to be controlled. Wilkinson writes about the Egyptian practice of circumcision, both male and female, as "a salutary precaution well suited to a hot climate" (317), a sanitized expression of the common nineteenth-century myth that Egyptian women were highly sexual because their clitorises expanded in the hot climate of North Africa (Moscucci 70).

Eliot's awareness of both the power and the threat of ancient Egyptian women is important, since although she and the other women writers discussed in this book were not what we would call "women's rights activists" today, all were aware of the debates surrounding the "Woman Question" and were concerned about their own status as women in a culture that had clear expectations about women's roles in the domestic sphere and placed certain restrictions on women's participation in the public sphere. Still, to draw on representations of ancient Egyptian women would have challenged the boundaries for ideal British womanhood, so women writers instead incorporated more familiar representations of Greek and Italian women into their literary work, and this imperialist approach resulted in visions for emancipation that were not inclusive, since they did not envision emancipation for most Eastern women. British women writers, then, developed a *nationalist*, but not an *internationalist*, form of feminism as they presented their visions for emancipation.

This book highlights the distinct experiences of Nightingale, Eliot, Field, and Glyn as they encountered ancient Egyptian women, making clear how imperialist discourse about Eastern women manifested itself in specific ways in their literary work. In Chapter 1, I lay out the important contexts for understanding the encounters British women writers had with ancient Egyptian women. I discuss why ancient cultures, especially Greek and Roman cultures, were compelling to nineteenth-century Britons, and as the century progressed, ancient Egyptian culture was increasingly of interest as travel to Egypt became more accessible. I detail how British women writers accessed knowledge of ancient Egyptian culture, particularly through the periodical press, highlighting articles that emphasized the role of ancient Egyptian women as creators and shapers of culture. I then turn to the nature of imperialist discourse about Britain's presence in Egypt during this period, since this discourse discouraged British women writers from fully engaging Egyptian culture and encouraged a turn to ancient Greek culture instead, and I show how, when British women writers did engage Egyptian culture, they typically followed the denigration of contemporary Egyptian women perpetuated by imperialist discourse but sometimes found inspiration in the roles played by ancient Egyptian goddesses. Finally, I show how other British writers not discussed in this book represented ancient Egyptian women according to the imperialist discourse that influenced Nightingale, Eliot, Field, and Glyn, as a way to compare representations across a wider group of writers.

After discussing the contexts necessary for understanding these women writers' encounters with representations of ancient Egyptian women in Chapter 1, I discuss their individual encounters in Chapters 2–5. In Chapter 2, I argue that Nightingale—whose treatise about emancipation *Suggestions for Thought* (1860) was written shortly after her return to England from Egypt in 1850—encountered and assessed women of color in Egypt according to ideals for women she had developed by viewing art in Italy in 1847–1848, ideals that assumed Eastern women could be emancipated only by adopting Western Christianity. In Italy, Nightingale was exposed to artistic works that affirmed her Christian spiritual beliefs and helped her work through her emerging religious philosophy, in which artists played an important role in revealing God's perfect form to humans and in which women's spiritual development was the result of struggle to recognize this perfect form. Nightingale was particularly struck by Correggio's *The Magdalen* (c. 1518–1519), an image of Mary Magdalen in the desert after she has repented of her sins, and she later incorporated this image into the draft version of *Suggestions for Thought*, in which abstract religious ideals were written about in fictionalized form.

Nightingale's reactions to Italian art reveal how her emerging religious philosophy relied on race hierarchies (the privileging of one race or ethnicity over another), and her reliance on hierarchies developed more fully in Egypt, where she experienced a more intense intermingling of Eastern and Western cultures. She negotiated this experience by assessing Egyptian culture—and Egyptian women—according to her religious philosophy, which acknowledged the role of Eastern religions in the development of Christianity but assumed a progression toward a Christian view of God. The visual representations of Egyptian women she saw, such as those of Nefertari at Abu Simbel, presented women as integral to the expression of God's perfection, and Nightingale drew parallels between the status of women in Western and Eastern religion, parallels that were important to her thinking about women's emancipation as she wrote *Suggestions for Thought*. However, while Nightingale retained some references to Egyptian culture in *Suggestions for Thought*, she favored Italian Renaissance representations of women over Egyptian ones, resulting in a vision for emancipation that excluded Eastern women, unless they embraced Christianity.

Like Florence Nightingale, George Eliot traveled extensively on the Continent, viewing art in France, Germany, and Italy and incorporating her knowledge of the visual arts into her writing, but unlike Nightingale, Eliot did not travel beyond the boundaries of the Continent to view representations of

Eastern women that might have influenced her work. Though she wished to travel east in the 1870s to gather material for her most Eastern novel, *Daniel Deronda* (1876), she was unable to go because of George Henry Lewes's ill health, so her knowledge of the Eastern world was developed through books she read rather than firsthand observation. Chapter 3 examines Eliot's deep reading of linguistic, historical, religious, and mythological theories that emphasized the Egyptian origins of Greek culture and presented ancient Egyptian women as experiencing better privileges than women of other ancient cultures. Still, while Eliot clearly understood the power of ancient Egyptian women, she also understood that they were viewed as dangerously transgressive. Although she used direct references to Cleopatra to characterize the plotting poisoner Bertha in *The Lifted Veil* (1859), she typically avoided associating Western women seeking emancipation with these powerful women, since to do so would have been perilous in British culture, which still sought more familiar models for women's emancipation.

In *Romola* (1862) and *Daniel Deronda* (1876) Eliot engages the position of Eastern women by placing Western women characters in relationships with men who have ties to the East, but she stops short of directly showing how Eastern attributes might provide a direction for Western women as they contemplated their desire for emancipation. In *Romola*, the primary women characters have access to the East through their relationships with the pagan scholar Tito Melema, but Eliot does not give these women the attributes of powerful Egyptian women, and Romola, in particular, is represented as upholding Western, Christian ideals after she converts from paganism to Christianity. In *Daniel Deronda*, controversial among Christian readers for Eliot's attention to Jews in English culture but well received by the Jewish community, Daniel's character is developed through positive references to Egypt via Moses's role as a leader for the Jewish community, and Gwendolen Harleth is described in derogatory terms, as an unattractive Egyptian mummy with a "rag face and skeleton toes peeping out" (372). Although Eliot sometimes uses open-ended symbolism that allows readers to infer a more positive Egyptian context for interpreting Gwendolen's actions, she develops Gwendolen's character primarily through direct references to Greek rather than Egyptian mythology. Eliot avoids directly associating Gwendolen with Egyptian goddesses, a decision that points to the perceived "danger" of the East, particularly when the Eastern woman might provide a model for Western women's emancipation.

Chapter 4 shows how Katharine Bradley, who also had the opportunity to travel to Egypt but did not, and Edith Cooper, writing together as "Michael Field," approached their encounters with Eastern women according to the artistic principles they learned through strict training in European, especially

Italian Renaissance, art. Their affinity for Victorian aestheticism, which privileged Greek culture over that of Egyptian culture, also contributed significantly to their approach to these encounters. Although Bradley and Cooper were aware of the Egyptian presence in art, since they commented on photographs of Egyptian temples and paintings with Egyptian subjects in their collaborative journal, they more closely followed the European ideal of beauty established in their conversations with the art critic Bernhard Berenson, who used his instruction of Bradley and Cooper as the basis for his books about Italian Renaissance art, such as *The Florentine Painters of the Renaissance* (1896). As a result of their training with Berenson, Bradley and Cooper adopted a Graeco-Italian ideal for beauty, which they used in their 1892 collection of poetry *Sight and Song*.

Using an Italianized version of the Greek goddess Venus to challenge traditional Victorian notions about sexual desire in *Sight and Song*, Bradley and Cooper developed a method for expressing same-sex desire that still was not too threatening to their European audience. They retained this ideal as they more fully engaged Egyptian culture in their verse dramas, especially *Queen Mariamne* (1908), in which the Graeco-Italian qualities of Mariamne are privileged over the Egyptian qualities of Cleopatra. Although Cleopatra is characterized in relation to the Egyptian goddess Isis in the play, she is a thoroughly unsympathetic character, and it is Mariamne, referred to in relation to the Greek Venus in the play, who is the true heroine. Like Nightingale and Eliot, Bradley and Cooper were unable to fully embrace the positive qualities of ancient Egyptian women, and their attachment to all things Greek contributed to their negative representation of women from the deep East.

Chapter 5 examines the romances of Elinor Glyn, which were produced when the British Empire was at its height and about to begin its descent. Glyn—who traveled to Egypt regularly and saw the romance as a model for emancipation, since it was a genre that could emphasize "spiritual" rather "physical" unions between men and women—used her knowledge of ancient cultures to develop these romances as cross-cultural narratives, in which experience with other cultures was a key element in relationships between men and women. As an early-twentieth-century, aristocratic Englishwoman, Glyn did not have access to the formal education enjoyed by her male peers but did have access to more informal methods of educating herself about ancient cultures, including her family's library during childhood and the company of upper-class men such as the Viceroy of India Lord Curzon and the Oxford philosophy professor F. H. Bradley during adulthood. As a result, the literary sources for her romances were popular rather than scholarly sources, such as Charles Kingsley's children's narrative *The Heroes* (1856), and Glyn developed a commodified view of ancient cultures, in which her knowledge of Greek and Egyptian culture was shaped by the conversation she encountered at the social gatherings she attended.

In *Three Weeks* (1907), controversial because of its acknowledgment of sexual relations outside marriage as part of the process of establishing a spiritual union, Glyn intermingles aspects of Greek and Egyptian culture, representing the lead woman character, "the Lady," as an imaginary Eastern goddesses who influences her English lover, Paul Verdayne, without threatening his British masculinity. Cognizant of earlier representations of Cleopatra as manipulative, especially Shakespeare's characterization of her in *Antony and Cleopatra*, Glyn significantly revises these representations by positively associating the Lady with the more loving qualities of Cleopatra. Yet, she ultimately returns to more familiar Greek and British ideals for womanhood over the course of the novel. By the end of the romance, the Lady has not only been recast as a Greek goddess, who has the softer qualities of Hera than the more threatening qualities of the Egyptian goddess Hathor, but she becomes a procreative mother modeled on a British ideal rather than an Egyptian or Greek ideal. In doing so, Glyn returns to a physical rather than spiritual version of the romance and, like the other women writers discussed in this book, provides a limited view of women's emancipation, possible only through imaginative romance and not sustainable once her characters return to their daily lives.

All of these women writers, then, were influenced to some degree by nineteenth-century imperialist attitudes toward Egypt, and only in the latter half of the twentieth century did visions of women's emancipation come to include Egyptian women, as Egyptian women writers undertook the important task of "writing back" against the British empire and creating more inclusive visions for emancipation. As Bill Ashcroft, Gareth Griffiths, and Helen Tiffin write in their influential book *The Empire Writes Back: Theory and Practice in Post-Colonial Literatures* (1989, rev. 2002), postcolonial literature, which ultimately can represent "indigenous" cultures that have been controlled by imperialist nations, develops in stages, and it is only through the "appropriation of the power of writing" that postcolonial literature can represent indigenous culture (4–5, 77). Ashcroft, Griffiths, and Tiffin recognize the role feminism plays in the development of postcolonial literature, writing: "the history and concerns of feminist theory have strong parallels with post-colonial theory," since both approaches to literature "seek to reinstate the marginalized in the face of the dominant, and early feminist theory, like early nationalist post-colonial criticism, sought to invert the structures of domination" (173). In Chapter 6 of this book, I use the parallel between postcolonial and feminist theory to trace the development of feminist awareness in Egypt in the late nineteenth and early twentieth centuries, with emphasis on Egyptian women writers' representations of themselves before the mid-twentieth century, which included references to ancient Egyptian goddesses. I then focus on Latifa Al-Zayyat's important contribution to Egyptian feminism with her 1960 novel *The Open Door*, the story of a young woman whose emancipation comes from her participation in the political resistance to England's control of the Suez Canal in the 1950s. Employing a social realist style, Al-Zayyat represents Egyptian women as thoroughly engaged in *modern* Egyptian culture, through their interest in Egypt's political and economic independence from Britain, rather than turning back to ancient Egyptian history for inspiration.

Yet, in the late twentieth and early twenty-first centuries, Al-Zayyat and other Egyptian women writers have recognized the advantage of drawing on ancient Egyptian "heritage imagery," as Marilyn Booth refers to imagery from ancient Egyptian history that expresses Egyptian women's desire for emancipation ("Introduction," *Open Door* xxvii). I briefly discuss the work of women writers such as Sahar Tawfiq, Alifa Rifaat, and Nawal El Saadawi, who have used heritage imagery via second-wave feminist views, and then turn to more extensive discussion of the work of Ahdaf Soueif, Radwa Ashour, and Iman Mersal, who also use heritage imagery but whose poststructuralist understanding of identity especially clarifies the limits of nineteenth-century British women writers' *nationalist* visions for emancipation. By contrasting the more inclusive visions of these women writers to the more exclusive visions of nineteenth-century British women writers, we have a better understanding of the imperialist pressures under which writers such as Nightingale, Eliot, Field, and Glyn wrote—and a more thorough understanding of the development of *internationalist* feminism by twentieth- and twenty-first-century Egyptian women writers.

*   *   *

The theoretical assumptions of my argument include assumptions about (1) literary expression in the nineteenth and early twentieth centuries; (2) the influence of gender, class, and race on this form of expression; and (3) the role of historical context in literary analysis. First, I assume that there is something unique about fictional forms of literary expression, and these forms of expression can be distinguished from nonfictional forms. While I do not hold that fictional expressions (such as the novel, poetry, and drama) should be privileged over nonfictional forms (such as travel narratives, journalism, and letters), much has been done to analyze the role of nonfictional forms of expression in the British imperialist project, and a return to the study of fictional forms (or, in the case of Nightingale, the fictional draft of what became a nonfictional treatise) may further illuminate how British women writers reflected upon and contributed to romanticized visions of the East as British imperialism reached its height. Marilyn Butler, in her important response to Said's *Orientalism*, argues that Western fictional narratives about the East are "rich in metaphor, allegory and myth" (398), and even as they present romanticized visions of the East, they nevertheless show the complexity of those visions because they use to their advantage the unique qualities of fictional forms of expression. My study still values nonfictional forms of expression, since I use these forms as sources for understanding the fictional examples that are the focus of this book: for example, Nightingale's letters about her travel to Egypt are a source for understanding the choices she made when writing the fictional draft of *Suggestions for Thought*. Still, there is something unique about the translation of British women's encounters with ancient Greek and Egyptian women into fiction: focusing on fiction allows for a more thorough discussion of specific narrative strategies such as plot, character development, imagery, and other strategies that, while sometimes present in nonfictional forms, do not dominate in such forms.

I also assume that class, race, and gender influenced how writers expressed themselves in literature in the nineteenth and early twentieth centuries. All of the British women writers discussed in this book benefited from the privileges of class and race, which allowed them to express themselves through literature, a privilege possessed only by a very few women of color before the mid-twentieth century. Nightingale's advantages due to class and race are best known; while she received official governmental support for her work with injured soldiers during the Crimean War, her black counterpart, Mary Seacole, was denied the opportunity to go to the Crimea as a government-supported nurse, most likely because of her ethnicity (Salih, *Wonderful Adventures* xxviii). While Seacole managed to travel to the Crimea by raising her own money for the trip and published a memoir upon her return to England, Nightingale's post-Crimea career, which included writing numerous reports about health and sanitation for the British government, resulted in authority with the general public Seacole never garnered. The privileges experienced by Eliot, Bradley, Cooper, and Glyn are perhaps more subtle but, nevertheless, gave these women access to opportunities to express themselves in literary form. Eliot's position as a section editor of the *Westminster Review* established her in the London literary world and allowed her to make the transition to fiction in the mid-1850s (Haight 97–102). Bradley and Cooper's financial stability, which allowed them to take university-level courses in art and literature and travel abroad with Berenson, gave them authority in artistic circles, where they interacted with proponents of aesthetic ideals such as Oscar Wilde, Charles Ricketts, and Charles Shannon (Thain and Vadillo 24, 29–30). Finally, Glyn's connections in British high society, including connections with military officials as prominent as the Viceroy of India Lord Curzon, gave her a certain caché that prompted the American film industry to bring her to Hollywood to write screenplays in the 1920s (Barnett 283).

These privileges due to class and race may very well have been what encouraged these women to take up the issue of gender inequality in their literary work, since their privileged positions gave them access to debates about the position of women. While I do not hold, as Hélène Cixous does, that women's experiences are innately different from men's and that women writers, because they have a different understanding of language, use different narrative strategies when expressing themselves in literature (Cixous 418–20, 422), I do believe that the cultural circumstances of women's lives in the nineteenth and early twentieth centuries made them particularly aware of gender issues and influenced the topics about which they chose to write. All of the writers included in this study experienced some degree of gender inequality and expressed frustration about this inequality. Nightingale faced pressure from her family to marry rather than take up a profession (Woodham-Smith 23, 32), and Eliot was initially ostracized by London society after she lived openly with George Henry Lewes without marrying him, though she and Lewes later "outlived" this ostracization and found acceptance in "an exclusive urban and international circle" (McCormack 1). Bradley and Cooper were unable to be entirely truthful about their relationship, which had a romantic dimension, due to biases against homosexuality in late-nineteenth-century society (Donoghue 29–31, 65), and Glyn faced harsh criticism from her friends, and official censorship of her work, because she acknowledged sexual relationships outside marriage in her romances (Glyn, *Elinor Glyn* 127).

Although none of these women writers participated directly in political movements to establish equality between women and men, and Glyn even considered herself anti-suffrage (Linett 183), they all were aware of the debates that raged in Parliament, newspapers, the periodical press, and other venues, and they seem to have approached their encounters with Eastern women with at least some sense of the inequalities they had faced as women and an interest in ensuring that other women did not face the same inequalities. Still, because their encounters with Eastern women were influenced by imperialist discourse, they often were unable to articulate a vision for equality that could include all women. In focusing on these authors' gendered, classed, and raced experiences and on the literary representations that emerge from these experiences, this book reflects first- and second-wave feminism's understanding that agency was central to women's emancipation, even if we now recognize that agency is a social construct set up by individuals to feel powerful rather than a tangible measure of that power. With this recognition, this book also draws on the third-wave feminist principle that identity is more fluid than first- and second-wave feminists realized, and the work of critics such as Judith Butler, who showed in *Gender Trouble* (1990) how the flexibility of language facilitates gender performativity, has been helpful to me in understanding that there is infinite variety in narratives about women's emancipation; the ones I analyze in this book are just some of the possibilities, and all of them might be interpreted in multiple ways. In approaching this topic, I also have paid special attention to the way in which third-wave feminists—such as Gayatri Spivak, in "Three Women's Texts and a Critique of Imperialism" (1985)—have shown how discourse about race influences gender identity. Spivak points out the constraints placed on the colonial subject by such discourse, arguing that Jean Rhys's novel *Wide Sargasso Sea* (1966) is a "reinscription" of Charlotte Brontë's *Jane Eyre* because it does not escape imperialist discourse in its presentation of non-English women, favoring the white creole Antoinette over the "native" Christophine (244, 253). Such readings have helped me understand that British women writers contributed to these constraints through their discourse about women's emancipation.

My methodology is a historically informed variation of formalist feminism, a critical approach that has at its root the analysis of narrative and gender. Formalist feminism builds on third-wave feminist principles about subjectivity, emphasizing the blurring of gender boundaries through the analysis of binary opposites, but also recognizes that the third-wave approach of emphasizing binary opposites as a means for questioning gender inequality might be limiting, since the narrative strategies used by writers interested in questioning gender inequality are more nuanced than even binary opposites sometimes can express. Although the term "formalist feminism" does not emphasize an historical approach to literary analysis, some of its practitioners successfully analyze literature from this perspective without abandoning their commitment to analyzing the specific cultural and material conditions that affect narrative and gender in particular historical periods. For example, at a plenary panel at the 2011 British Women Writers Conference, speakers Caroline Levine, Sandra Macpherson, and Robyn Warhol offered very different approaches to the question, "What is formalist feminism?," but all illustrated how historical and cultural contexts intersect with narrative and gender when analyzing nineteenth-century British literature. Levine focused on "how gender takes form" and the need for a "third form," something to supplement the two forms covered by a binary opposite, to understand how gender operates. For example, Levine argued, looking at gender in Victorian literature via the separate-spheres model, which relies on the public/private binary opposite, is not sufficient; other "forms," such as the way in which

John Ruskin's complicated views about the public and private spheres were deployed in the nineteenth century, are needed to understand how gender operates in Victorian literature. Macpherson, on the other hand, argued that forms, or shapes, do, in some sense, contain people, and feminist criticism needs to be as aware of bodies as forms as well as language as form. In George Eliot's *Silas Marner* (1861), Macpherson argued, there is a proliferation of descriptions of "shapes" of characters, showing that "people are defined by their shapes." Finally, Warhol, using the work of Jane Austen as an example, indicated that formalist feminism must acknowledge the role of readers, who are forms, or "figures of person," just as characters in novels are not people but "creatures," shaped by the form of literary expression. All three speakers contributed important perspectives about how to approach gender issues in literary texts in a formalist manner, while still retaining historical awareness, in order to capture the specific lived experiences of the writers who produce narratives and the readers who consume them.

My methodology in this book retains a strong commitment to historical research but uses this research to contextualize the narrative strategies used by women writers to articulate their encounters with Eastern women in literary forms such as fictionalized treatises, novels, poetry, drama, and romances. The writers I have chosen for this book represent well the broader issues of imperialist influence on representations of women's emancipation in nineteenth-century literature. Though well discussed in other respects (for example, the religious context for Nightingale's *Suggestions for Thought*, the Jewish context for Eliot's *Daniel Deronda*, the lesbian context for Field's poetry collection *Sight and Song*, and the cinematic context for Glyn's *Three Weeks*), their work has not already been discussed in an Egyptian context, so choosing these writers encourages readers to entertain new perspectives about works they may have already studied in other contexts. This approach, I believe, shows how imperative it is to recognize representations of Eastern women, or more broadly women of color, even when they are represented in part through their absence. As the individual chapters in this book show, our understanding of the Egyptian "presence" in nineteenth- and early-twentieth-century fiction is dependent on analyzing what British women writers did *not* write about or wrote about in an *indirect* manner.

Ultimately, all of the women writers discussed in this book, though they had unique encounters with women of color through their knowledge of Egypt, were, in some sense, "bound by an English eye" as they wrote about women of color during the growth of British imperialism. Their understanding of Greece and Italy as gateways to Egyptian culture provided them with opportunities to engage the position of Egyptian women in relationship to their own positions in British culture, yet they did not always fully represent the powerful ancient Egyptian women that might have symbolized a more inclusive vision of emancipation. It was only once Egyptian women writers themselves began articulating their views about women's emancipation that imperialist ways of writing about Egyptian women were challenged and revised. Although a few Egyptian women writers had access to the publishing venues needed to represent their interest in emancipation before the mid-twentieth century, only after 1950 did Egyptian women writers gain widespread access to such venues and present more inclusive visions for emancipation as they "wrote back" against the British empire.

CHAPTER 1

Bound by an English Eye: Ancient Cultures, Imperialist Contexts, and Literary Representations of Ancient Egyptian Women

Subsequent chapters in this book will contextualize the specific knowledge Nightingale, Eliot, Field, and Glyn had about ancient Egypt, but here, it is important to lay out five broad historical and cultural contexts, which facilitate a clear understanding of how British women writers approached their encounters with representations of ancient Egyptian women. First, it is important to understand why ancient cultures, especially Greek and Roman cultures, were compelling to nineteenth-century Britons, and how as the century progressed, ancient Egyptian culture was increasingly of interest as well, particularly as travel to Egypt became more accessible. Second, it must be clear how British women writers accessed knowledge of ancient Egyptian culture, including through the periodical press, which typically focused on contemporary Egyptian political issues but also included articles that emphasized the role of women in ancient Egypt as creators and shapers of culture. Third, it is vital to examine the nature of imperialist discourse about Britain's presence in Egypt during this period, since this discourse discouraged British women writers from fully engaging Egyptian culture and encouraged a turn to ancient Greek culture instead. Fourth, we must understand that when British women writers did engage Egyptian culture, they typically followed the denigration of contemporary Egyptian women perpetuated by imperialist discourse but sometimes found inspiration in the roles played by ancient Egyptian goddesses—especially their involvement in love, marriage, and childbirth—roles that appealed to British women writers even as they worked to transform roles for women in their own culture. Finally, I want to highlight how other British writers, both women and men, represented ancient Egyptian women according to the imperialist discourse that influenced Nightingale, Eliot, Field, and Glyn, as a way to compare representations across a wider group of writers. Rather than exoticizing Egyptian culture as a way to tantalize their audience, as was more common among their male contemporaries and antifeminist female contemporaries, these women writers avoided references to Egyptian culture as a tactical maneuver to appeal to a British audience while still expressing their visions for women's emancipation.

Nineteenth-Century British Interest in Ancient Cultures

A number of critics already have laid out the influence of Greek and Roman ancient cultures on Britons. In *The Victorians and Ancient Greece* (1980), Richard Jenkyns details the development of English interest in ancient Greece, indicating that it began in the mid-eighteenth century, when men such as James Stuart and Nicholas Revett traveled to Athens to draw ancient ruins and brought Greek architecture back to England by building a Doric temple in Worcestershire in 1758 (1–2). Using the Turks' conquest of Greece as the rationale for this revival, since to be interested in ancient Greek culture was to resist the Turks (3), Stuart and Revett infused a Grecian perspective into the "Augustan Age," during which Roman models had prevailed in English architecture (2). This belief in Greek culture as "more authentic" than Roman culture was further developed by the end of the eighteenth century, when men such as the Dilettani member Robert Wood, who knew Stuart and Revett, traveled east with his library of Greek literature, so he could read this literature where it was originally written (7). This extended the scope of Stuart and Revett's Greek revival and fueled interest in Greek literature and the arts; early nineteenth-century male Romantic writers were particularly interested in the poetry of Homer, whom they admired for his epic narratives, even as they struggled to write epics that would live up to the standard set by Homer (8, 22–25). Once Greece gained its independence, interest in Greek culture waned, and the Victorians, in many ways, reacted against Hellenism through their revival of Gothic architecture. Yet, some Victorians—Algernon Swinburne and John Addington Symonds, for example—continued to look up to the Greeks, and even those who seemed to reject Hellenism—such as John Ruskin—exhibited the "tension" between admiration and dismissal, which Jenkyns sees as "central to Victorian Hellenism" (15–16). "Whatever a man's own opinion might be," Jenkyns writes, "it was hard for him to avoid the awareness that Greek influences were all around him" (16). Thomas Arnold's introduction of Greek into the curriculum at Oxford helped solidify this influence (60–61), and through the early twentieth century, Greek (as well as Latin) was a central part of upper- and middle-class men's education in England. As Charles Freeman indicates in *Egypt, Greece, and Rome: Civilizations of the Ancient Mediterranean* (2004), Freeman's own great-uncle took examinations for a "prestigious prize" at his college at the start of the twentieth century, and all but one of the papers "had some connection with Latin or Greek" (1).

Yet, both Freeman and Jenkyns acknowledge that nineteenth-century women did not benefit from the classical education given to men and, therefore, did not have the same level of access to ancient Greek culture that men had (Freeman 2; Jenkyns 63). Still, some women did manage to learn the classics, through informal means such as tutors and reading in family libraries. Only recently have critics devoted book-length studies to this topic, responding well to Yopie Prins's point, in "Greek Maenads, Victorian Spinsters" (1999), that "[w]hile recent critics have emphasized the construction of masculine identities and the mediation of masculine desire in Victorian England through an idealized vision of ancient Greece, the place of women within Victorian Hellenism remains largely unexplored, despite the fact that an increasing number of women were learning Greek" (43). Isobel Hurst's *Victorian Women Writers and the Classics* (2006) brings attention to these women, arguing that although nineteenth-century women who studied Greek spent more time translating than composing Greek verse, and that their literary representations of learning Greek emphasize the struggle faced by women who tried to do so, their involvement in the publication of translations and Greek-inspired literature did much to "empower" Victorian women and girls (2–3). Hurst extends previous analysis of women writers who learned Greek, discussing not only the work of Elizabeth Barrett Browning and George Eliot, who were "granted an exceptional status as female classicists" (4), but also the work of less prominent women writers—Eliza Lynn Linton, Amy Levy, and Augusta Webster—who did not study Greek intensely but still incorporated Greek imagery into their work (10). Shanyn Fiske, in *Heretical Hellenism: Women Writers, Ancient Greece, and the Victorian Popular Imagination* (2008), adds Charlotte Brontë and Jane Harrison to the list of women who developed a knowledge of Greek language and culture, despite lack of support for their desire to learn about it. Arguing that learning about Greek language and culture "provided a means of telling very different stories about themselves than the narratives prescribed by their own society" (8), Fiske provides detailed analysis of Brontë's references to Greek culture in her juvenile essays and her 1853 novel *Villette* and traces the development of Harrison's career as a "prominent lecturer in Greek art and archaic religion" (21). Still, the relatively sparse access that nineteenth-century women had to direct study of ancient

Greek culture is important in understanding the work of the writers I include in this book. Certainly, Eliot was the exception to the rule; Nightingale, Field, and Glyn did not study Greek culture as thoroughly as Eliot did, though all had access to information unusual for women of their time.

Just as women of higher-class standing had some access to information about ancient Greek culture, they also had access to ancient Roman culture, even if they did not engage it as thoroughly as did their male counterparts. A natural extension of nineteenth-century interest in the Greeks, interest in ancient Roman culture was important, and modern-day Rome often functioned as a way for Britons to connect with ancient Greek culture and as a gateway to the East, including Egypt. As Jenkyns explains, even in the eighteenth century, when Roman models were more prevalent in English architecture than Greek models, there was the recognition that the Romans, in a variety of fields, had simply been imitating the Greeks (2). "The Roman poets never forgot that they stood in the shadow of a giant; their fingers were always pointing behind them to the glories of the Greek past, and an admiration for Latin literature leads naturally to a respect for the authority of the Greeks" (2). For eighteenth- and nineteenth-century travelers, then, going to modern Italy was a way to access not only ancient Roman but also ancient Greek culture (41–42). Jenkyns writes, "In the Mediterranean world antiquity seemed to be still present. Many a northern traveller in Rome was impressed, like [the landscape painter] Clive Newcome, by the 'great silent population of marble'. . . . As the Englishman journeyed south, he seemed to travel backwards in time" (44). Norman Vance, in *The Victorians and Ancient Rome* (1997), confirms that even those travelers who went to Rome primarily to access Renaissance history could not help but feel the impact of its ancient aspects as well: "they could not fail to notice the ruins of the Colosseum, observed in the moonlight by Goethe as well as Byron, or the fragments of Roman magnificence which littered the Roman Campagna all round the city" (19).

Travel to modern-day Rome also provided "a readily accessible and not too disquieting Orient," where travelers had an "exemption from the familiar and the possibility of 'other' experiences" (1–2), as Robert K. Martin and Leland S. Person show in their collection, *Roman Holidays: American Writers and Artists in Nineteenth-Century Italy* (2002). Robert S. Levine's essay in this collection, "Road to Africa: Frederick Douglass's Rome," indicates that, for the more adventurous traveler, Rome was the midway point between England and Africa, the Near East, or the Far East. Frederick Douglass's reaction to Rome, while on his way to Egypt in 1887, is particularly relevant, since Douglass's understanding of race issues in the United States allowed him to see Rome as the beginning of a process of encountering people he believed looked more like him and other African Americans. Even on the way to

Rome from Paris, Douglass notes a change in the physical appearance of the people he sees, writing, "As the traveler moves eastward and southward . . . he will observe an increase of black hair, black eyes, full lips, and dark complexions" (Douglass qtd. in Levine 232). By the time Douglass reaches Egypt, he believes "he has entered a realm of greater, but not 'pure,' blackness" (Levine 238). Though Douglass would use Rome as a more innocuous setting in the revised version of his autobiography *Life and Times* (1892), at the time he visited the Italian city in 1887, it was meaningful to him, functioning as a "stopping point on the road to Africa in his eastward journey from lighter skinned to darker skinned peoples and nations" (241).

Even travelers to Rome who did not have Douglass's experience of what it meant to be black in America thought about Rome in relation to what they expected to see or had already seen in the East. For example, Herman Melville took an eastward rather than westward route during his travels in 1856–1857 and came to Rome only after seeing Egypt and the Holy Land, where he had experienced "an almost panicked sense of physical and psychological suffocation" and a sense of disgust at the "clamorous disharmony" he observed there (Milder 209). Egypt, in particular, left Melville "deeply ambivalent" about metaphysical questions (212), and when he arrived in Italy, he was so weary from his journey to the East that he was more "stunned" by the experience than appreciative of the "stunning" qualities of the city, though he did recognize the "massive" and "majestic" qualities of ancient Roman architecture (218). Henry James, too, was disappointed in 1869, in part because he expected to "receive the revelations of antiquity" in Rome and instead found a city on the verge of "modernity" (Powers 65–66).

Still, many men and some women found travel to Rome creatively invigorating. The American sculptors Hiram Powers and William Wetmore Story, both of whom drew on classical subjects for their work, had fruitful careers there (Powers 53), and, as Alison Chapman and Jane Stabler show in their collection, *Unfolding the South: Nineteenth-Century British Women Writers and Artists in Italy* (2003), women writers and artists who went to Rome found a place where they could be artistically productive, though they sometimes experienced "complex and painful anxieties about professional identity and vocation" there (8). Certainly, many nineteenth- and early twentieth-century British women writers set their literary narratives in Italy and drew on its ancient aspects in constructing their narratives: Elizabeth Barrett Browning's *Aurora Leigh* (1856) and Eliot's *Middlemarch* (1871) come to mind immediately. Although many nineteenth-century women never had the chance to travel to Italy, the women discussed in this book were among those who did, and this travel gave them greater access to ancient cultures than the average nineteenth-century woman had.

British Women Writers' Access to Ancient Egyptian Culture

For men and women of a certain class, then, both modern-day Italy and modern-day Greece functioned as gateways to the East, and although more nineteenth-century Britons traveled to Greece and Italy, people of a certain class also increasingly traveled to Egypt. John Pemble, in *The Mediterranean Passion: Victorians and Edwardians in the South* (1987), includes travel to Egypt in his discussion of Britons' interest in the Mediterranean and details how Thomas Cook's travel agency made Egypt more accessible to Britons by the mid-1860s, when ships docked at Alexandria on a weekly basis (23). Even in the 1840s, when Nightingale made her trip, Alexandria could be accessed by ship on a monthly basis (23), and after Britain occupied Egypt in 1882, Britons were further encouraged to travel to Egypt, since they no longer needed a passport to travel there (35). Once in Egypt, Britons coming before the 1880s traveled by horse or by boat on the Nile, but beginning in the 1880s, they also could travel between major cities, such as Alexandria and Cairo, by railway (29). By the mid-1880s, 5,000–6,000 Britons were traveling to Egypt through Cook's agency each year (47), and by 1898, the agency included in its advertisements a list of "Royal and Distinguished Persons" who had traveled there through the agency (3). Although reasons for traveling to Egypt varied, one draw was the country's connection to Christianity, a theme evident in Nightingale's writing about her travels and also in Eliot's work, where the importance of Egypt in connecting Christianity and Judaism is recognized.

Travelers to Egypt of course returned with "souvenirs": in the early 1860s, a young man traveling with the historian Henry Thomas Buckle admitted to his mother that he had "broke a bit off" the neck of the Sphinx to bring home with him, and Buckle, in fact, brought back "enough antiquities to equip a private museum" (5). Others followed suit, including the "amateur Egyptologists" Greville Chester and Amelia Edwards, who founded in 1888 the Society for the Protection of the Monuments of Ancient Egypt, despite gathering their antiquities "by less than scrupulous methods" (6). Through these methods of "acquisition," Britons who could not travel came to learn about ancient Egypt. Eliot, Bradley, and Cooper were among those who saw Egyptian antiquities in the British Museum, which already had significant Greek and Roman collections by 1830 and developed its Egyptian collection during the Victorian period (4). Egyptian antiquities, both real and fake, became part of the European landscape as ancient Egyptian architecture, art, and customs were incorporated first into Greek and Italian culture and then across Europe. In *The Egyptian Revival: Ancient Egypt as the Inspiration for Design Motifs in the West* (2005), James Stevens Curl shows how symbols associated with the Egyptian goddess Isis were incorporated into ancient Greek sculpture; Egyptian design features made their way into Roman architecture; Egyptian obelisks, including Cleopatra's Needle in London were brought to Europe; and Victorians re-created ancient Egyptian art and architecture, such as the Egyptian Court at the Crystal Palace, which "brought the Egyptian style before a wide public" (321). Jeffrey Richards elaborates on "Egyptomania" in Victorian England in *The Ancient World on the Victorian and Edwardian Stage* (2009), discussing the Egyptian Court as well as other venues in which Egyptian culture was brought to the general public, such as The Egyptian Hall at Piccadilly (which initially featured art exhibitions and later musicals and magic shows) and the British Museum's Egyptian gallery (which allowed the public to view thousands of objects from Egypt after the museum created a separate Department of Egyptian and Oriental Antiquities in 1866) (16–18). Still, Richards points out that Victorian interest in Egyptian culture was not simply for entertainment; Victorians looked to ancient Egypt as an "empire" with "lessons to offer on the rise and fall of imperial powers" (17).

The role of ancient Egypt as an empire to emulate, as well as the role of the British empire in contemporary Egypt, were regular topics of discussion in Victorian newspapers and periodicals, important venues through which Britons who could not travel to Egypt learned about the country, albeit from an imperialist perspective. My own review of the *Wellesley Index to Victorian Periodicals* indicates that most articles about Egypt in the period 1840–1910 focused on contemporary Egyptian politics and Britons' concern about their nation's role in the often tense political situation there, but there were also a significant number of articles about ancient Egyptian archaeology and mythology, which referred to the role of ancient Egyptian goddesses as creators and shapers of culture. For example, as early as 1836, *The Foreign Quarterly Review* ran reviews of books with discussion of representations of women in ancient Egyptian temples. The reviewer of Jean-François Champollion's *Monuments de l'Egypte et de la Nubie* (1836) describes Hathor, whom I will discuss as one of the important creation goddesses later in this chapter, as she appears in her temple: "The figure has a cow's head surmounted by a lotus; and the name, Athor,—which signifies House or Womb of the Sun, the Egyptian Messiah, or Bethshemesh . . . —is clearly visible above the head of the broken and decayed statue" (Anonymous, "Art. V." 113). The reviewer also compares Hathor to the Greek Venus and identifies the temple builder Sesostris's wife as the subject of two "colossal statues" inside the temple, in which she is portrayed "in the character of Venus or Athor" (114). In fact, Sesostris's wife, whom Champollion refers to as Nofre-ari, a spelling the reviewer rejects, is the "presiding divinity" at the temple (112), suggesting she shaped Egyptian culture in the same way Hathor, who often appeared as a nourishing cow, shaped the world by providing a foundation between mortals and immortals (Hart 76).

Comparison of goddesses across ancient cultures also appears as late as 1883, in an article in *The Contemporary Review*, "The Gods of Canaan," in which the Hebrew goddess Ashtoreth, the Phoenician goddess Aphrodite, and the Egyptian goddess Isis are conflated (386). Focusing on the centrality of sun worship in ancient Phoenician culture, these goddesses are highlighted for their role in supporting the male gods associated with the sun while still demonstrating their own power (Sayce 387). For example, Ashtoreth, as the moon goddess, is the "female power" who stands next to the male god Baal, but "Ashtoreth was not only the face or reflection of Baal; the pious Phoenician saw in her also the crescent moon, the pale reflection of the sun" (388). Further, Isis is highlighted for her role in piecing together her brother/husband, the sun god Osiris, after he was destroyed by his brother Seth; according to this article, the Phoenicians compared Osiris to one of their own sun gods, Tammez, who was followed into the underworld after his death by his wife, the Isis-like goddess Ishtar (393–94).

Isis's role in putting Osiris back together also appears in an 1870 article in *Blackwood's Magazine*, "About How the Old Egyptians Lived and Died," in which Isis and Osiris are presented as "more celebrated than all the rest of the ancient Egyptian gods" (307). In addition to her role in Osiris's recovery, she is described as "the land of Egypt," a complement to Osiris, who is described as "the Nile" (308); this characterization of Isis confirms the complementary role ancient Egyptian goddesses played while still being celebrated for their own qualities. Interestingly, this article immediately follows an installment of Robert Edward Francillon's serialized novel *Earl's Dene*, in which the vices of Cleopatra, as Caesar's lover, are contrasted to the virtues of Octavia, Caesar's wife, but in which Cleopatra also is presented as more appealing to men than Octavia's virtues (Francillon 202). As we shall see later, the contrast between the positive power of Isis and the negative power of Cleopatra was common in nineteenth-century writing about Egypt and would have been recognized by readers as they read Francillon's novel and then the article about how "Old Egyptians" lived and died. The negative but still alluring aspects of Cleopatra's character typically are what are emphasized in Victorian periodicals, and an 1894 review of an exhibition titled "Fair Women," which appeared in *The National Review*, confirms this characterization, since the reviewer comments that one of Lawrence Alma-Tadema's paintings of Cleopatra shows well the "wiles and voluptuous charm . . . of the Serpent of the Old Nile" (Anonymous, "About" 614).

This characterization, written in the 1890s, is not surprising, given the development of decadence at the end of the Victorian period, but even a much earlier article, from the 1872 volume of *The Dublin University Magazine*, paints Cleopatra in a manipulative light. Focusing on her biography, the author, Dr. H. A. Dick, argues that Cleopatra's life serves as one of the "extreme cases of the action of principles common to all mankind" (229). Citing Shakespeare as the source for contemporary understanding of Cleopatra, which acknowledges the role "love played in [her] life," Dick argues that Cleopatra's biography "shocks our modern notions of morality" but also "attracts us by its splendor" (229). Still, around the same time Dick was writing in *The Dublin Magazine*, another writer, for *The Cornhill Magazine*, argued for a more complex view of Cleopatra, since she (as Shakespeare portrayed her) and Goethe's Mignon were "the two feminine impersonations" who "betoken the most intimate and refined knowledge of human nature" (Anonymous, "On the Character" 344). To this writer, Shakespeare's Cleopatra is "fully developed and revealed . . . open as day . . . wear[ing] her heart upon her sleeve. . . . She knows herself and she knows others" (345). As my chapters about Field and Glyn will demonstrate, Shakespeare's representation of Cleopatra was an important source in nineteenth-century British women's writing about Egyptian women, but there also was the opportunity for revision of his portrayal of her, whom not everyone viewed in the same manner as this writer.

Still, it is clear from articles that appeared in the periodical press that Britons adapted Cleopatra and other Egyptian women for their own purposes. For example, in *The National Review* in 1894, there are two distinctly different uses of ancient Egyptian women to comment on Egypt's relationship to England. In the first article, "Our Cleopatra," H. D. Traill, who had traveled to Egypt for seven weeks to study the political situation there, argues that Egypt is Cleopatra to England's Antony (127). Responding to Wilfred Blunt's article in *The Nineteenth Century*—in which Blunt, who traveled to Egypt regularly, writes favorably about the last Khedive of Egypt, Abbas II (1892–1914)—Traill expresses more skepticism about the Khedive, who had recently made negative comments about Egyptian troops and suggested that the British Commander-in-Chief Herbert Kitchener resign (124). Using Cleopatra as a metaphor for Egypt's relationship with England, Traill expresses skepticism about the future of Egypt without England's involvement:

> It may be that we shall have to break off the *liaison*. . . . [I]ndeed, it is certain we shall have to do so. . . . [W]hen we have to part company with our Cleopatra, let those believe who can that she will prove capable of living as a *femme sole*. . . . To me . . . there seem but three lines of future open to her when we depart [:] . . . slave-mistress of the Turk [,] . . . new *liaison* with some new Western lover, in all probability France [,] . . . [or an] arrangement with the European Powers [,] . . . political polyandria of the most odious and demoralizing kind. (127)

This portrayal of Egypt as Cleopatra, who is always in alliance with some European power, often as its "slave-mistress," draws heavily on the stereotypical view of Cleopatra as Eastern seductress, who can only bring trouble to England. The second article in *The National Review*, a fictional piece by the Australian artist Mortimer Menpes titled "The Actualists. Some Impressions of Shilito Jessop, Artist," portrays an unidentified ancient Egyptian object in the British Museum as the "one dear and true friend" who can bring Jessop comfort when he becomes obsessed with artistic technique and loses sight of "real" art—something that connects "the artistic and the human" (563). Jessop describes this Egyptian art object as "a little black woman's head, placed on a pedestal close by one of the windows" and says of her: "I have known Her in ages past, perhaps on the banks of the mysterious Nile, perhaps in further ages still. I have loved Her, and I shall love Her again in ages to come. . . . On [Her] forehead is the serpeant symbol of wisdom. She is of the Sphinx type which died before the Romans went to Egypt—the type which belonged to a past when there were gods among men" (564). Jessop goes on to describe the physical qualities of this women that are Sphinx-like (her "brow," "nostril," "lip," "chin," and "smile") and asserts that she gives him "comfort," "knowledge," and "strength" (564). This use of an ancient Egyptian art object as the source of strength for an uninspired artist living in London clearly draws on romanticized representations of ancient Egyptian women, which were also common in the period.

As Ailise Bulfin has shown in "The Fiction of Gothic Egypt and British Imperial Paranoia: The Curse of the Suez Canal" (2011), popular fiction of the 1890s particularly drew on representations of Egypt as romanticized by the British but increasingly presented Egypt as hostile toward Britain as the century progressed and the British became more "paranoid" about the political situation in Egypt, especially regarding control of the Suez Canal, which threatened Britain's access to important trade routes (414–16). Bulfin does not discuss the work of women writers, focusing instead on late-Victorian male authors such as Guy Boothby, Arthur Conan Doyle, Richard Marsh, and Bram Stoker, but her analysis provides a helpful framework for understanding how British imperialist views shaped fictional representations of Egypt as Britain's interest in Egypt increased. She focuses on the appearance of the "curse tale," in which Egyptians function as "foreign invaders," in popular fiction; this type of tale appeared occasionally before the late 1860s, increased in appearance after the late 1860s and began to carry the "threat of retribution" to Britain for its involvement in the Suez Canal, and became widespread in its appearance in the 1890s (417–18). The romanticized vision of Egypt, especially ancient Egyptian women, found in Menpes's fictional piece, then, is one view of Egypt that appeared in newspapers and periodicals, but as seen in the piece about the relationship between Egypt and Britain by Traill, writers of nonfiction also recognized the "threat" Egypt presented to Britain that Bulfin has thoroughly analyzed in late-Victorian popular fiction.

Although ancient Egyptian women clearly were discussed in newspapers and periodicals, and although women readers were an important constituent in the reading public, many recent critical studies about Britain's understanding of ancient Egypt do not consider the degree to which women accessed these materials. Curl and Richards, whose work I already have discussed, do not explicitly address women's participation in Egyptomania, and Tim Jeal's *Explorers of the Nile* (2011), which traces the travels of David Livingstone, Richard Burton, and other men on the Nile, does not acknowledge that British women participated in the imperialist project in Egypt, either by traveling there or contributing to imperialist thought through their writings about Egypt. Still, some recent women scholars have acknowledged women's participation in the imperialist project through travel to Egypt. Deborah Logan, in *Harriet Martineau, Victorian Imperialism, and the Civilizing Mission* (2010), writes about Martineau's excitement about traveling down the Nile, especially after thinking that it would not be possible to go (185), and Lynn Parramore's *Reading the Sphinx: Ancient Egypt in Nineteenth-Century Literary Culture* (2008) analyzes the work of Lucie Duff-Gordon, who in *Letters from Egypt* (1865) wrote about her experience living in Egypt in an attempt to cure her tuberculosis, as well as Amelia Edwards, who went to Egypt in 1873 "on a whim," published *A Thousand Miles up the Nile* (1876) upon her return, and became one of the leading figures in London's late nineteenth-century Egyptology circle. Parramore's analysis of Edwards, in particular, takes up the ways in which gender, class, and race might influence a woman traveler's experience in Egypt: she highlights how Edwards and her companion, Lucy Renshawe, were interrogated about their reasons for visiting the country because they were women (139), and she discusses Edwards's reactions to the images of ancient Egyptian women she saw in tombs and temples during her visit, including an image of Cleopatra wearing a headdress that incorporates aspects of the important creation goddesses Maat, Hathor, and Isis (142; see Figure 1.1).[1]

Still, Logan's and Parramore's analyses focuses on travel narratives rather than the fictional representations that I focus on in this book, and my choice to focus on fictional representations helps to construct a larger body of analysis about how British women writers of a certain class encountered and responded to representations of ancient Egyptian women. As indicated in the introduction to this book, Nightingale and Glyn traveled to Egypt and drew on these experiences in their writing; and Bradley, Cooper, and Eliot, who had opportunities to travel to Egypt but did not go, had good access to information about ancient Egypt through texts such as John Gardner Wilkinson's *Manners and Customs of the Ancient Egyptians* (1836), the "most influential book" on the topic in the nineteenth century (Richards 17). Still, it is clear that attention to other ancient cultures, such as Greek and Roman cultures, took precedence over discussion of ancient Egyptian culture, and the discussion that did take place was rooted in imperialist views. Given the difficulty that women faced in gaining access to information about Egypt that might counteract imperialist perspectives, it is remarkable that the women writers discussed in this book knew as much as they did about Egyptian culture. That Eliot read Herodotus's accounts of Egypt in the original Greek (Wiesenfarth 142), and that Bradley and Cooper viewed Egyptian artifacts at the British Museum in the company of the poet Robert Browning (Ms. 45853), an encounter I will discuss in more detail in Chapter 4, made them unusual for women of their time. As the individual chapters of this book will show, Nightingale, Eliot, Field, and Glyn drew on this privileged knowledge of ancient Egypt to develop themes related to British women's emancipation, even if they often do not explicitly refer to this knowledge in their fictional representations.

Imperialist Discourse About Britain's Presence in Egypt

The imperialist discourse that informed British women writers' perspectives about Egyptian culture is part of a larger discussion among postcolonial theorists about Westerners' encounters with Eastern cultures in the nineteenth century because, as Bulfin indicates in her article about popular fiction of the 1890s, Egypt was a "focal point" for British discourse about the East (416). Edward Said's *Orientalism* (1978), which highlighted surface-level Orientalism and established the framework for examining nineteenth-century British literature's reliance on the West/East binary, is, of course, central to this discussion, as are the works of those critics who have critiqued, expanded, and complicated Said's theories, especially Gayatri Spivak's "Can the Subaltern Speak?" (1988), Sara Suleri's *The Rhetoric of English India* (1992), and Homi Bhabha's *The Location of Culture* (1994).[2] What is necessary here is not to replay the development of postcolonial theory, but to show in some detail how Egypt became a focal point for Britain and how the imperialist discourse used to discuss Egypt in Britain influenced British women writers' perspectives about Egypt. Britain's presence in Egypt in the late nineteenth and early twentieth centuries is well summarized in Jason Thompson's *A History of Egypt: From Earliest Times to the Present* (2008), which, along with Bulfin's account of how these events influenced popular fiction, can provide a framework for understanding how Nightingale, Eliot, Field, and Glyn would have been influenced by the developments in British imperialism in Egypt.

Thompson explains how Napoleon Bonaparte's 1789 "expedition" into Egypt marks the beginning of modern Egypt, since Napoleon wanted to interrupt British contact with India, even though he presented himself as there to liberate Egypt from the Mamluks (219). And Bulfin indicates that the occasional appearance of Egyptian themes in popular fiction at midcentury can be attributed to "the cultural fascination with Egypt stimulated by Napoleon's 1798 expedition" (417). Certainly, we see that cultural fascination in Nightingale's writing about Egypt as she prepared for her 1849 trip there. As I will detail in my chapter about her, her preparation for the trip was extensive. She read many of the key British texts about Egypt and took certain books with her, so she could refer to them while traveling. But unlike the popular fiction produced by the male authors that Bulfin discusses, the women writers I discuss do not always translate their fascination with Egypt into their literary work, precisely because their understanding of women's emancipation did not include Egyptian women. Napoleon's 1798 expedition and subsequent events in Egypt's history were important to them, but their interest in women's emancipation shaped different literary responses than those found in male-authored popular fiction.

Thompson details the arrival of British troops shortly after Napoleon, Napoleon's retreat in August 1799, and Britain's decision to remain in Egypt after the final French defeat in March 1801 (220–22). While the British withdrew according to the Treaty of Amiens in March 1803, taking with them many of the Egyptian archaeological treasures found by the French (including the Rosetta Stone), they would return in 1807, in order to ensure grain supply would not be cut off, due to a deteriorating relationship with the Ottomans (222–23, 225). The Ottomans were in control of Egypt via Muhammad Ali, whose ability to play competing groups (the Mamluks, the Albanians, and the Ottomans) against each other had gained him the position of pasha, second in command to the sultan in Istanbul (224). Although the British invasion in 1807 was unsuccessful, England again exerted its influence on Egypt in the 1820s and 1830s, first by helping the Greeks gain independence from the Ottomans (who relied on Egyptian troops in their battles) in 1827 and then by pushing back Egyptian troops from Syria in 1839, when Ali, angered that the Ottomans had not granted him Syria in return for supplying troops during the Greek crisis, fought the Ottomans for Syria (232–33). After pushing back troops, Britain established itself in Alexandria and continued to use its influence when it thought necessary as three pashas (Ali's grandson, Abbas Hilmy I; Ali's fourth son, Muhammad Said; and son of Ali's general, Ismail Ibrahim) took varying approaches to modernizing Egypt in the mid to late 1800s (235–41). Under Said, who facilitated the building of the Suez Canal through his friendship with the French consul Ferdinand de Lesseps, Britain was careful to monitor the progress of a structure that would be key to its access to the Far East (237), and under Ibrahim, who was the most "pro-Western" of the three pashas, Britons were attracted to Egypt along with other Europeans by Ibrahim's attention to cultural development (241). Inspired by Napoleon III's new Paris, Ibrahim tried to make Cairo into a "Paris along the Nile," demolishing homes to build wide boulevards and bringing opera to the theatres in the 1860s (241). Many Europeans who came to Egypt during this time, Thompson argues, came "because of the Bible," believing that "scenes in Egypt [were] somehow more convincingly biblical than the ones they saw in Palestine" (241).

This is the Egypt to which Nightingale and her contemporaries traveled, and as I already have indicated, as the century progressed, many Europeans took advantage of commercial travel packages through agencies such as Thomas Cook, which made travel to Egypt more convenient (242–44). The biblical draw of Egypt that brought earlier writers such as Nightingale to the country also would be relevant to later writers such as Eliot, whose interest in the Judaic roots of Christianity made Egypt enticing. Though Eliot never traveled to Egypt (despite a desire to do so), she and her generation understood the imperialist advantages of British involvement in Egyptian politics, which were often articulated via religious discourse. As Susan Meyer explains in "'Safely to Their Own Borders': Proto-Zionism, Feminism, and Nationalism in *Daniel Deronda*" (1993), one aspect of the biblical draw of Egypt was tied to Britain's interest in advocating for a Jewish homeland in Palestine, after the British pushed Egyptian troops back from Syria in 1839. As Meyer indicates, other European powers, especially France and Russia, had established themselves as "protectors" of "particular populations" of the Ottoman Empire (i.e., the French advocated for Catholics and the Russians advocated for Greek Christians), and Britain used advocacy for Jews as a way to "check another Egyptian invasion" of Syria (748–49). Though English Jews remained skeptical about Britain's motivation for such advocacy and did not embrace Zionism until the early 1880s, when anti-Semitism in Russia heightened concern among English Jews about their community's future, this context certainly played a role in the literary work produced in England at the time, as we will see in my chapter about Eliot. Still, the impact of Egypt's political situation is not always the incorporation of Egyptian themes, as Bulfin has argued for late Victorian, male-authored popular fiction. As Meyer convincingly argues, the political situation for Jews in England at this time results in the suppression of certain representations. In her view, "female transgression," as embodied by Daniel Deronda's Jewish mother, is "suppressed" in Eliot's novel (743), and I will argue that this context also suppresses the use of ancient Egyptian women to represent female transgression in the novel.

While many Europeans were attracted to Egypt because of Ismail Ibrahim's incorporation of European culture in the 1860s, his "lavish" spending sent the country into debt in the early 1870s, and by 1875, Egypt was bankrupt (Thompson 248). The Caisse de la Dette Publique, an organization consisting of representatives from Britain, France, Italy, and Austria, stepped in to control the debt, and Ibrahim was eventually sent into exile (249). With a new leader, Khedive Tewfiq, in power and Evelyn Baring (Lord Cromer) in Egypt on behalf of Britain, Egyptian nationalists were unhappy, and the Egyptian cabinet declared war on Britain in 1882 (250–51). The British promptly defeated nationalist troops and began what turned out to be a 70-year occupation (253). Although the "Protectorate" would be lifted in 1922, Britain retained many of its powers until 1936, when the Anglo-Egyptian Treaty finally removed most of the "Reserved Points" that had ensured the British government's power in Egypt (280). The Egypt known to Bradley and Cooper, as well as to Glyn, then, was one in which British officers controlled the Egyptian government, and the Egyptian khedive followed Britain's lead. Every Egyptian government minister had a British adviser (255), and much of the decision-making occurred in exclusive British clubs, such as the Gazira Sporting Club and the Turf Club (260). Cromer's attitude toward Tewfiq and other Egyptian officials, Thompson explains, was one of contempt, a belief that Egyptians could not govern themselves, and this view was disseminated to the British public (254). Furthermore, British officials saw Egyptian society as land to be used but not improved in other ways: money went toward agricultural projects, while improvements in manufacturing and education were purposely halted (258).

Although little of this world would be seen directly in the work produced by Bradley and Cooper because, I argue, their own European aestheticist interests outweighed their interest in fully engaging Eastern culture, much of this world would be seen in the work produced by Glyn. Though Glyn did not share the obsession for the Egyptian mummy held by the late-Victorian male authors discussed by Bulfin, much of what Bulfin argues about popular fiction, especially with regard to the "mummy romance," in which "an encounter between a beautiful female mummy and some variety of imperial Englishman awakes an eternal but ultimately doomed passion" (419), can be applied to Glyn's work. In Glyn's cross-cultural romance, *Three Weeks* (1907), an Eastern goddess encounters an Englishman who loves but cannot keep this goddess in the material world. The Egyptian qualities of this goddess are replaced with Greek and British qualities over the course of the novel, but the Egyptian scenes in the novel are drawn directly from Glyn's own experiences in the British high-society circle that populated Egypt in the later years of British occupation.

It is not surprising, given the imperialist attitude of Britain toward Egypt, that British women writers had a limited perspective of Egypt and turned to representations of ancient Greek women rather than Egyptian women, since ancient Greek women were more familiar and less threatening within British culture. While Eliot's interest in religion, history, and linguistics led her to pursue a more complex understanding of Egypt than many of her contemporaries, other women writers did not (or could not) pursue the same level of understanding. Bradley and Cooper's lack of interest about Egypt, especially next to their passion for Greek and Italian culture, is striking but does make sense, given the historical context of Britain's occupation of Egypt. And, by the time Glyn, who had close ties to British administrators, was visiting and writing about Egypt, the separation between British leaders and Egyptian government officials, not to mention the Egyptian public, was so strong that Glyn could not experience Egypt as a rich and varied culture. As I explain in my chapter about Glyn, though she often believed she was having authentic cultural experiences in Egypt, the Egypt she experienced was mostly an imitation of British society life, corresponding very closely to Thompson's description of 1900s Egypt: "As ever-increasing numbers of British official arrived in Egypt, they crystallized into a separate community. Many among the earlier generations of British travelers . . . had at least superficially delved into Egyptian society. . . . No longer. The new British administrators had almost no contact with Egyptians apart from the men they worked with at the ministries" (259). Even Glyn herself recognized this as problematic, writing of her own attempts to experience Egyptian culture in a way her friends did not, and yet she still was "bound by an English eye" as she incorporated her knowledge of Egypt into her literary work, presenting a view of the country that was thoroughly romanticized.

Women Writers' Perceptions of Contemporary and Ancient Egyptian Women

When the women writers discussed in this book did engage Egyptian women, they gravitated toward representations of ancient Egyptian goddesses rather than real-life, contemporary Egyptian women, who had been thoroughly denigrated by British culture, which saw the influence of Arab/Muslim culture in Egypt as threatening. As Jill Matus points out in "The 'Eastern-Woman Question': Martineau and Nightingale Visit the Harem" (1999), Edward Lane's *An Account of the Manners and Customs of the Modern Egyptians* (1836) had a strong influence on British perceptions of contemporary Egyptian women, since it was "required reading for many travellers" (70). Lane, whose book was read by both Nightingale and Eliot (Vallée, *Florence Nightingale on Mysticism* 124; Wiesenfarth, *A Writer's Notebook* 110, 207–08), presented Egyptian women as sexually corrupt, in part because their husbands encouraged such behavior, and Lane argued that the *Arabian Nights*, one of Glyn's favorite books (Glyn, *Romantic Adventure* 105), was a realistic depiction of Egyptian life (Matus 70). Matus's characterization only partially captures the sentiment with which Lane writes about Egyptian people. In the chapter about "Character," Lane argues that although modern Egyptians possess some positive qualities, such as "religious pride" (377), "cheerfulness" (393), "hospitality" (394), "gradicude" (396), "filial piety" (400), and "love of country" (401), they also are "indolen[t]" (402), "obstinate" (402), and "libidinous" (403)— which, like Wilkinson, Lane credits to their "hot climate" but also "the institution of polygamy" (403).

Lane cites the Koran as the source for the idea that, even in ancient times, Egypt was "the abode of the wicked," and he applies this characterization to modern Egypt (403). In modern Egypt, writes Lane, the "most immodest freedom of conversation" exists in "both sexes," even among "the most virtuous and respectable women," who use language in the company of men that "many prostitutes in [England] would abstain from" (404). Further, Egyptian women are "the most licentious in their feelings of all females who lay claim to be considered as members of a civilized nation" (404). They have so much "liberty," they "are not considered safe, unless under lock and key," and they "possess a degree of cunning in the management of their intrigues that the most prudent and careful husband cannot guard against" and "the husband himself is made the unconscious means of gratifying his wife's criminal propensities" (404). Lane admits the belief held by urban men—that almost all the women "would intrigue if they could do so without danger," a view parallel to that expressed in the *Arabian Nights* (404)—is "over-severe," since women of the middle or upper classes cannot allow lovers in their homes and cannot go to the home of married or unmarried men without attracting attention (405). Still, according to Lane, "many of the women of Egypt engage in intrigue notwithstanding such risks. . . . Among the females of the lower orders, intrigues are more easily accomplished, and frequent" (405).

By reading the views of writers such as Lane, Matus argues, women travelers were "primed" for an imperialist perspective about Egyptian women before they even arrived in the country (70). Further, Matus asserts that travel narratives by nineteenth-century women writers such as Harriet Martineau's *Eastern Life: Past and Present* (1848), which Nightingale read while traveling in Egypt (Vallée, *Florence Nightingale on Mysticism* 238), do not reverse Lane's representation of modern Egyptian women as "libidinous and lascivious"

(Matus 70). Martineau's narrative simply "changes the emphasis," by focusing on "the enormous costs of living in thrall to sex" (70). Martineau focuses on the "boredom" and "passivity" evident in the women who live in harems, and she characterizes the Egyptian harem itself as "hell upon earth" (70, 68). Matus does see Martineau as indirectly making the "feminist argument linking social health and the position of women," since Martineau recognizes that the "boredom" seen in harem women is an example of how women's intellect becomes "stunted" because they are "valued only for their bodies" (71). Still, Martineau struggles to see harem women as anything more than prostitutes (71), confirming that she only slightly revises Lane's characterization of Egyptians as worse than prostitutes. Also, though Matus does not highlight this, Martineau's entire discussion of harems is framed as an experience that affects Martineau so significantly, she comes away from her visits to two harems with "a heaviness of heart greater than [she] has ever brought away from Deaf and Dumb Schools, Lunatic Asylums, or even Prisons" (259). Clearly, Martineau still possesses an imperialist view that prevents her from seeing women who inhabit harems as anything more than slaves. Further, Martineau cites as authorities both Wilkinson, who was "by his books, a daily benefactor to us in Egypt" (iv), and Lane, whose "generosity" as a "public benefactor" through his scholarship she valued (258).

Martineau's characterization of the Egyptian harem as "hell upon earth" is echoed by Nightingale in her letters, when she contrasts a dispensary run by nuns to Said Pacha's harem, both of which she visited on the same day: "[I]f heaven and hell exist on this earth . . . it is in the two worlds I saw on that one morning: the dispensary and the hareem" (Nightingale, *Florence Nightingale on Mysticism* 462). In addition, Nightingale also characterizes the contemporary Egyptian women she comes across in her travels as nonhuman: the poor Egyptian women helped by the Sisters of St. Vincent de Paul are "mere beasts" (147); one working Egyptian woman "looks for all the world like an elephant; her hideous black veil fastened on the top of her nose is just like a trunk" (153); and "in their great black shrouds, twining their wild arms about," the Arab/Muslim women at the mosques that Nightingale visits "look like everything but a human being!" (165). Seeing these women as nonhuman, Nightingale also cannot see these women in the roles that most British women occupy: twice, she comments that the Arab/Muslim Egyptian woman is "not a wife, nor a mother" but a "servant" to her husband, who is her "master" (157, 338). In contrast, Nightingale believed that ancient Egyptian women "had a vocation, a profession, provided for them in their religion, independent of their wifedom" (338), and it is to representations of ancient Egyptian women that writers such as Nightingale, Eliot, Field, and Glyn turn when they do represent Egyptian women.

Unlike representations of contemporary Egyptian women, which regularly appear with negative connotations attached, representations of ancient Egyptian women could be referenced at a safer distance, from a perspective that did not require direct engagement with the current politics of imperialist Britain, such as the 1876–1877 Constantinople Conference at which the Great Powers attempted to resolve recent rebellions against the Sultan, which Eliot references as "the terrible Eastern question" in her letters (6:343). Most twenty-first-century readers will be familiar with the Greek goddesses referenced by the writers discussed in this book,[3] but readers may be less familiar with the key goddesses of ancient Egypt, so it is worth providing background information here about those known to Nightingale, Eliot, Field, and Glyn and also referred to by the modern Egyptian women writers I discuss in Chapter 6 of this book. Like ancient Greek goddesses, these ancient Egyptian goddesses are associated with love, marriage, and childbirth, but their creation abilities are more strongly emphasized than those of ancient Greek goddesses, whose roles in these areas were limited to their own families. The creation goddesses Maat, Nut, Hathor, and Isis—who not only contributed to the creation of their own families but also to the creation of the whole world—are referred to frequently, as are the wives of ancient Egyptian rulers, such as Nefertari, who often was depicted making offerings to the creation goddesses. Maat, wife of the god Thoth, is central to the creation myth in that she helped stabilize an unstable universe (Lesko 268–69), and Nut, as goddess of the sky, is central because she protects both heavenly gods and earthly beings by providing a buffer between the two worlds (Hart 145). Nut is depicted as both a human and a cow (Hart 144), which connects her to Hathor, the goddess of love, beauty, and motherhood whose work in these areas connects the mortal and immortal worlds (Hart 76, 80). Like Nut, Hathor can appear as either human or animal, and she often appears with aspects of both: a human face with cow horns or ears (Barrett 59). Hathor and Isis, who is also associated with motherhood and often shown "suckling" the falcon-god Horus with "divine milk" (Hart 102), are the goddesses to whom the wives of ancient Egyptian rulers, such as Nefertari, typically make sacrifices (Lesko 121–22). Further, although Cleopatra lived more than a thousand years after Nefertari, she is also important, since writers such as Field and Glyn understood ancient Egyptian culture primarily through their knowledge of Cleopatra. Cleopatra, a mother herself, drew on images of ancient goddesses, especially Isis, to present herself as life-giving rather than life-taking in Ptolemy-ruled Egypt. She more commonly came to be depicted as a seducer and manipulator, first by Graeco-Roman historians and later by literary writers, who tended to follow Shakespeare's depiction of her in his 1606 play *Antony and Cleopatra* (Witt 223; Tyldesley 150; Wyke 251; Bate and Rasmussen 157–59). But, she originally presented herself as life-giving, precisely because she wanted to link herself to ancient Egyptian goddesses.

Although Egyptian goddesses had a more important role in the mythology about the creation and protection of the world than did Greek goddesses, there are connections between these two groups of women. Egyptian goddesses became important in Greek culture beginning in the seventh century BCE, when Greek explorers were encouraged to come to Egypt by King Psammetichus (Psamtek) and took back both material goods and cultural traditions (Freeman 158). In *Isis in the Ancient World* (1997), R. E. Witt explains that not only did the Athenians build temples to Isis (113), but symbols associated with Isis, such as the sistrum and the hydreion, were used in sculptures of Greek women, especially Demeter, goddess of the harvest (75; see Figure 1.2). Still, Witt also explains that not every Egyptian goddess could be incorporated into Greek culture easily. Isis was relatively easy to incorporate, since she ensured Egypt was a productive land by shedding tears and causing the Nile to rise, a narrative that meshed well with Greek narratives about Demeter (14–16). On the other hand, Hathor, with her animal features, was more difficult to reconcile with the Greek ideal of beauty, as seen in Venus; it also was difficult to reconcile Hathor's orientation toward the sky with the sea-oriented character of Venus (123). As a result, it was not uncommon to see Isis incorporated into ancient Greek art, whereas it was less common to see Hathor incorporated. Isis even makes it into ancient Roman art, with images of her appearing in Italian frescoes in the ruins of Vesuvius (81–82).

Certainly, there are other ancient women used by nineteenth-century writers not discussed in this book, but these are the figures that emerge in the work of the writers I discuss, suggesting that powerful women who still retained the feminine characteristics of life-giver were appealing to British women authors as they negotiated how to write about their own emancipation. Still, as I have shown in the introduction to this book, "color" remained an important factor in how British women responded to ancient cultures. As I discuss in the next section, British women writers often perceived Greek culture as "purely" white and Egyptian culture as composed of "mixed" races, another factor that encouraged British women writers to represent Greek goddesses rather than Egyptian ones when writing about their own emancipation.

Other British Writers' Representations of Ancient Egyptian Women

The visions for emancipation produced by Nightingale, Eliot, Field, and Glyn should be seen in the context of other nineteenth-century British literary writers, both women and men, who incorporated ancient Egyptian imagery into their work. Not surprisingly, those who incorporated ancient

Greek imagery have been more fully discussed than those who used ancient Egyptian imagery. Linda Dowling's *Hellenism and Homosexuality in Victorian Oxford* (1994) was key in establishing a body of criticism that understands ancient Greek culture as a site for expressing sexual desire, especially homosexual desire. Dowling, who traces how the study of Greek through the tutorial system at Oxford University in the 1830s opened a space for "homosocial bonding," examines the use of Greek ideals in the work of a later generation of Oxford students, especially John Addington Symonds, Walter Pater, and Oscar Wilde. More recently, Stefano Evangelista and T. D. Olverson, whose critical work I discuss in more detail in my chapter about Field, have extended Dowling's work, discussing ancient Greece as a site for expressing sexual desire in the work of Pater and Wilde but also late-Victorian women aesthetes, such as Field, Vernon Lee, and Amy Levy. As previously mentioned, Olverson's work is especially helpful in understanding why British women writers often use ancient Greek imagery rather than that of ancient Egypt, since they were inculturated into believing that Greek "heritage" was "purely Caucasian . . . unmixed with Egyptian or Semitic influences" (9). While some women writers recognized this "racist imperialist agenda" as problematic, others were "enamoured" by the "white light" of Greek sculpture (9).

Victorians' tendency to separate Greek and Egyptian culture is also discussed in Simon Goldhill's *Victorian Culture and Classical Antiquity: Art, Opera, Fiction, and the Proclamation of Modernity* (2011), which shows the problem with separating these two cultures, since Egyptians clearly were a part of Greek culture. For example, Goldhill analyzes Edward Bulwer Lytton's *The Last Days of Pompeii* (1834) for its engagement with the various ethnicities, nationalities, and religious groups present in first-century CE Rome (195). The "Greeks, Romans, Egyptians, and Christians" in the novel are first shown to be distinctly "separate," but ultimately, "the Greeks transcend all the other groups by becoming a new sort of Christian" (195). The primary Egyptian in the novel, Arbaces, "fits easily into the standard novelistic stereotypes of ancient Egypt . . . dangerous, tyrannical, and corrupt," but Arbaces's character also "makes the claim for the primacy of Egypt . . . Egypt as the true origin of Western culture" (197). Although Goldhill brings attention to the presence of Egyptians in ancient Greek and Roman culture, his examples focus primarily on male Egyptian characters in British novels, so more discussion of British writers' representations of ancient Egyptian *women* still is needed. In light of this, it is worth briefly discussing some of the authors who have engaged this topic but are not included in the chapters in this book, as a way to contextualize the work of Nightingale, Eliot, Field, and Glyn.

Victorian male writers, who sometimes engaged Egyptian culture more fully than the women writers discussed in this book, produced representations that were strongly Orientalist, exoticizing Egyptian culture as a way to tantalize the audience. H. Rider Haggard's novel *Cleopatra* (1889) and Gerald Massey's poem "The Aryan Mother" (1870) deserve consideration here, since their representations of Eastern women shaped the broader debate in Victorian culture about appropriate roles for British women—or, as it was commonly called, the "Woman Question." Haggard's *Cleopatra*—which details Cleopatra's death after the Battle of Actium from the perspective of one of Isis's priests, Harmachis—is particularly relevant, since it was written shortly after the publication of *She* (1887), Haggard's most direct response to the debate over the position of Victorian women. Patricia Murphy, in "The Gendering of History in *She*" (1999), characterizes *She*, in which a "white" (Arab) queen named Ayesha rules over African tribes but also dominates over the British male explorers who encounter her in Africa, as "a thinly disguised allegorical admonition to recognize and dispel the threat that the New Woman posed to late-Victorian society" (747), and Andrew Stauffer, in the introduction to the 2006 Broadview edition of *She,* links Haggard's famous "femme fatale" to Cleopatra, writing that Ayesha is yet another threatening woman figure in "a long tradition of male fantasy that includes Homer's Circe, Shakespeare's Cleopatra, and Keats's 'La Belle Dame sans Merci'" (22).

To write *Cleopatra*, Haggard traveled to Egypt in January 1887, visiting sites that would provide the inspiration for his novel. Writing about this experience in his autobiography, *The Days of My Life* (1926), Haggard recalls visiting the tomb of Seti, where bats flying about the tomb like "dancers in a ghostly dance" provided inspiration for the "great bat" depicted in *Cleopatra*: "I incarnated them all in the great bat that was a spirit which haunted the pyramid where Cleopatra and her lover, Harmachis, sought the treasure of the Pharaoh, Men-kau-ra" (260). Certainly, Haggard's Cleopatra possesses the same seductive but threatening qualities Ayesha possesses, and in an article about the influence of Haggard's *Cleopatra* on Edgar Rice Burroughs's *A Princess of Mars* (1917), Richard Kyle confirms this likeness, arguing that Haggard's Cleopatra is manipulative in her seduction not just of Antony but also of Harmachis, since Cleopatra's sexuality causes Harmachis's—and Egypt's—downfall (117). Sarah Hatchuel also emphasizes Haggard's representation of Cleopatra as threatening in *Shakespeare and the Cleopatra/Caesar Intertext: Sequel, Conflation, Remake* (2011), asserting that Haggard depicts Cleopatra "as a powerful and extraordinary woman, but also as a decadent imposter and deceiver, a cunning thief and effective poisoner" (29–30).

While Haggard presents Cleopatra as yet another seductive and threatening woman who might symbolize the emancipated "New Woman" in Victorian Britain, Gerald Massey's poem "The Aryan Mother" (1870) presents a European matriarch as a powerful force in the world because of her ties to ancient Egyptian women. The poem opens with the Aryan Mother characterized as a "phantom-form, majestic in its gloom" (1), who worries over the state of the world, "Mournfully [looking] across a Chasm deep as doom" (2). Massey's emphasis on the important role the Aryan mother plays in the future of the world reflects Massey's belief, articulated in his 1907 study *Ancient Egypt: The Light of the World*, that women figures in Aryan folktales possessed life-giving qualities, which could be directly traced to similar qualities possessed by ancient Egyptian goddesses. For example, Massey argues that the tale of "Sleeping Beauty" can be seen as parallel to the story of Hathor, one of the many life-giving women figures in Egyptian mythology: "The Moon-Goddess is the lovely young lady sleeping in Amenta waiting for her deliverer, the Young Solar God, to come and wake her with the Lover's kiss. She was Hathor, called the Princess in her Lunar character; and he was the all-conquering Horus" (24). In Massey's poem, the link between the Aryan Mother and ancient Egyptian women is explicit when Massey writes that the Aryan Mother "is the Ancient Mother rising, sphinx-like . . . To plead with those who will not hear" (5). Like ancient Egyptian women, the Aryan Mother has life-giving qualities because she "brought forth" men of diverse ethnic backgrounds, both "Her dusky Indians and her great white Heroes of the North" (7–8).

As with Haggard's representations, Massey's representations appear intended to shape discussions about the "Woman Question," since Massey expressed strong opinions about the appropriate roles for women during his British and American tours in the late 1880s (Shaw n. pag.). In "The Coming Religion" (1887), one of his published lectures, Massey rejects the idea that women were responsible for men's downfall, as Haggard suggests in *Cleopatra*, but still places the responsibility for men's well-being on women, writing: "So far from Woman having been the cause of any pretended Fall of man, she has been the true Saviour of humanity; or rather, the main instrument for saving because more open to the Divine influence, which I hold to be for ever working to prevent the propagation of man's worser moods and personification of his baser self" (n. pag.). Though David Shaw comments in his biography of Massey, *Gerald Massey: Chartist, Poet, Radical, and Freethinker*, that "Women's liberation movements would have been proud of [Massey]," since "he considered that the Fall of Man was being gradually superseded by the Ascent of Woman" (n. pag.), Massey's thoughts about woman's ascent in "The Coming Religion" are followed by comments that urge women to follow a traditional role, that of devoted motherhood. Writes Massey, "The truth is, that woman at her best and noblest must be monarch of the marriage-bed. We must begin in the creatory if we are to benefit the race, and the woman has got to rescue and take possession of herself, and consciously assume all the responsibilities of maternity, on behalf of the children" (n. pag.). While Massey made some statements about woman's suffrage that could be interpreted as supporting the cause, he clearly believed that a woman was, first and foremost, meant to be a man's "helpmate" (Flower 14–15).

Though Massey's and Haggard's representations of ancient Egyptian women helped shape debate about the "Woman Question," their contributions primarily uphold stereotypes about powerful women—that their power is typically negative, since they act mainly as seducers of men, or when their power is positive, it is a result of their status as procreative mothers. Further, their tendency to approach ancient Egyptian women in a similar light, with Isis and Cleopatra representing the polar opposites of good mother and bad mistress, illustrate their patriarchal and imperialist approach to Egyptian women, since they map already existing conceptions about British women onto Egyptian women. Still, Haggard's and Massey's representations do provide a framework through which to consider the works of women writers, since women writers were immersed in the same patriarchal and imperialist discourse. Nevertheless, the women writers discussed in this book were more invested in breaking from stereotypes about women, even if they did not always succeed in doing so. Because women writers had a vested interest in breaking stereotypes about roles for women in nineteenth-century culture, it is important to consider some of the women writers not included in this book who represented ancient Egyptian women, in order to see how their representations followed or departed from those by Haggard and Massey. As I have already mentioned, critics have focused attention on women such as Lucie Duff-Gordon, Amelia Edwards, and Harriet Martineau, who wrote nonfictional accounts about their experiences traveling in Egypt, which brought them face-to-face with their social position as British women, but there also are fictional representations by women writers such as Charlotte Brontë, Elizabeth Barrett Browning, Mathilde Blind, and Marie Corelli, whom critics have argued engaged ancient Egyptian women in more provocative ways than Haggard and Massey did.

Charlotte Brontë's novel *Villette* (1853) and Elizabeth Barrett Browning's long narrative poem *Aurora Leigh* (1856) are perhaps most relevant to providing a framework for the women writers discussed in this book, since both Brontë and Barrett Browning had an interest in what we now call women's agency. Criticism of their work covers well the ways in which Cleopatra was a figure that both discouraged and encouraged British women to consider their own cultural position as they built the argument for more agency for nineteenth-century British women. The comments made by Lucy Snowe about Cleopatra's portrait in Brontë's *Villette* have already been well discussed in Jill Matus's "Looking at Cleopatra: The Expression and Exhibition of Desire in *Villette*" (1994), Siân Griffiths's "Dissolving Pearls: Charlotte Brontë's Textual Hieroglyphics" (2007), and Aimillia Mohd Ramli's "From *Pasha* to Cleopatra and Vashti: The Oriental Other in Charlotte Brontë's *Villette*" (2010). Matus provides important comparisons between Lucy's description of Cleopatra's portrait; Edouard de Bievre's *Une Almé* (1842), the portrait upon which Brontë based Lucy's description; and other nineteenth-century paintings of Cleopatra. Matus argues that Brontë "magnifies and intensifies" the more "contained" portrayal of Cleopatra by de Bievre by "returning to earlier associations of exotic sexuality with the East" (354–55), but Matus also recognizes that Brontë did not necessarily perceive Cleopatra as a "coarse" woman, citing references to Cleopatra in Brontë's *Juvenilia* in which she is characterized as "majestic" and "learned" (355). Still, as Matus argues, Lucy does see Cleopatra as a "dark, indolent, gipsy-queen," linking her to "nineteenth-century stereotypes of Egyptian women" (355).

Building off Matus's criticism, Griffiths lays out well the ways in which Lucy's characterization of Cleopatra as lazy is indicative of Lucy's immersion in Victorian gender roles (53), and Ramli shows how these gender roles rely on Orientalist principles, especially when these principles are articulated by the dominant masculine figures in the novel (123). My own reading of Lucy's description of Cleopatra's portrait follows Matus, Griffiths, and Ramli in that I believe Lucy has a complex view of Cleopatra, since she both identifies with her and rejects her, but my reading puts more emphasis on the fact that her description is followed by a scene in which Lucy observes men looking at the portrait, a framework that resonates with my discussion, in Chapter 4, of Bradley and Cooper's experiences with male mentorship in their own viewing of artistic representations of women, including Eastern women such as Cleopatra. In *Villette*, after Lucy describes the portrait of Cleopatra as "represent[ing] a woman, considerably larger, I thought, than the life . . . half-reclined on a couch . . . [without] decent garments" (275), Lucy watches Colonel de Hamal, her friend Ginerva's suitor, who looks at the painting. Ramli quotes the line that sums up Lucy's impression of de Hamal's response to the painting—"[W]ith what admiration he gazed upon Cleopatra!"—and also mentions Lucy's comment that Cleopatra is "dusky," a characterization that situates Cleopatra as "a racialized 'other'" (Ramli 122–23). But Ramli does not discuss Lucy's thoughts about de Hamel's response to the painting: "I observed him for ten minutes, and perceived that he was exceedingly taken with this dusk and portly Venus of the Nile" (281), a description of Cleopatra that recognizes the connection between Greek and Egyptian cultures and one that presents Cleopatra as powerful in her effect on others. As the "Venus of the Nile," she holds de Hamal's attention.

Lucy continues to watch, as de Hamal is joined by Dr. Bretton (who also courts Ginerva but marries Polly instead). Lucy does not think the painting is "to [Bretton's] taste," since he "did not simper" as de Hamal does when he looks at it (281). Lucy walks the gallery with Bretton, with whom she enjoys talking about art and literature, since "without pretending to be a connoisseur, he always spoke his thought," "listened so kindly, so teachably," and "communicated information" with "lucid intelligence" (282). As they leave the gallery, Lucy asks Bretton "what he thought of the Cleopatra," to which he responds, "Pooh! . . . My mother is a better-looking woman. . . . I can only say, 'le volupteux' is little to my liking. Compare that mulatto with Ginerva!" (282). As Ramli points out, the final line spoken by Bretton is "chauvinistic," but what Ramli does not discuss is the mentor/mentee relationship between Bretton and Lucy here, which anticipates Bradley and Cooper's observations of European painters' representations of Eastern women, including Cleopatra, under the tutelage of Bernhard Berenson, who admittedly was more of a connoisseur than Bretton is. Neverthless, as I argue for Bradley and Cooper's situation, I believe Lucy is guided by male aesthetic principles, since she suggests that she has regularly discussed art and literature with Bretton, and this aesthetic training contributes to her imperialistic perspective about Cleopatra. Yet, Lucy's description of de Hamal's response to the painting also mocks the very act of observation, or the "male gaze" as Matus refers to it in her reading of the novel (354). The narration reads: "I had caught a glimpse of a head too pretty to belong to any other than the redoubted Colonel de Hamal. What a very finished, highly-polished little pate it was! What a figure, so trim and natty! What womanish feet and hands! How daintily he held a glass to one of his optics! With what admiration he gazed upon the Cleopatra! Oh, the man of sense! Oh, the refined gentleman of superior taste and tact!" (281). This feminizing of de Hamal—as well as Lucy's comment that even as Bretton doesn't like the painting, he finds "pleasure in looking over [de Hamal's] head; Dr Bretton, too, gazed on the Cleopatra" (281)—calls into question the aesthetic training Lucy receives from Bretton, suggesting she recognizes the problem of viewing Cleopatra through a solely masculine, imperialist perspective. As Matus, Griffiths, and Ramli argue, Lucy's negotiation of her own cultural position as a woman is complex, since it involves both identification with and rejection of ancient Egyptian women such as Cleopatra, something the representations by Haggard and Massey I have already discussed do not show.

Elizabeth Barrett Browning's representations of ancient Egyptian women in her long poem *Aurora Leigh* (1856) have been discussed indirectly or briefly by critics such as Susan Stanford Friedman, Gail Turley Houston, and Simon Avery and Rebecca Stott, though these references should be analyzed in more detail, since this poem also shows the complex manner in which women writers engaged ancient Egyptian women, especially in comparison to their male counterparts. Barrett Browning's interest in traveling to Egypt is confirmed in a letter to Robert Browning, in which she writes: "Why should we not see Athens, and Egypt too, and float down the mystical Nile, and stand in the shadow of the Pyramids?," to which Browning replied that they could go wherever Barrett Browning (or "Ba," as she was called) wanted (Browning, *Letters of Robert Browning* 444, 453). Further, Barrett Browning's nickname "Ba" has been interpreted by Julia Bolton Holloway, a medieval scholar and custodian of the English Cemetery in Florence, Italy, where Barrett Browning is buried, as equivalent to the Egyptian word for the portion of the soul that makes up individuality and is represented in Egyptian hieroglyphics as a bird with a human head (Holloway n. pag.).

Friedman's analysis of Barrett Browning's poem in "Gender and Genre Anxiety: Elizabeth Barrett Browning and H. D. as Epic Poets" (1986), a comparison of *Aurora Leigh* and H. D.'s *Helen in Egypt* (1961), does not discuss the explicit references to Egypt, including one to Cleopatra, in *Aurora Leigh*, but her presentation of Barrett Browning's poem next to H. D.'s suggests that there are implied references to Isis in the poem. Arguing that both H. D. and Barrett Browning use the lyric (a genre accessible to women writers in the nineteenth and early twentieth centuries) in order to revise the masculine tradition of the epic, Friedman shows how H. D.'s Helen is presented as the "incarnation of Isis" (220) and how both Helen and Aurora "return to the mother as symbol of love, sexuality, and the female body" to achieve their own emancipation from "patriarchy" (221), suggesting that the narrative of Aurora's emancipation should be understood in the context of British women comparing themselves to ancient Egyptian women as they assert agency.

Gail Turley Houston, in *Victorian Women Writers, Radical Grandmothers, and the Gendering of God* (2013), confirms that Barrett Browning takes a multicultural, even "polytheistic," approach in *Aurora Leigh*, by using diverse women figures such as Medusa and Lamia to examine Aurora's "want" for a mother figure (74, 90). Houston argues this use of diverse women figures is similar to the approach taken by earlier women writers, "radical grandmothers" such as Eliza Sharples, who merged "symbolic goddesses" such as Eve and Isis in her writing, suggesting the need for "female prophets" (90).[4] Like Friedman, Houston does not discuss the direct references to Egypt in the poem, and Simon Avery and Rebecca Stott, in *Elizabeth Barrett Browning* (2003), discuss only the passage in Book Three, where Aurora refers to Egypt in her description of London "at the day's decline," when the city "perish[es] in the mist / Like Pharaoh's armaments in the Deep Red Sea" (Barrett Browning 3:195–96). At this moment, Aurora asserts, "You feel as conquerors though you did not fight, / And you and Israel's other singing girls, / Ay, Miriam with them, sing the song you choose" (3:201–03). Avery and Stott rightly read this passage as one empowering British women, since "Miriam is given especial significance in Barrett Browning's recasting of the flight from Egypt narrative, supplanting her brother Moses, for she is the truth-teller, the narrator/observer, and she is also both sister and mother, the redeemer who placed Moses in the bull-rushes, thereby saving him from death and thrusting him into a new role as savior" (196).

My own reading of *Aurora Leigh* follows Avery and Stott's interest in the Egyptian context for reading Barrett Browning's poem, but I believe the imperialist aspects of these references are important to acknowledge and shape how we interpret Aurora's emancipation at the end of the poem. Avery and Stott overlook the fact that Aurora's use of Egypt in her description of London represents Egypt as an enemy, as the Pharaoh's armaments perish in the Red Sea, a line Barrett Browning draws from Exodus 15:4–5, and the other Egyptian references in the poem support the idea that Barrett Browning, like other nineteenth-century women writers, took an imperialist view of Egyptian women, even as they used these women to articulate their own emancipation. The first reference to Egypt in the poem is articulated by Romney, Aurora's cousin and suitor, when on Aurora's birthday, he tells her she may write as "well" or as "ill" as other women, but she cannot become a poet because "We want the Best in art now, or no art" (2:144, 149). He believes that no one has time "to sit upon a bank / And hear the cymbal tinkle in white hands," but when the hard work is done, "when Egypt's slain, I say, let Miriam sing" (2:169–71). This statement lays the groundwork for Aurora's later characterization of the Pharaoh's armaments in Book Three, and Aurora also rejects Egypt as a site for women's empowerment in Book Seven, when she characterizes her aunt, who watches over her every action and who is as much an obstacle to Aurora's emancipation as Romney is, as the "sucking asp to Cleopatra's breast" (2:863–64). While this characterization suggests that Aurora's aunt is only the asp and Aurora is Cleopatra, who might be liberated from the asp, Barrett Browning never returns to this image in her representation of Aurora's emancipation, and in Book Four, her characterization of English marriage as an institution in which women sacrifice themselves as "Indian widows" do upon pyres (4:195–202) suggests Barrett Browning follows the typical thinking, even among progressive nineteenth-century thinkers, that Eastern women are oppressed.

It is no surprise, then, that Barrett Browning does not directly develop Egyptian imagery to articulate Aurora's emancipation, using instead Greek, Roman, and Judeo-Christian imagery to articulate this emancipation, as Joyce Zonana has aptly shown in "The Embodied Muse: Elizabeth Barrett

Browning's *Aurora Leigh* and Feminist Poetics" (1989). As Zonana argues, Barrett Browning uses a range of admittedly "traditional, highly bifurcated images" of women from "Western literature" (248)—including Eve, Venus, Miriam, Psyche, Medusa, Lamia, Madonna, Danae, and Io—to chart how Aurora comes to recognize the various qualities of womanhood in other women (her aunt is Medusa, Lady Waldemar is Lamia, and Marian is the Madonna [250]) and then in herself, so she can become her own "muse," or source of empowerment at the end of the poem (259). Yet, by looking at Barrett Browning's use of references to Egypt, and especially at the reference to Aurora as a potential Cleopatra, we can see more fully how imperialist views influence which representations of womanhood are fully developed and which ones are not, despite Barrett Browning's knowledge about Egyptian culture. As Friedman and Houston have suggested, Barrett Browning does use implicit references to Isis, but her direct references to Cleopatra clearly are negative. My own view is that Barrett Browning's overall representation of ancient Egyptian women is more imperialist than Brontë's, but I do believe it is more complex than the representations seen in Haggard's and Massey's work.

Brontë's and Barrett Browning's representations indicate how women writers incorporated ancient Egyptian women into their visions for emancipation in the mid-nineteenth century, when British imperialism was still growing but not yet at its height. Toward the end of the century, writers such as Mathilde Blind and Marie Corelli also drew on Egyptian imagery in a manner that reflects a more thoroughly developed imperialist discourse about Egypt. Robert Fletcher's compelling essay on this issue in Blind's work, "'Heir of All the Universe': Evolutionary Epistemology in Mathilde Blind's *Birds of Passage: Songs of the Orient and Occident*" (2005), articulates well many of the same principles I use in this book, since he argues that Blind's writing about Egypt confirms her "participat[ion] in ideologies of imperialism" and how this participation helped to shape "the subjectivity of an 'independent woman' in the Victorian period" (436). Drawing on some of the same theoretical sources I use in this book, such as Inderpal Grewal's *Home and Harem: Nation, Gender, Empire, and the Cultures of Travel* (1996), Fletcher's reading of Blind's 1895 *Birds of Passage* collection is particularly helpful in understanding how late-Victorian women writers, who seem to be even more fully "bound by an English eye" than earlier women writers such as Brontë and Barrett Browning, represented ancient Egyptian women.

Fletcher asserts that Blind, who traveled to Egypt for brief visits to cure bronchitis in 1892 and 1894, "not surprisingly participates in . . . Orientalist historiography" by "assign[ing] Egyptian culture the status of ancient, static, pre-modern Other" in *Birds of Passage* (451–52). Blind's interest in ancient

Egyptian culture was fueled, in part, by her concern about the effects of British modernization on the country. She was among those opposed to the Aswan Dam proposal, which Cromer approved in 1898 despite knowledge it would flood the ancient monuments at Philae, and many of the poems in the first half of Blind's *Birds of Passage* focus on "deciphering the meaning" of sites such as Philae (444–45). Still, in the poems that focus on women, Fletcher argues that Blind moves toward Western concepts rather than developing Eastern ones as fully as she might. In "The Mirror of Diana," Blind favors ancient Greek women over ancient Egyptian women, since the Greek Diana remains "vital," while the "buried gods of Egypt lose their significance" (446). And, in "The Moon of Ramadân," those priests who served Isis in ancient Egypt have been eclipsed by Islamic priests (447). Islamic understanding of nature, as opposed to the poet's understanding of it, is presented as "naïve" and a "form of idolatry" (447), showing how Blind's imperialist view, albeit a revisioned Romantic Orientalism, affected her representation of ancient women. Further, as Fletcher shows, Blind's understanding of Muslim beliefs proves to be underdeveloped; in "Mourning Women," a sonnet about Muslim women, Blind draws on "an ahistorical and totalized understanding of Islam" (451) to characterize Islam as a religion that requires women "To take love's penalties without its prize!" and views their "souls" as "none fit for Paradise" (Blind 10, 14).

My own reading of the poems confirms Fletcher's interpretation, but it is worth noting that Fletcher does not comment directly on the lines about Isis in "The Moon of Ramadân" that appear before the lines about her priests, perhaps because they appear to be merely descriptive: "And Isis, Queen, whose sacred disk's / Horned splendor crowned her brow" (Blind 57–58). While the lines are descriptive, the straightforward quality of them provide a contrast to the indirect references to Isis in Barrett Browning's *Aurora Leigh* and the clearly negative references to Cleopatra in Barrett Browning's and Brontë's work. Given the imperialist discourse that had developed around a figure such as Cleopatra, the choice to refer to Isis instead of Cleopatra and to describe her in nostalgic but positive terms is significant. Still, it is notable that, across Blind's collection, the ancient Egyptian monuments play a significant role in Blind's representation of Egypt, which Fletcher points out was shaped by her tourist perspective on the country; she "comfortably traveled in Egypt under the care of Thomas Cook's steamers and modern tourist hotels, such as the landmark Shepheard's" (439). Though Blind was known for her "radical politics" and "feminism," I would agree with Fletcher's assessment that her presentation of the "independent woman" in *Birds of Passage* is "reliant nevertheless on binaries of 'East' and 'West' fundamental to imperialist ideology" (436).

In other words, Blind was "bound by an English eye" as fully as the women writers discussed in this book, and her work suggests that as British imperialist interest in Egypt grew, the absence of ancient Egyptian women was an important marker of the influence of imperialism on representations of British women's emancipation. As I have already noted, Bulfin's work shows how male-authored popular fiction responded to the Egyptian political situation in the late-Victorian period, and Blind's work follows trends in that genre more fully than those seen in earlier women writers such as Brontë and Barrett Browning, who used references to ancient Egyptian women very sparsely and within more European contexts, such as a Shakespearian context (Brontë) or a biblical context (Barrett Browning). With Blind's work, the Eastern context is more explicit via the title of the collection, as well as in poems in the collection that draw on the Romantic Orientalism of earlier male poets such as Lord Byron and Percy Shelley, whom Fletcher identifies as Blind's primary literary influences (438).

Egypt is prominent from the outset, with the poem "Welcome to Egypt" opening the collection and featuring, as Fletcher indicates, "the fertility of the contemporary Nile delta" and "the figure of a *live* Egyptian," which is the exception rather than the rule in the collection (439, emphasis mine). Though Blind makes Egypt central in a way not seen in the work of earlier British women writers, she also departs from the male-authored popular fiction of her own times by making Egypt a "life-giving" rather than threatening place. According to Fletcher, this life-giving quality is part of Blind's turn to Romantic Orientalism, "one of those Byronic moments, if you will, where the Orient's difference is attractive as a sign of dissatisfaction at home" (440). Yet, there still is a displacement of ancient Egyptian women in favor of other types of women, including contemporary Islamic women, as seen in "Mourning Women," a trend Bulfin also sees in male-authored popular fiction of the 1890s. Discussing Guy Boothby's *Pharos of Egypt* (1899), for example, Bulfin writes that Pharos, a fictional version of the Pharaoh of the Exile Merenptah's high priest Ptahmes, can be identified as a "disaffected modern Egyptian" because of his dress, which "bear[s] no resemblance to the dress of ancient Egypt" but "with the religion of Egypt's modern citizens," Islam (427). That Blind's work follows the trends found in male-authored popular fiction suggests the widespread influence of British imperialism by the mid-1890s, and the degree to which women writers were "bound by an English eye" as they wrote about their own emancipation.

Perhaps even more fully bound was Marie Corelli, whose work is known for being antifeminist at times and whose representation of ancient Egypt in her novel *Ziska* (1897) reflects the highly romanticized image of Egypt resulting from increased imperialism in latter part of the nineteenth century.

Ziska features an Egyptian woman whose exotic beauty leads European men to compete for her love, only to discover that she is a reincarnated ancient Egyptian courtesan who seeks, in the protagonist Armand Gervase, a contemporary version of her lover Araxes. Although Bradley Deane, whose work Bulfin draws on, mentions *Ziska* only briefly in "Mummy Fiction and the Occupation of Egypt: Imperialist Striptease" (2008), Deane suggests a way of reading this novel in its Egyptian context, since it is clear that Corelli's novel fits the criteria he establishes for mummy fiction, in which a woman wrapped like a mummy uses her "preserved . . . youthful beauty" to attract the "libidinous attention of modern British men," who are in Egypt as administrators of the protectorate during British occupation (384). Attracted to these mummy women, British men pursue cross-cultural romances that cannot be "consummated," says Deane, precisely because the British protectorate benefits from continued discussion of the "Egyptian Question" rather than its resolution (385).

Catherine Delyfer, in "New Woman Fiction, Gender and Empire: Egyptian Encounters and Subversions in Marie Corelli's *Ziska* (1896) and Victoria Cross's *Six Chapters of a Man's Life* (1903)" (2011), has extended Deane's work, though Delyfer argues that the relationship between Ziska and Gervase ultimately subverts traditional discourse about race and gender, challenging the notion that European men have the "right," and even the duty, to "dominate and control others" (160). While I find Delyfer's reading of the novel overly allegorical in its linking of colonial and gender narratives, Deane's analysis provides a strong framework for reading *Ziska* in its Egyptian context, though there is more that might be done with this context, since the novel also illustrates British women writers' tendency to use ancient Greek imagery as a contrast to ancient Egyptian imagery. Early in the novel, Ziska's "extraordinary" Egyptian beauty is contrasted to the "ordinary" Greek beauty of her rival, Helen Murray (17). At a costume ball not unlike those Glyn attended during her visits to Egypt during British occupation, Helen appears as "a Greek vestal," a virgin priestess of the goddess Hestia or Vesta, wearing "white, with a chaplet of silver myrtle-leaves round her hair" (34), while Ziska wears the ancient Egyptian costume of Charmazel, the mistress of the warrior Araxes. She is "clad in gleaming golden tissues and veiled in the old Egyptian fashion up to the eyes, with jewels [including an 'emerald-studded serpent'] about her waist, bosom and hair" (25, 27). At the ball, Helen doubts her ability to keep the primary male character Armand Gervase's attention when someone as striking as Ziska is present, but as the novel progresses, it is clear that the "extraordinary" Egyptian beauty of Ziska also is threatening. When Ziska kills Gervase at the end of the novel, so he can be reborn as her former lover, Araxes, she is described as completely "othered" because of her Eastern qualities. She is "thin and skeleton-like . . . no creature of flesh and blood . . . but some mysterious bodiless horror of the Supernatural" (151). This contrast between Helen's ordinary Greek beauty and Ziska's extraordinary ancient Egyptian beauty and the othering of Ziska for her Eastern difference is yet another manifestation of the romanticized view of Egypt presented by Corelli, a view I will take up in more detail in my chapter about Glyn, since Glyn read and commented on Corelli's novels.

Ultimately, the representations seen in the work of writers not included in this book provide an important framework for understanding those found in the work of Nightingale, Eliot, Field, and Glyn. Like their female peers, these women writers recognized that ancient Egyptian women could be an important source when articulating ideas about British women's emancipation, but they also remained "bound by an English eye" as they incorporated their knowledge of ancient cultures into their works. While their representations are not as strongly Orientalist as those found in the work of their male peers, their representations certainly reflect the influence of British imperialism on writers of both genders, and as we turn to discussion of the work of Nightingale, Eliot, Field, and Glyn, we will see the specific ways in which British imperialism shaped their nationalist, but not internationalist, visions for women's emancipation.

CHAPTER 2

Acting as "the right hand . . . of God": Christianized Egyptian Women and Religious Devotion as Emancipation in Florence Nightingale's Fictionalized Treatises

As described in the introduction to this book, Florence Nightingale's letter to her family as she approached Alexandria, Egypt, by sea in November 1849 highlights the imperialist tendency to separate East from West but also recognizes the intermingling of cultures across the Mediterranean, especially when Victorian travelers looked at these cultures as ancient civilizations that provided the foundations for contemporary British society. Similar to the travelers to Greece and Italy described by Jenkyns and Vance, who could not help but feel as though they were "travel[ling] backwards in time" as they encountered Mediterranean cultures (Jenkyns 44), Nightingale saw in Egypt the opportunity to gain greater understanding of the foundations of her own culture, and just as she had compared and contrasted Greece and Egypt on her way to Egypt, she would compare and contrast these countries on her return home in April 1850, when she spent nearly two months in Athens before heading to Italy for a short stay and then going back to England. Setting forth a number of contrasts between the two cultures in letters written to her family, Nightingale characterizes the Peloponnesian women she meets in Greece as a stark contrast to the women she had seen in Egypt: "dwarfs" compared to "the gigantic Egyptian race," but their "excessive cleanliness and attention to dress . . . is wonderful after Egypt" (McDonald, *Florence Nightingale's European Travels* 368). She also differentiates the "genius" of the two peoples, commenting that the Egyptian genius is one of "exalt[ing] God" while the Greeks' is their ability to "deif[y] man"

(378). Finally, the landscape of the two places differs significantly: Corfu is "the most lovely island in the world," with "colouring . . . like Guido's of St. Michael [a painting at the Church of the Immaculate Conception in Rome]," and "the solemnity of Egypt consists in its being all one uniform colour, all one light or one dark, while here the immense variety makes it look three times as big as it is" (363).

Nightingale's inclination to compare and contrast specific aspects of Greek and Egyptian culture is a clear marker of British women writers' struggle to negotiate the boundaries of West and East that were central to British imperialism, and this chapter shows how Nightingale encountered and assessed these boundaries as she traveled through countries where, perhaps for the first time, she recognized that the relationship between West and East was more complicated than it initially appeared. Gérard Vallée, in his introduction to Nightingale's letters about Egypt, indicates that Nightingale had some preparation for the intermingling of cultures she encountered, since her trip to Egypt was framed, in part, by her "knowledge of Greek art and mythology" (Vallée, *Florence Nightingale on Mysticism* 119). Further, Nightingale made a concerted effort to understand Egyptian culture on its own terms before she arrived, by consulting a number of books before embarking on her journey, including Lane's *An Account of the Manners and Customs of the Modern Egyptians* (1836), Wilkinson's *Manners and Customs of the Ancient Egyptians* (1837), and Martineau's *Eastern Life: Past and Present* (1848), all of which I have discussed in Chapter 1.[1] She also met with the German scholar Christian Carl Josias von Bunsen, who gave her the "*dernier mot*," or last word, on Egyptology before she left (118).

Nightingale went to Egypt, it seems, as well prepared as someone of her class, race, and gender could have, and Michael Calabria, in *Florence Nightingale in Egypt and Greece: Her Diary and "Visions"* (1997), articulates the impact of her experience in Egypt, arguing that Nightingale's writing about it on her return trip in 1850 laid the groundwork for her ideas in her best-known treatise, *Suggestions for Thought*, which Nightingale began drafting in 1852 and published privately in 1860 (McDonald, *Florence Nightingale's* Suggestions for Thought 23, 27). Analyzing a letter Nightingale wrote from Thebes in February 1850, which Calabria refers to as *Vision of Temples*, Calabria states, "At first glance, the *Vision* appears to be little more than an imaginative tale of ancient Egypt wrought by an enthusiastic tourist," but, in fact, it "serves as a vehicle by which Nightingale conveys the metaphysical essence of her own radical spiritual views" (8). For Calabria, *Vision of Temples* is a working out of two of the central ideas in *Suggestions for Thought*: "1) that humanity's concept of God is imperfect and 2) that humanity's comprehension of the divine nature increases through an evolution of consciousness" (121).

Together, *Vision of Temples* and *Suggestions for Thought* reveal that Nightingale "was essentially a mystic. At the heart of her spiritual creed was a belief in an omnipotent spirit of righteousness (God) whose very thoughts were manifest as immutable laws" (8).

Certainly, Nightingale's trip to Egypt was a pivotal point in the development of her spiritual journey, not just in terms of her development of an abstract spiritual creed but also in terms of the specific actions she would take as she lived according to this creed. The expectation placed on Nightingale by her family to marry rather than take up a profession is well known and has been discussed thoroughly by other critics. Cecil Woodham-Smith and Mark Bostridge, in their biographies of Nightingale, have articulated the relentless pressure Nightingale felt from her family, including the details surrounding Nightingale's reluctance to marry her cousin Henry Nicholson or her friend Richard Monckton Miles (Bostridge 77–78, 126; Woodham-Smith 36–38). Further, critics interested in feminist recovery of *Suggestions for Thought* as a treatise comparable to Victorian men's religious treatises, such as John Henry Newman's *Apologia Pro Vita Sua*, have shown how this familial pressure influenced Nightingale's writing of *Suggestions for Thought*. In one of the first feminist recovery essays about Nightingale's work, "Florence Nightingale's Feminist Complaint" (1981), Elaine Showalter argues that Nightingale presented the Victorian family as a "prison" where women are "enslaved to their mothers" (409), just as Nightingale had been enslaved by her "socially ambitious, intellectually lazy, and emotionally infantile" mother, Fanny (397). While this characterization of Nightingale's mother likely is meant to be provocative, more recent critics such as Claire Kahane, in "The Aesthetic Politics of Rage" (1996), and Ruth Y. Jenkins, in "Rewriting Female Subjectivity: Florence Nightingale's Revisionist Myth of 'Cassandra'" (1994), have affirmed that Nightingale's treatise should be read, at least to some degree, in the context of Nightingale's family history and certainly within the cultural context of the Victorian family. Given these familial contexts, it is easy to see that traveling abroad allowed Nightingale the chance to formulate the principles by which she wanted to live her life, independent of her family's expectations.

Calabria's attention to Nightingale's experience in Egypt as a significant influence upon the ideas central to *Suggestions for Thought* is important, since this context makes Nightingale's treatise, which seems abstract to many modern readers, more accessible. But, what the letter Calabria calls *Visions of Temples* does not reveal is the role that ancient Egyptian goddesses played in Nightingale's understanding of the parallels between ancient Egyptian religion and Christianity. In *Visions of Temples*, Nightingale briefly mentions the Luxor and Koorna temples, which were built for the goddesses representing

Mother Nature (123), but other letters from the Egyptian leg of Nightingale's trip better articulate the role these goddesses played in Nightingale's thinking. Furthermore, while Calabria and coauthor Janet Macrae show how Nightingale's experience in Egypt influenced certain sections of *Suggestions for Thought* in their edition of the treatise,[2] they do not take up the ways in which Nightingale's knowledge about ancient Egyptian goddesses influenced her writing about women's emancipation in *Suggestions for Thought*. Their discussion of the key passages about women's emancipation in the treatise, such as the well-known section about the stifling of women's creativity by English society's insistence that they work on creative projects at "odd moments" (110), are contextualized strictly within the Western tradition, particularly through the work of John Stuart Mill and Virginia Woolf.

Nightingale's writing about women's emancipation should be contextualized more fully in terms of West/East relations, and this chapter places *Suggestions for Thought* in a West/East context that more thoroughly acknowledges its Egyptian context in particular. I argue that Nightingale's trip to Egypt, sandwiched between travel to Italy and Greece, shaped the manner in which Nightingale presented women's emancipation in *Suggestions for Thought*. In particular, the visual representations of women Nightingale found first in paintings and sculptures in Italy and then in ancient temples in Egypt became sites for Nightingale to negotiate the intermingling of cultures she noticed as she sailed through the Mediterranean toward Alexandria. In Italy in 1847–1848, Nightingale was exposed her to artistic works that affirmed her Christian spiritual beliefs and helped her work through her emerging religious philosophy, in which artists played an important role in revealing God's perfect form to humans and in which women's spiritual development was the result of struggle to recognize this perfect form. Still, Nightingale's discussion of specific works of art during this leg of her trip reveals the ways in which her emerging religious philosophy relied on race hierarchies (the privileging of one race or ethnicity over another). Nightingale's reliance on these hierarchies developed more fully once she arrived in Egypt, where she experienced the intermingling of what she perceived as distinctly Western and Eastern cultures, and she negotiated this experience by assessing Egyptian culture—and Egyptian women—according to her religious philosophy, which acknowledged the role of Eastern religions in the development of Christianity but assumed a progression toward a Christian view of God. Nevertheless, the artistic representations she encountered in Egypt contributed significantly to her religious philosophy, since these representations paid homage to Egyptian gods in ways that were both similar to and different from the homage paid in European artistic representations to the Christian God that Nightingale worshipped. Further, the visual representations of ancient Egyptian women she saw presented women as integral to the expression of God's perfection, and this allowed Nightingale to consider the parallels between the status of women in Western and Eastern religion, parallels that were important to her thinking about the problem of women's emancipation as she wrote *Suggestions for Thought*.

Upon returning to England, Nightingale incorporated the artistic representations she encountered during her travels into the draft manuscript of *Suggestions for Thought*, which was written during a difficult time with family members, since they continued to resist her desire to follow her religious calling and work as a nurse. In the treatise, Nightingale refers to Egyptian culture when discussing the formation of religious belief, but the artistic representations she uses to articulate her religious philosophy through women characters are drawn primarily from the European legs of her trip. Although the fictional aspects of the draft manuscript were stripped from the 1860 privately printed version of the treatise, remnants of Nightingale's understanding of artistic representations of women during her travels can be found in the final version, which presents liberation via devotion to God as attainable only by certain kinds of women: white, upper- and middle-class women who possessed the biblical knowledge needed to be inspired by religious art, but also working-class English women and Eastern women who were able to embrace Christianity and exhibit the qualities expected from religiously devoted women. By rereading *Suggestions for Thought* with Nightingale's Egyptian experience in mind, we can better understand how Nightingale suppressed this experience as she wrote and why the vision of emancipation she articulates in *Suggestions for Thought* excluded most Eastern women, unless they were able to integrate into white, European culture via a Christian religious perspective.

*   *   *

While Nightingale has been discussed only selectively in critical studies about nineteenth-century women travelers—such as Billie Melman's *Women's Orients: English Women and the Middle East, 1718–1918* (1992), Maria H. Frawley's *A Wider Range: Travel Writing by Women in Victorian England* (1994), and Lynne Withey's *Grand Tours and Cook's Tours: A History of Leisure Travel, 1750–1915* (1997)—she was in many ways a typical nineteenth-century woman traveler. As Frawley indicates, women travelers went abroad with the expectation that they would obtain "a measure of cultural competence that derived not from education but from experience" (24), and Nightingale began her trip to Italy, Egypt, and Greece in 1847 with the expectation that she would see a variety of social institutions, especially religious institutions, as well as experience the art and culture of the countries she visited (McDonald, *Florence Nightingale's European Travels* 3). Nightingale perhaps differs from other women travelers in that she came to Mediterranean countries with a stronger interest in religious vocation as an alternative to marriage and an openness to learning about various world religions in an effort to work out her own religious philosophy. As Devon Fisher has shown in *Roman Catholic Saints and Early Victorian Literature: Conservatism, Liberalism, and the Emergence of Secular Culture* (2012), many British travelers to Italy in the nineteenth century felt anxiety about visiting Rome in particular because they would "confront . . . the Catholic question that England faced" (32), and McDonald confirms that "[c]onversion to Roman Catholicism, or 'going over to Rome,' was a subject of anguished consideration" for Nightingale (*Florence Nightingale's Theology* 326). Unlike her contemporaries, Nightingale was much more interested in what Roman Catholicism had to offer (she believed its strength was its articulation of the belief that "God still inspires mankind"), though she believed the Catholic Church lacked the "freedom of thought" that Protestantism advocated so strongly (McDonald, *Florence Nightingale's European Travels* 79). While she visited many Catholic churches in Italy and retreated to the Convent of the Sacred Heart (63), she did not consider converting to Catholicism during her trip, despite the fact that others in her circle, such as Henry Manning and Elizabeth Herbert, did consider it (81).

Nightingale's interest in Catholicism, and more broadly in all world religions, would influence her representation of Egyptian women, as we shall see, for though she wanted to learn about other world religions, like many women travelers, her British imperialist perspective prevented her from fully understanding some religions, especially Islam, a topic I will discuss in more detail later in this chapter. Still, as she traveled to Italy in 1847, she had a better appreciation of the art and culture she encountered than she had in 1837, when she first traveled there with her family. This time, she was more mature, had read more widely, and was better prepared to understand other cultures than she had been during her earlier trip (McDonald, *Florence Nightingale's European Travels* 3). Further, she had with her two invaluable resources for understanding culture, friends Charles and Selina Bracebridge, who not only understood the familial pressure Nightingale felt at the time (Bostridge 108–09) but also could help negotiate the cultural experiences she had on the trip. Selina seems to have been an especially helpful resource for appreciating art; while Nightingale sketched and had taken watercolor classes, Selina was a more accomplished visual artist, having studied with the watercolorist Samuel Prout.[3] Even without advanced artistic skills, Nightingale understood the power of the visual arts in recording travelers' experiences, and she often drew diagrams of particular places she had visited in her letters to her family, which accompanied her more detailed written descriptions. For example, when looking for a Minerva statue that her aunt Julia Smith wanted her to see, she included a detailed map of the Vatican, which she hoped would prompt her aunt's memory about the exact location: "I have looked at every Pallas statute and bust in the Vatican and cannot detect the expression she alludes to" (McDonald, *Florence Nightingale's European Travels* 250).

Nightingale's desire to see the statue that Smith had referred to because of its distinct "expression" is notable, since Nightingale's analysis of art in her letters from Italy often emphasizes how expression reveals a particular emotion, a key component in Nightingale's religious philosophy. Her philosophy acknowledged the process an individual undertook in developing devotion to God, and struggle, something Nightingale had experienced in her own spiritual journey, was an important part of the process. Nightingale preferred artistic depictions of people who had struggled but overcame their difficulties and, as a result, were closer to God. Christ's struggle was an obvious model for Nightingale to follow, and in her letters, she analyzes images of Christ according to whether they captured this emotional process. For example, she does not like Michelangelo's *Christ* in the Minerva because it is a "very irreverential Christ, a full-length statue holding a cross" (111), but she does appreciate Guido Reni's *Crucifixion* at San Lorenzo in Lucina because it depicts Christ as "him who had overcome, not him who was still suffering" (110).

In addition to images of Christ that depicted his triumph over suffering, Nightingale liked images of other biblical people who appeared secure in their emotions. She points out the "security of inspiration" seen in Isaiah's expression in Michelangelo's Sistine Chapel (151), and even when she views non-Christian works of art, she appreciates these works as long as they depict emotions related to overcoming struggle, as in an "Assyrian idol," who is "the very ideal of calm force" (68). Still, she dislikes the Laocoön, which she saw in Rome, because "eternal marble ought to perpetuate only eternal feelings and here it is perpetuating a transitory expression of physical pain" (112). Similarly, she critiques a head of Cicero in Cavalier Campana's Etruscan collection because she would prefer a calmer emotion depicted: "it is really the man speaking, adjuring the gods against Catiline. I would rather have had him in the sublime humility of his tribute to Plato" (141). This commentary reveals that Nightingale cannot help but impose a Christian interpretation to the sculpture. The calmer emotion she desires is associated with the *Christian* quality of humility, as Nightingale sees it.

In discussing the art she encountered on her European travels, Nightingale was developing a religious philosophy that emphasized the process of becoming secure in one's devotion to God, a concept that would become central to her ideas about women's emancipation, and as she shaped this philosophy through artistic observation, she articulated specific judgments about the images artists created. These judgments were directly related to her religious philosophy, which saw artists as akin to prophets, since they could directly represent God's perfection to humans. Writing about Michelangelo's Sistine Chapel, she asserts that God would not have revealed such a great work to Michelangelo if he were not close to God:

> Oh how Michelangelo must have prayed, how he must have filled himself with the spirit of the prophets, before he could have had these forms revealed to him. . . . He has performed that wonderful miracle of giving form to the breath of God, chiselling his inspiration, wonderful whether it be done by words, colour or hard stones. (151–52)

Repeatedly in the letters, Nightingale refers to Michelangelo as a seer or some other enlightened figure, with encomiums such as "Oh M. Angelo, arch-priest of the divinity, thou real priest and minister of the Most High, art thou now an Archangel Michael, even as he was perhaps once a mortal like thee?" (202). In such statements, she assumes the special ability of the artist to connect mortals with the divine.

To stress this point even more fully, Nightingale contrasts the artist's special ability with her own inability to understand the art she views. Part of the reason she returns to the Sistine Chapel so often while in Rome is because she is overwhelmed by Michelangelo's work there and needs more time to understand all aspects of it (201). She attributes her inability to understand his work fully to her incomplete spiritual journey, and she trusts Michelangelo as a prophet who has received God's vision (150). When she is "startled" by his depiction of Isaiah as "so young," she reasons that Michelangelo "knew him better" than she does because Isaiah was revealed to him directly by God (153–54). Still, Nightingale recognizes that to accord artists the status of prophet can be problematic, since it does not account for subject matter that might not reveal God's vision. Accordingly, when artists depicted subject matter Nightingale did not like, she attributed it to a lapse in their closeness to God. She rationalizes Raphael's *La Fornarina* (c. 1518–1519), an image of Raphael's mistress Margherita Luti, as such a lapse, pointing out that "of all the acts he committed upon earth, this is the one he most wishes to recall" (158). In an act of mitigating cultural difference, she insists that he "must have repented of it," or God never would have revealed the Dresden Madonna to him (158).[4]

This comment in particular reveals that as Nightingale viewed art, she was developing a religious philosophy that would address women's role in society.

Though her commentary about repentance is aimed at Raphael, one imagines it also is aimed at Luti, given other comments Nightingale makes about women in art: she consistently prefers depictions of women who uphold Christian ideals, or at least repent when they fail to uphold these ideals. Describing Michelangelo's representation of God's creation of Adam and Eve in the Sistine Chapel, Nightingale emphasizes women's unique qualities, particularly intuition, by pointing out the differences in Adam's and Eve's reactions to God upon their creation. Adam "looks at Him and is not ashamed. There is however nothing of the inward consciousness of the divine presence in it, no speaking purely from *heart* to *heart*" (202). Eve, on the other hand, "kneeling in perfect love and devotion, receives with entire submission the commands of her Creator, which come straight from His *spirit* to hers, without any material manifestation of power" (202). This is a more intuitive reaction, and in Michelangelo's depiction of Adam's and Eve's fall, Nightingale notices that "the difference between man and woman, between reasoning and inward perception, is still preserved. Adam's thoughts are towards the favoured paradise and the avenging angel. . . . Eve, crouching and heart-stricken . . . is an image of the anguish of the soul—the long spiritual inward writhings of remorse, which receive no alleviation and no embitterment from external things" (203). Women, Nightingale implies, feel sin more keenly than men do, and this belief in the intensity of women's emotions in relation to their spiritual journeys will resurface in *Suggestions for Thought*, where Nightingale argues that what society needs is a female Christ who can experience the kind of suffering that will transform women's place in society.

Nightingale iterates women's ability to feel sin more keenly in her discussion of Correggio's *Magdalen* (c. 1518–1519), which she saw at the very end of her trip, in July 1850 at the Dresden Gallery in Germany. Describing Correggio's depiction of Mary Magdalen in the desert after she has repented for her sins, Nightingale writes,

> It is the most religious picture as Σ [Nightingale's nickname for Selina Bracebridge] says—all the world is dark behind her. In that gloomy background there is nothing bright, no one ray of light—she does not look back. . . . In her expression is deep peace, for she has ceased to sin. There is now no more struggle. . . . There has been deep suffering, but it is over. . . . The whole interest centres in her expression. . . . She has gone through the stage where "Rest, rest, passions that once stirred my heart had ended in that word, my one desire to be at rest" and she has found her rest. (457)

This description of Mary Magdalen, who exhibits the same secure emotion Nightingale had seen in male biblical figures, becomes the foundation for

Nightingale's description of women's emancipation through religious devotion in *Suggestions for Thought*. By describing a woman who has sinned as secure in her emotions because of her spiritual experiences, Nightingale suggests that women have the potential to become prophets, just as men do.

Nightingale further develops the idea that women have the potential to become prophets when she discusses Raphael's Dresden Madonna, which she also saw in July 1850. Previously, Nightingale had not been impressed with Raphael's painting, but she insists that "Raphael at Dresden is a different man" (455). Though many other painters have depicted the "purity" of Mary,

> Raphael alone has succeeded in giving her intellect with purity—that far-seeing eye, that expression of forethought and power. . . . Mary in this picture is altogether a woman—there is no Mariolatry here. It is the most living reality I ever saw and I seem to have seen her alive and not in the picture. As to the figure, there is a grand simplicity about it, so unlike all his other Madonnas, who are merely pure from foolishness. (455)

Nightingale goes on to link what she sees in the picture to a model for real-life women, stating, "It is to me a grand prophecy of what will be when we have discovered God's laws and the way to keep them: of what woman will be and is intended to be, uniting purity with power" (455). Again, Nightingale's commentary about European artistic depictions of women anticipates the key concept in *Suggestions for Thought*: if people understand God's laws, the problems of society, including the oppression of women, will be solved, and women will be able to meet their full potential.

*   *   *

These comments about women as they were depicted in European art—as possessing unique abilities, capable of spiritual transformation, and central to the transformation of wider society—set the standard for Nightingale's judgments about women when she arrived in Egypt. Although Nightingale appreciated the important role that ancient Egyptian goddesses played in their society, evident in her praise of Isis as she approached Alexandria (Vallée, *Florence Nightingale on Mysticism* 141–43), once Nightingale encountered Egyptian women—both through artistic representations and real-life situations—she applied a Christian, European standard. While traveling in Europe, Nightingale had used race hierarchies, often presented as hierarchies based on nationality and religion, to assess certain cultural situations,[5] and once in Egypt, she continued developing her religious philosophy through artistic observation that revealed her reliance on these hierarchies. I already have detailed Nightingale's preparation for her trip to Egypt via an extensive reading list and consultation with Bunsen, and Vallée explains that this trip was a more intense cultural experience than what Nightingale experienced in Europe, since not only had she never encountered the East but also because it was unusual for white women to travel on the Nile at this time (118).

Still, Nightingale seems to have recognized that travel to Egypt was an opportunity to see things in a new light, and particularly to widen her understanding of world religions (119). In a letter written after her arrival in Alexandria, she comments on the presence of various religious types in the city: "This place is full of Roman Catholic sisters and Lazarists, Greek church, Armenian church, Mussulman [Muslim] mullahs, Protestant Waldenses, Alexandria the Cosmopolite" (146). Yet she also writes from a clearly hierarchical perspective about the work of religious people in Egypt. From Qena, 500 miles down the Nile from Alexandria, she writes about the religious changes over time in Egypt, noting that "in the fourth century, all Egypt was Christian," whereas during her travels, the only "good" Christians in Egypt seem to be the Roman Catholic sisters, who are "the only people whom we have seen in all this miserable land attempting to do the slightest good," while other Christians "seem to use their residence in the East not . . . for doing any earthly good, but merely for the sake of using the customs of the country to justify their own vices and profiting by their sojourn among Musselmen to live like Musselmen" (215–16). Nightingale goes on in dismay about the "de-Christianizing" of Egypt: "Has Islam usually obtained such *complete* possession of a formerly Christian country?" (216). Clearly, Nightingale struggled to accept Islam, and even at the end of her trip, despite encountering Muslims she found to be more devout than many Christians (451), she could not accept Islam as an entirely legitimate religion and believed Egypt was in need of "deliverance" (453). Describing Cairo for the last time, she writes: "as I looked upon that vast city which did not know its right hand from its left . . . I thought how Christ, if he had been there, would have felt—how he would have yearned over Cairo and how he would have been straitened till his task was accomplished. Behold that great city, how would he have set about her deliverance?" (453–54).

Nightingale's bias against Islam may have been enhanced by her interest in Coptic Christianity, the "descendants of the pharaohs" she regretted had been "reduced" in number significantly because of Muslims' persecution of them (155). When able, she attends Coptic churches in Egypt, stating, "One's feelings toward the Anglican Church are very different when she is hiding in corners, struggling with the devil and still adhering to her own beloved ritual" (170), and she expresses strong interest in ancient Egyptian religion, perhaps because of its connection to Coptic Christianity. She touts the contribution of ancient Egyptian beliefs to the broader development of religion, though she believes this development results in a superior form of religion, Christianity. She puts special emphasis on the Egyptian sun-god Osiris's likeness to Christ (222–23), and in Osiris, she recognizes the spiritual process—"victory, after struggle" (304)—she appreciated in the suffering but ultimately triumphant biblical figures she had seen in Italian art.

Still, like other members of the British upper and middle classes, she could not have helped but view Egyptian culture with an "English eye," and she consistently contrasts what she sees in Egypt to the European experiences with which she is more familiar. For example, she immediately notices that the landscape is distinctly different from what she has experienced in Europe. I have already mentioned her awareness of a change in landscape as early as Malta, where she feels as though she is "stepping from the West to the East at a stride" (138), and her characterization of Cairo as "beautiful" but "unnatural" (181). Once traveling down the Nile, Nightingale seems to appreciate Eastern coloring more fully, since she describes it as akin to "precious stones," but she still focuses on its "unnatural" contrast to how things appear in Europe. "All the colours of Africa," she writes, "are those of precious stones, the colours of Revelations [sic], while those of Europe are like flowers. . . . The whole Nile is so unnatural—if one may use the expression—so unlike nature" (177). Still, Nightingale's descriptions of the Egyptian landscape show that Eastern coloring is not always distinctly different from that of the West. At Alexandria, Nightingale writes that the Eastern morning reminds her of her favorite Italian painter Guido Reni's *Aurora* (1614), a ceiling fresco in Rome about the coming of dawn as represented in Graeco-Roman mythology (143). Further, the Valley of the Kings at Thebes (Luxor), which comes closest to the Western landscape Nightingale knows well, is described as "a plain . . . surrounded by . . . lovely hills," with "a river . . . about twice as wide as the Thames at Westminster" (330). Nevertheless, while Thebes resembles a European landscape, Nightingale iterates her overall preference for real Western landscapes when she writes, "In Italy there are crimson lights and purple shadows; here there is nothing in earth, air, sky or water which one can compare in any way with Europe" (240).

Nightingale's preference for Western landscapes is linked to her religious philosophy, which, as I have already discussed, focused on developing an understanding of and devotion to a perfect God. When she visits the Eastern (Arabian) Desert to see the quarries and catacombs, the religious symbolism Nightingale uses to describe the landscape privileges Western religious belief. In the "dead desert" of Egypt, Nightingale sees "an awful devil at work, making this kingdom his own," and she speculates that it is "the contrast of the sky with the earth which makes the terror of the desert" (184). While the relationship between earth and sky in England favors a "rich and variegated" earth over the "deadness" of the sky, the dominance of the sky in Egypt is so strong that God cannot produce anything, and the devil is able to have his way in such a place (185). Nightingale applies the devil's influence in Egypt to its people, writing, "The struggle between God and the devil is perpetually visible before one's thoughts . . . and you do not wonder at orientals being the mystical people they have become, nor at the Europeans, where all beauty is of the earth and the thoughts turn to the earth, becoming a practical, active people" (185). While Nightingale does not go so far as to say that Egyptians are inactive here, referring them to "mystical" instead, the contrast is implied, and in other letters, she argues that Egyptians, particularly Egyptian women who are sheltered in harems, are inactive.[6]

As Jill Matus points out, in "The 'Eastern-Woman Question': Martineau and Nightingale Visit the Harem" (1999), Nightingale follows the typical English response to harems, focusing on the inactivity of women when she visits Said Pasha's harem, where "the *ennui* of the palace made her want to cry" (74). Nightingale characterizes herself in opposition to this inactivity, as "no dahabieh bird, no divan incumbent" (74), but the longer Nightingale is in Egypt, the more she feels as though she is becoming inactive: "A sort of torpor crawls over one in a dahabieh. You feel, as you lie on the divan and float slowly along and the shores pass you gently by, as if you were being carried along some unknown river to some unknown shore, leaving forever all you had ever known before" (Vallée, *Florence Nightingale on Mysticism* 182). This comment is not unlike that made by Lucy Snowe about Cleopatra's reclining position in Brontë's *Villette*, which I already have discussed, and Nightingale extends this feeling to losing one's identity (183), a key concept in nineteenth-century Englishwomen's ideas about emancipation. The notion of losing identity when placed in the position occupied by Eastern women will inform *Suggestions for Thought,* where Nightingale argues that English-women can achieve liberty by rejecting the patriarchal aspects of English culture that function similarly to the patriarchal aspects of Eastern culture. It is the confinement of women to their drawing rooms, the insistence that women develop skills such as reading, drawing, and playing music rather than skills that will help them find a vocation, that turns Englishwomen into the inactive women Nightingale sees in Egypt.

Nevertheless, while in Egypt, Nightingale finds ways to regain her sense of identity, by visiting temples that enhance her devotion to God, the solution to British women's oppression articulated in *Suggestions for Thought.* Nightingale feels particularly spiritual in temples that still retain the marks of *ancient* Egypt rather than those that reflect more contemporary Egypt, which in Nightingale's opinion had been denigrated by the influence of

Arab/Muslim culture. Nightingale is particularly impressed by Abu Simbel in Nubia because it is free of "that horrible Egyptian present" (262), which is Arab/Muslim. Built by Ramesses II, who defended Egypt against the Nubians and the Hittites, Abu Simbel features representations that make Nightingale feel close to God. Nightingale focuses on the representations of Ramesses II and his wife, Nefertari, who embody the Christian ideals of husband and wife, but she frames this discussion with comments about the qualities possessed by ancient gods and goddesses, to whom Ramesses II and Nefertari made offerings. Abu Simbel's architecture is "innocent," "childish," and "simple," much like the ancient goddess Hathor, whose name means "the habitation of Horus," the ancient god Nightingale equates with her Christian God (257). Nightingale immediately connects Hathor to other Egyptian goddesses (Isis, Neith, and Bubastis) and to Greek goddesses (Aphrodite, Athena, and Diana), conflations meant to emphasize the primary role of goddesses in ancient society. They represent "Nature," or the "matter formed" by God, who is consistently represented by a male figure—Horus or Osiris in the Egyptian tradition and Zeus in the Greek tradition (225, 304, 310). All of the ancient goddesses "enable Zeus to walk," acting as "the right hand . . . of God" (310).

No doubt, Nightingale's understanding of the representations of ancient Egyptian women she sees in the temples is shaped by her own religious views. At one point in the trip, Nightingale compares the status of women across religions, noting that in many religions women have something to support them through difficult times. "The Roman Catholic woman has a religion, the Protestant has an intellect. In the early Christian, in the old Egyptian time, women had a vocation" (338). While she sees parallels between the status of women in Christianity and in ancient Egyptian religion, she does not see a parallel to their status in contemporary Egypt, writing that "woman is nothing but the servant of a man" in Islam (338). Nightingale's recognition of the parallels between Christianity and *ancient* Egyptian religion, but not Islam, shapes how she reacts to the representations of ancient Egyptian women in the temples. For Nightingale, Osiris and Isis represent the ideal husband and wife, an idea Nightingale articulates more fully when she writes about the temples at Philae. There, Nightingale writes, Isis "signifie[s] . . . that nature reveals God in *all* His forms, sometimes in one of His attributes, sometimes in another but *always* the wife of the *Goodness* of God" (304).

Like Osiris and Isis, Ramesses II and Nefertari, as they are depicted at Abu Simbel, are ideal mates and function as historical equivalents of mythological figures, a collapsing of myth and history by Nightingale that perhaps helps her make the link between what she recognizes in powerful Egyptian women and a potential solution to the real-life oppression of British women, who need earlier role models to follow. In one of the images inside Abu Simbel, Ramesses II is shown making a sacrifice to God without the expectation of anything in return, which makes him "a perfect intellectual and spiritual man who feels his connection with that God, whose first and last lesson through His Christ has been, 'Be *one with* me,' not be my instrument nor my worshipper nor my petitioner" (Vallée, *Florence Nightingale on Mysticism* 266). Nefertari, "whose portrait is all over the temple," is shown by Ramesses's side, "the most lovely countenance, her black hair gathered together with a golden fibula on the side of her forehead and then falling on her shoulders" (269). Everywhere in the temple, Nefertari "occupies the place which the most advanced Christian civilization gives to woman: always the one wife, nowhere the face veiled, often the regent, the sovereign or the co-ruler with a brother" (269; see Figure 2.1). This presentation of Nefertari as a woman who has power as a coruler in her culture, just as the ancient goddesses hold similar powers, leads Nightingale back to the parallels she sees between ancient Egyptian religion and Christianity, for she concludes, "Woman may be quite satisfied with her *Christian* position in old Egypt" (269).

Nightingale's comments about Abu Simbel, then, indicate she appreciates the temple because it displays images compatible with her Christian beliefs, and she appreciates the temple Beit el-Wali in Nubia for many of the same reasons. There, one image of Ramesses and Nefertari shows them together at a sacrifice, and Nightingale again emphasizes the appropriate roles for men and women displayed in the image: Ramesses is "a fond and faithful husband," and Nefertari is one of the "happy women" of "olden times" (279). Still, Nightingale stresses it is *ancient* Egyptian religion that is parallel to Christianity, and even in the temples containing images that place women in a powerful position, one can see the "corruption" of that religion, since later rulers such as Ramesses III and the Ptolemies added to these temples their own interpretations of the relationship between mortals and the ancient gods and goddesses. The Temple of Hermonthis at Armant, for example, displays this corruption, since the ruins include "Egyptian, Roman, Christian, and Muslim" buildings. The "rise and fall of nations" seen in this "succession of ruins" is "almost painful," according to Nightingale, since the "sanctuary is now the prison of the pachas" (243–44). You also can see the effect of "That disgusting Cleopatra," Nightingale says, who made "herself, Julius Caesar and their son the triad of the place" (244). For Nightingale, a particular kind of morality is an important quality in those who rule Egypt, and although Nightingale acknowledges that any religion—Catholic, Protestant, or ancient Egyptian—risks "corruption" when it becomes "an instrument of power" (309), she objects when she perceives that rulers are not upholding her own moral values, a concern no doubt influenced by the imperialist view that British values were superior to those of other countries, especially countries the British classified as "Eastern."

Nightingale also dislikes Medinet Habu, the Mortuary Temple of Ramesses III in Luxor, because it does not reflect her moral values. "Ugly Medinet Habu," Nightingale begins a letter from February 12, 1850, "how I hate you with your gaudy colors, your squat columns as rough as they were high, your coronation scenes more vulgar than [Sir George] Hayter's . . . '*Coronation of Queen Victoria*'" (356). Nightingale contrasts this temple to Abu Simbel, saying that it is "not like the work of the great Ramesses but that of a common pacha tyrant" (356), and she compares it to Napoleon's neo-Greek temple in Paris, the Madeleine: "If Karnak is the St Peter's of Egypt, Medinet Habu is its Madeleine" (356). Nightingale particularly objects to the depiction of women in Medinet Habu, for she states,

> It is the very sanctuary of low oriental despotism, baseness and pomp. It reminded me of Napoleon throughout, with his Josephine and Marie-Louise, his notions of women and his coronation of his wife. You see Ramesses surrounded by his ladies (how unlike the loving Nefertari and her hero at the Ramesseum: 'lovely in their lives and in their death they were not divided'). You see the queen put out of the way, on a shelf, in the coronation scene, like the miserable wife of a Louis Quatorze. The empire was falling and barbarism beginning, which could produce a Medinet Habu. (357)

For Nightingale, Medinet Habu is indicative of all the problems Egypt faced after Ramesses II, for she continues, "From the time of Ramesses III (1290 BCE) art and power suddenly declined and the glory of Egypt departed forever. It is no wonder: the connection between freedom and art, between purity of morals and religion, and the high state of moral prosperity, seems very evident" (357). There is no direct reference to the connection between the kind of government a country has and the freedom of its women, but it seems clear from Nightingale's characterization of Ramesses III's and Napoleon's attitudes toward women as objects rather than partners that this link exists. Despot governments, whether they are Eastern or Western, disregard women.

Nightingale iterates the impact of governments and religions that do not value women's abilities when she describes a woman she sees in a Cairo market toward the end of her trip. The woman, who is selling her belongings because she has separated from her husband, is described as follows: "In the little goldsmith's shop . . . sat . . . a woman wrapped in her black silk habarah all but one eye which was a very pretty one, who had brought all her diamonds and . . . even her silver goolleh tops for sale. . . . She asked no questions, showed no interest, but sat, the picture of meekness and despair and resignation, while her things were offered to us by the goldsmith" (438). This is one of the last images of Egypt Nightingale provides her friends and family before summing up her trip by connecting the condition of this woman to the general condition of Egypt:

> Alas! we have now done with Egypt. Cairo is not Egyptian, it is Arabian. . . . The only thing which now remains to us of Egypt is the pyramids. . . . It is perfectly distinct from that in Rome or in any of our living countries. . . . It had a race, of which not one remains. . . . Egypt to an European is all but uninhabited, the present race no more disturbs this impression than would a race of lizards, scrambling over the broken monuments of such a star. You would not call *them* inhabitants, no more do you these. So farewell, dear beautiful, noble, dead Egypt, the country which brought forth a race of giants. (439)

Despite these damning remarks about "Arabian" Egypt, Nightingale recognized that she did not fully understand one aspect of some Arabs' lives, Islam, stating, "I never could understand, never could feel any interest in, never look upon as a religion at all" (440). Still, she did think she had gained insight into Islam by going to Egyptian mosques (444), and she appreciated Muslims' devotion to learning their religion, which "put [Christians] to shame" (451). Nevertheless, in assessing what she had learned from her experience in Egypt, she says that she felt most "at home" when she felt a connection between Egyptian beliefs and Christianity. "In Karnak I felt that their God was my God" (440), she writes, confirming that as open as she was to learning about other religions and nationalities, she still employed an English eye when assessing Egyptian culture, including the status of Egyptian women.

* * *

Back in England in 1850, Nightingale abandoned the powerful representations she had seen of ancient Egyptian women for those of Italian women seen in the European legs of her travels as she articulated her ideas about British women's oppression (and religious devotion as a solution to this oppression) in *Suggestions for Thought*. Since many of the direct references to artistic works did not survive Nightingale's revision process, looking at the draft manuscript of *Suggestions for Thought*, which is reprinted in Lynn McDonald's *Florence Nightingale's* Suggestions for Thought (2008), is central to understanding how Nightingale's religious philosophy is meant primarily for upper- and middle-class Englishwomen but did accommodate working-class Englishwomen and Eastern women who were able to embrace a Western, Christian lifestyle. Still, the final version of the book, three volumes privately printed in 1860, contains some artistic references, so I will first examine these references and then turn to the draft manuscript.

The artistic references in Volume 1 of the 1860 version are situated within a larger discussion about spiritual belief, which Nightingale offers to working-class readers of the text not so they will have an "authority" on religion but so they can be guided by the "Spirit of Truth" and find "unity of faith" (59–60), a term Nightingale used in her letters from Egypt to suggest that various world religions are connected, even if Christianity is the highest stage in spiritual development. "Belief" is difficult to define across cultures, since as Nightingale puts it, a theologian from an African tribe might think belief is "jumping over a stick," while Samuel Johnson defines it in the *Dictionary of the English Language* as "credit given on account of authority" (61). Drawing on her experience in Egypt, Nightingale explains that belief should be defined as a "sense of certainty" in God, since Moses played a key role in moving religion toward the "highest state of belief," in which a "perfect God" is honored, even though his "savage Hebrew tribe" was unable to recognize this (62–64). As a result, Nightingale says, belief "degenerated" in Egypt, since "[w]henever one man has endeavoured to impose the more perfect idea of a supreme being . . . upon a nation less developed than himself, we see it degenerate" (62).

Nightingale thinks people must rely on their own senses in order to believe, rather than accepting imposition of belief, and the struggle to understand the "nature of God" can be facilitated by going to places, such as the Sistine Chapel, where God reveals his perfection to humans (81), a comment that recalls Nightingale's discussion of the Sistine Chapel in her letters to family members. Again, Nightingale's hierarchy of religion developed in Egypt plays a role, for she writes that while the Egyptian Hebrews couldn't quite grasp the "nature of God," anyone who goes to the Sistine Chapel should be able to "imagine the nature which painted that roof. There was a will without which that roof would not have been; that will determined each stroke of the pencil—but the first stroke had regard to the last and to every intermediate one" (80–81). From Nightingale's perspective, it is a Western piece of art, made possible by God's will, which encourages belief in a perfect God rather than the misguided belief of Hebrews in Egypt, confirming that Nightingale relied on hierarchies based on religion, nationality, and race as she articulated her religious philosophy.

Still, just as Nightingale recognized the role of the artist in revealing God's perfection, she stresses that the artist must exercise his creativity, a form of free will, in concert with God's will, writing, "The artist who begins upon twelve pictures to fulfill one purpose has one will throughout, by which will they are developed into being. He [God] *is* not those pictures, but they are the manifestation of his will when done. . . . If we had seen Michelangelo at work, we should have been quite sure that there was a conception in his mind of what was to appear on his canvas, a purpose he meant to fulfill" (81–82). Still, one need not be a painter to reveal God's perfection; people with other occupations can and should rely on their senses to develop belief in God (85). Nevertheless, Nightingale says that the senses must be "healthy" in order for the methodology to work (95), and in *Suggestions for Thought*, she sees an "unhealthy" eye as the sign of a lower form of religious belief, held by Hebrews in Egypt and Australian tribes (62).

Having established some of the key concepts for understanding religious belief in Volume 1, Nightingale turns to discussion of British women's oppression in Volume 2, where she again uses artistic observations from her travels to advocate religious devotion as a solution to this oppression. Here, she avoids discussion of the artistic representations she saw in Egypt, focusing instead on those she saw in Italy. Drawing on the comments in her letters about Michelangelo's God-given abilities, she argues that Englishwomen are oppressed by their families, who do not respect their God-given abilities. Nightingale points out that while Englishwomen are told to make the most of "odd moments" in the day to pursue their passions, no one would ever suggest that an artist such as Michelangelo do the same thing. "Can we fancy Michelangelo running up and putting on a touch to his Sistine ceiling at 'odd moments'? . . . We know what can be done at odd times, a little worsted work, acquiring a language, copying something, putting the room to rights. . . . Nothing requiring original thought" (320–21). Because women are limited to working at odd moments, rather than given the support to develop their abilities, they cannot become serious artists. To illustrate her point, Nightingale refers to a "lady friend" who had the same "turn for architecture" Michelangelo had, yet never had the opportunity to pursue this interest. "The one had no possibility given her, the other had" (323), she writes, recalling an earlier discussion in *Suggestions for Thought* about free will, where she asserts that everyone has the *freedom* to do something, but not everyone has the *power* to do it (237).

Still, as we see toward the end of Volume 2, where Nightingale recycles this idea in a discussion of how the seventeenth-century artist Bartolomé Esteban Murillo became a professional while another friend, "Mrs. A.," did not, it is not God who is sexist but Victorian culture, which does not provide women the support they need to fulfill their potential, instead insisting they spend time on meaningless activities (555). Victorian culture needs a different model, one that will honor the intellectual, artistic, and moral capabilities of women (556), and Nightingale envisions a woman who can bring progress for the entire sex: a female Christ, "a woman, who will resume, in her own soul, all the sufferings of her race, and that woman will be the Saviour of her race" (584–85). But until a female Christ emerges, women remain unable to fulfill their potential. Using a specific reference from the Italian leg of her travels, Nightingale writes that "woman" is like the statue of the Archangel Michael at the top of Castel Sant'Angelo, which is connected to St. Peter's Basilica: "She has an immense provision of wings, which seem as if they would bear her over earth and heaven, but when she tries to use them she is petrified into stone; her feet are grown into the earth, chained to the bronze pedestal" (585–86).

This reference to a woman with immovable feet recalls other references in the so-called "Cassandra" section of *Suggestions for Thought*, which affirm the race hierarchies seen in Nightingale's Egyptian travel letters. Twice, Nightingale refers to the bound feet of Chinese women as a metaphor for the situation faced by British women, who are restricted by society's refusal to let them develop their capabilities fully. At the beginning of the section, when Nightingale describes the "suffering" of Englishwomen when they are taught to have "no passion," she compares their emotional repression to the physical repression of Chinese women (549). Then, toward the end of the section, Nightingale again relies on this metaphor, when "Cassandra" complains that even if women have the support to develop their capabilities, they will not be able to make use of this opportunity, for they are "[l]ike the Chinese woman who could not make use of her feet if she were brought into European life" (574). This comparison between the emotional repression of Englishwomen and the physical repression of Chinese women, which was not uncommon in the nineteenth century, suggests that women of different nations suffer a similar oppression, yet only Englishwomen are accorded emotional complexity in the first reference, suggesting that Nightingale was not able to see Chinese women as equals.

The second reference does suggest that Chinese women can be brought into English life, even though their bound feet would prevent them from fully participating in this life, and the notion that foreign women might be brought into English life is worth further analysis, since it points to a more complex view of women of different classes and ethnicities than we might expect from Nightingale. Nightingale's ambivalent attitude toward Mary Seacole, the Jamaican doctoress who traveled to the Crimea to help soldiers at the same time Nightingale did, is well known,[7] and Nightingale expresses a similar attitude toward working-class English women, which Mary Poovey highlights in *Uneven Developments: The Ideological Work of Gender in Mid-Victorian England* (1988).[8] But Nightingale's views about Indian women, which have not been discussed as fully by critics, complicate her position on women she perceives as unlike herself, while still confirming that Nightingale was "bound by an English eye" when thinking about emancipation for all women.

Inderpal Grewal's *Home and Harem: Nation, Gender, Empire, and the Cultures of Travel* (1996), which covers a wide range of writers who exemplify the tension between British and Indian women's notions of domesticity, is helpful for seeing how Nightingale often expressed a typical British view of Indians. Discussing Nightingale's relationship with the Indian national Behramji Malabari, who campaigned against child marriage and widow sacrifice, Grewal argues that Nightingale, who wrote the preface for Malabari's biography, articulated the typical British view of Indians, by characterizing Malabari as a "native" in need of British help in this preface (148). Indeed, Nightingale states that Malabari's biography is valuable because it "give[s] us a peep into an Indian home—that of Mr. Malabari and his family" and that readers will "see how much he owed to his mother, a remarkable woman, of strong will, masterful mind, and irresistible energy; yet a simple, homely housewife, with the tenderest heart" (Nightingale v), comments Grewal rightly finds offensive because they present Malabari as "an exemplary native" and his mother as the one responsible for ensuring his "civilized" status (Grewal 149). Still, in the preface, Nightingale goes on to express faith in Indian women to help change their own culture, offering a more complicated view of their role in reform.

> [T]he women of India possess influence the most unbounded. In their own households, be it in hut or palace, . . . they hold the most important moral strongholds of any women on earth. . . . How may we hope to reach this great influence, and utilize it for the cause of social progress? The answer seems to be that the women of India *can only* be reached by educated ladies of their own country. . . . They have ready access to their poorer sisters—*they* understand their circumstances and feelings. It is to *them*, therefore, that we must appeal to convince their countrywomen, by example and precept, of the evils of the present marriage system, and to suggest the remedy. (Nightingale vii–viii)

Granted, Nightingale's call for *educated* Indian women, who likely gained knowledge through the British educational system, to take the lead in social reform of India reveals her class biases, as does her comment that women might exert their influence, even if they live in a "hut." Yet, the fact that Nightingale was calling on women to be more active shows a certain amount of respect for Indian women that Grewal indicates was not always shown by Indian national men, including Malabari himself (146–47).

It is clear that Nightingale assumes women who embraced English ways of living would be most helpful in creating social change, but whether Nightingale herself embraced the women who became "more English" is unclear.

I have not come across evidence that Nightingale knew Pandita Ramabai, a Hindu woman who, according to Grewal, converted to Christianity and was exactly the kind of woman Nightingale calls on to help other Indian women in her preface to Malabari's biography. But Ramabai clearly knew about Nightingale, since she refers to Nightingale as a model for other women to follow in her 1889 *The Peoples of the United States* (Ramabai, *Pandita* 193). Further, it is likely Nightingale at least knew about Ramabai, since as Max Müller indicates in his memoir, *Auld Lang Syne*, Malabari and Ramabai were the "chief actors" in the widow reform movement (113). Ramabai testified about the lack of women doctors to the Hunter Commission, which led to the establishment of Lady Dufferin's National Association for Supplying Female Medical Aid to the Women of India (Ramabai, *Letters and Correspondence* xii), an organization Nightingale supported by advising Lady Dufferin about hygiene books for Indian women (Vallée, *Florence Nightingale on Social Change* 730–38). Yet, when Ramabai traveled to England in 1883 as part of the process of embracing Christianity and expected to find acceptance among English women, she was treated as though she was a "child" in need of guidance from the Anglican sisters with whom she stayed (Grewal 190–94). One imagines that if Nightingale knew Ramabai, her reaction likely was similar to that of the Anglican sisters Ramabai encountered, given Nightingale's ambivalent attitudes toward religion, nationality, class, and race.

* * *

The cultural contexts I have laid out in this chapter should enable us to clearly see that Nightingale has a particular kind of woman in mind as she writes about women's emancipation in *Suggestions for Thought*, and this perhaps explains—but does not excuse—Nightingale's suppression of her Egyptian experience as she wrote *Suggestions for Thought*. The vision she articulates in the treatise is intended primarily for those like herself, upper- or middle-class English women who can marry and do not need to work but want some vocation instead of marriage. Still, this vision also has the potential to include English working-class women and foreign women who can be brought into this life through their devotion to a Christian God. If we turn to the draft manuscript of *Suggestions for Thought*, reprinted in Lynn McDonald's *Florence Nightingale's* Suggestions for Thought (2008), this focus on a particular kind of woman as ready for emancipation through religious devotion becomes even clearer. Nightingale again avoids the artistic representations of women she saw in Egypt, focusing on Italian representations instead. Italian representations are seen especially in what McDonald refers to as the "English family novel" section of the draft, the section toward the beginning of Volume 2 in which three sisters (Portia, Columbia, and Fulgentia) struggle to overcome restrictions placed on them by society (McDonald, *Florence Nightingale's* Suggestions for Thought 7), and the "Cassandra" section, which comes at the end of Volume 2 and features a Cassandra-like figure, named Nofariari in the draft.

In the "English family novel" section of the draft, Fulgentia, the sister McDonald identifies as most like Nightingale (299), is described by the narrator not in relation to Egyptian women such as Isis or Nefertari, who had garnered Nightingale's approval for virtues similar to those found in Christianity, but as Correggio's *Magdalen*, the image of Mary Magdalen Nightingale had seen in Dresden and admired for its depiction of the end to Mary's struggle after she repents for her sins (McDonald, *Florence Nightingale's European Travels* 454, 456, 486).

> Fulgentia, white as the pearl which glistened in her dark hair, looked that night like Correggio's Magdalen. As she stood for one moment at the door of the London palace, the resemblance struck me particularly. Like that picture there was nothing but the dark background behind her, typifying the darkness of the past. She had gone through nothing but darkness—the sharp stones of the courtyard were in front—for there was nothing before her but a hard, sharp, struggling life. The light was upon her face and she looked straightforward, far out into the night as upon a distant point on which all her faculties were concentrated, all her thoughts were absorbed. The future was everything to her. She had no other thought or hope. (McDonald, *Florence Nightingale's* Suggestions for Thought 426)

This description of Fulgentia, which echoes Nightingale's description of the painting in her letters very closely, puts emphasis on Fulgentia's readiness for the transition from darkness into light. While there is nothing overtly religious about the description of darkness and light, the comparison of Fulgentia to Mary Magdalen suggests a religious undertone to Fulgentia's transition, a transition that can be achieved not just by upper- and middle-class women but also those of the lower classes who have embraced Christianity. Still, the parallel between Fulgentia and Mary Magdalen excludes some women; one imagines that it does not include the Muslim women Nightingale encountered during her travel to Egypt, nor would it include any English woman who has not repented for her sins, as Mary has.

Still, Nightingale recognizes that even women who have not repented for their sins face difficulties because English society has not provided them with better support. As Fulgentia leaves the ball and the narrator asks her "why she did not like society," she replies,

> What has "society" done for us? What is the mission of society? of mankind? to civilize and educate us. How does it fulfill this mission? What does it do for "fallen women"? Those who have committed indictable crime, it takes possession of, and ordinarily condemns to a place where they must lose all hope as well as all desire of reformation. One would have thought that society, which had done so badly for them in their childhood, would now have wished to remodel them. (427)

Nightingale recognizes it is society's responsibility to support Englishwomen who may have "fallen" because of their class status but might repent for their sins. If they are able to repent with the help of social institutions, Nightingale suggests, they should have the same opportunities for emancipation upper- and middle-class Englishwomen such as Fulgentia have.

Nightingale's use of Italian, rather than Egyptian, artistic representations to define the type of woman who is ready for emancipation is continued in the "Cassandra" section of the draft, which features dialogue between the Cassandra-like Nofariari and her brother Fariseo. Nofariari, who takes the name Cassandra only toward the end of the narrative, is presented to readers as an ideal woman, not in relation to any of the artistic representations of women Nightingale saw in Egypt but from the perspective of the Italian painter. Pictured first on a terrace of a Venetian palace, Nofariari

> re-entered the palace and reached her balcony, where she threw herself down on its cold pavement, resting her forehead on the stone balustrade and her long hair, of the golden tint which the Venetian painter delight to honour, bound with gems, radiant gems, which sparkle in the moonlight, fell upon her bare arm onto rough stone. But hardly for a moment could her energetic nature acquiesce in the humiliated despairing posture. She started up like the dying lioness who fronts her hunters, and standing at bay, as it were, she bared her forehead to the night breeze, and stretching out her arms she cried: "God, to Thee alone can I say all—God, hear me." (548)

With references to the Venetian palace and Nofariari's sparkling gems, Nightingale presents a decidedly upper-class woman ready for the transition out of suffering and into religious devotion. Further, the reference to her "long hair of the golden tint" suggests that Nofariari is distinctly European, though the characterization of her as a "dying lioness who fronts her hunters" likely refers to an "Eastern" image, the "Dying Lioness" relief in the North Palace of Ashurbanipal at Nineveh, a characterization Nightingale might have known from reading about Assyria. Still, this is the only Eastern reference in this section, with European images dominating instead.

After presenting Nofariari as a woman ready for this transition, Nofariari asks God why he gave her "passion," "intellect," and "moral activity" if she isn't allowed to use them, and these key qualities, which Nightingale consistently emphasizes, remain in the 1860 version of the treatise, which reads: "Why have women passion, intellect, moral activity—these three—and a place in society where no one of the three can be exercised?" (548). Nofariari's question for God begins a section in which she expresses her "anguish" for women's suffering, much of which remains in the 1860 version. But, in the draft manuscript, Nofariari overcomes her anguish by looking to the moon, an act Nightingale describes through another Italian artistic reference, the Sistine Chapel. "She fixed her eyes upon the splendid moonlit expanse beneath her, when suddenly there came that darkening of the world, which we have all observed on a night when fleecy clouds veil unexpectedly the face of the moon, and which is like the wings of the Almighty . . . as in that inspired representation of Him in Michelangelo's Sistine Chapel" (552–53). It is in this moment that God comes to Nofariari, answering her "Is it Thou, Lord?" with "It is I" (553). In the 1860 version, the description of Nofariari looking at the moon is excised, and the line becomes simply: "'Is it Thou Lord?' And He said, 'It is I.' Let our hearts be still" (552).

This scene recalls Nightingale in the Sistine Chapel, which she described as "looking straight into heaven itself" (McDonald, *Florence Nightingale's European Travels* 150), and the ability of art to inspire devotion to God in a particular type of woman is reinforced in the following scene in the draft manuscript, when Nofariari and her brother talk "by the side of a fountain which shot up its single solitary spire toward heaven" (McDonald, *Florence Nightingale's* Suggestions for Thought 553). The fountain is not identified as a specific work of art from Nightingale's travel, but it functions much in the way Italian architecture does in Nightingale's letters, reaching up toward heaven and thus making it the best art form to connect people on earth to God in heaven (McDonald, *Florence Nightingale's European Travels* 99–100). In this setting, Nofariari makes her case for supporting women's creative faculties, something her brother doesn't understand, since he believes Nofariari has "everything to make a woman happy" (553). Still, Nofariari has spent seven years dreaming of a different kind of life—"I dreamed for an education. . . . I dreamed of experience, not patchwork experience, but experience followed up and systematized" (569–70)—and she argues that without an outlet for her faculties, she is "dead," with "no food for my head, no food for my heart, no food for my activity" (572–73). Although Nofariari's brother enjoys his leisurely life, Nofariari says that she "could not make use of leisure and solitude if I had it! Like the Chinese woman who could not make use of her feet if she were brought into European life" (574), a statement that remains in the 1860 version. Unable to enjoy the leisurely life, Nofariari dies, precisely because she "could do nothing," yet on her death-bed, she indicates death will emancipate her because she will be with God (592).

Nightingale's reference to the Sistine Chapel, then, is key in showing how women might be emancipated, and this reference, like the others I have discussed, suggest only a certain kind of woman can become emancipated according to Nightingale's religious philosophy: the woman who has access to the experience of the Sistine Chapel, can understand the significance of the images in the Chapel, and is patient with the process of how God reveals his perfection. The woman who can experience emancipation, then, becomes more narrow as *Suggestions for Thought* progresses—moving from any woman who can repent for her sins, as suggested by the depiction of Fulgentia as Correggio's *Magdalen*, to an upper-class European woman who has access to, and an understanding of, religious art. It certainly does not include contemporary Egyptian women, even though Nightingale recognized the similarities among ancient Egyptian goddesses such as Isis, historical Egyptian women such as Nefertari, and nineteenth-century European, Christian women such as Nightingale herself.

This narrow definition of the woman who can experience emancipation continues in Volume 3 of the 1860 version of the treatise, which is mostly summary of the key points from the first two volumes, including "God's law," "moral right," human will in relation to God's law, and how humans can achieve a "perfect moral nature" through this relation. Because Nightingale simply iterates earlier points in this volume, we assume these points apply to the kind of women established in the earlier volumes as well, and this is confirmed by one of the few references to the visual arts in the volume, which iterates Nightingale's hierarchical view of nationality, race, and religion. As part of the chapter on human will in relation to God's law, Nightingale argues that just because we recognize our wills are subject to God's law does not mean we become "indifferent" to "moral right" (648). While humans have failed to become more morally right in many areas, one area in which they have "advanced" is their understanding of the concept "God is love" (649). Contrasting images of "the mother of the ancient God of Love," who is "odious in her beauty," to the "Roman Catholic mother of God," who displays "purity" and "devotion," Nightingale argues that the ancient Greeks viewed the God of Love as "an embodiment of sensuality," while the Roman Catholic God of Love shows humanity's "improvement" about how it thinks about God (649). Nightingale's articulation of this advance in the area of moral right confirms her hierarchical view that Christianity—particularly Roman Catholicism, since she says that she will not make the "absurd mistake" of identifying the "Christian mother of God" as "pure" and "devoted" (649)—is the more advanced religious state, an argument that, as we have seen, also relies on hierarchies based on nationality, class, and race.

In thinking about the differences between the draft manuscript and the 1860 printed version of *Suggestions for Thought*, it is true that Nightingale excised many of the references to the visual arts that create specificity in the draft manuscript, and critics such as Showalter and Katherine N. Snyder have suggested the 1860 version of *Suggestions for Thought* is the more "impersonal" version of the treatise because of the elimination of specific autobiographical details. Though there is no clear evidence to indicate why Nightingale cut the details from the draft manuscript,[9] Showalter characterizes the final version as "gutted," "ruthlessly cut" because certain aspects of it were "too revealing, too forceful, or too 'crazy,'" (*Female Malady* 66), and Snyder asserts that the changes Nightingale made are a "cover-up . . . a form of protective self-censorship rather than liberated self-empowerment. . . . Aligning herself with the masculine authority that was the subject of her critique may have enabled Nightingale to accomplish the social reforms that were her goals, but it played havoc with the voice of 'Cassandra'" (35). I would argue that excising specificity from the draft manuscript is not simply a masking of autobiographical details that obscure the gender argument in the text; it also obscures the assumptions about religion, nationality, class, and race that Nightingale brought to her vision of women's emancipation, assumptions she developed during her Egyptian travels. Although Nightingale acknowledged that ancient Egyptian women possessed the virtues that Nightingale associated with her own Christian beliefs, she also thought Egypt had been denigrated by modern Arab culture, so she was unable to draw on what she saw as the positive aspects of Egyptian culture when composing *Suggestions for Thought*. Instead, when she incorporated Egyptian culture into her treatise, she emphasized what she saw as its negative qualities, and the result is a vision of emancipation that ignores Egyptian women. Recognizing that Nightingale's vision of emancipation was primarily for upper- and middle-class, European women, and that their emancipation was *contingent* on the restrictions placed on women from other class and ethnic backgrounds, exposes the illusion of emancipation and shows that even as Nightingale engaged Eastern culture through her travel to Egypt, she was still bound by an English eye, which prevented her from envisioning emancipation for all women.

CHAPTER 3

"[T]o give new elements . . . as vivid as . . . long familiar types": Heroic Jewish Men, Dangerous Egyptian Women, and Equivocal Emancipation in George Eliot's Novels

In February 1876, in the midst of writing *Daniel Deronda* and sending portions of it to John Blackwood to publish in *Blackwood's Magazine*, Eliot told Blackwood, who was "doubtful" about the Jewish character Mordecai, that she was trying "to give new elements" in the creation of this important character, to give readers something different in Mordecai than what author Benjamin Disraeli had given with Sidonia, the Jewish character in *Coningsby* (1844) (Eliot, *Letters* 6:223). Yet, Eliot recognized that giving new elements, using "elements not already used up—in forms as vivid as those of long familiar types," was "the most difficult thing in art," and she expected that "the wider public of novel-readers must feel more interest in Sidonia than in Mordecai" (223). In fact, *Daniel Deronda* was well received by the Jewish community (Himmelfarb 123–24), but its reception by the wider public was a real concern for Eliot during its serialization in *Blackwood's*. Eliot's anxiety is well documented in her letters and journal, and although her "husband" George Henry Lewes did what he could to protect her from the reviews, he, Eliot, and Blackwood regularly commented on the "unsympathetic" reaction to the "Jewish element" in the novel in their letters (6:294, 301, 305). Further, Eliot wrote in her journal in December 1876, after serialization ended, that she had been "made aware of much repugnance or else indifference towards the Jewish part of *Deronda*, and of some hostile as well as adverse reviewing" (6:314).

The reviews were damning with regard to Daniel's, if not Mordecai's, character. George Saintsbury, in the *Academy*, thought Daniel, an Englishman who discovers his Jewish heritage over the course of the novel, "a person so intolerably dreadful that we not only dislike, but refuse to admit him as possible. Only once, perhaps, is he human—when he persuades himself on all sorts of ethico-physico-historical grounds that he should like to be a Jew, solely because . . . he wishes to marry a fascinating Jewess" (373). Saintsbury believed such a character was fine for a "scientific monograph" but had no place in fiction: Eliot had "illustrated the immutable law that no perfect novel can be written in designed illustration of a theory, whether moral or immoral, and that art, like Atticus and the Turk, will bear no rival near the throne" (375–76). Even more hostile, the anonymous reviewer for the *Saturday Review* felt only a sense of "bewilderment and affront" when "a young man of English training and Eton and University education . . . finishes off with his wedding in a Jewish synagogue," and he wondered why Eliot had chosen to write about Jewish characters at all, stating: "[N]ot only are these personages outside our interests, but the author seems to go out with them into a world completely foreign to us. What can be the design of this ostentatious separation from the universal instinct of Christendom, this subsidence into Jewish hopes and aims?" (Anonymous, Rev. of *Daniel, Saturday* 377).

Though reviewers focused on Daniel's character and the "foreign" aspect of the novel because of its attention to Judaism, the novel pushes the boundaries of West and East even further, engaging not only Judaism inside and outside England but also Egyptian culture. The novel identifies Daniel as "an accomplished Egyptian" when he visits the Philosophers Club with Mordecai (563); the central woman character Gwendolen Harleth as both an Englishwoman who cannot "go in search of adventures" such as seeking "the source of the Nile" and as an Egyptian "mummy" with a "rag face and skeleton toes peeping out" (113, 372); Daniel's mother Leonora as experiencing the "desolation" of a Cleopatra because she fails to influence the men in her life (565); and Daniel's fiancée Mirah as having "fervid quality of emotion sometimes rashly supposed to require the bulk of a Cleopatra" when she realizes the depth of Daniel's friendship with Gwendolen (628).

The Egyptian references in the novel have not been discussed by scholars but should be, since they provide a clear context for understanding how Eliot more fully engaged the East with *Daniel Deronda* but was equivocal in her representation of British women's emancipation, via Gwendolen Harleth's character. In May 1874, just as Eliot was beginning to write the novel, she and Emily Strangford (who had traveled east herself and whose book *Egyptian Sepulchres and Syrian Shrines* went into a second edition in 1874), exchanged letters about the possibility of Eliot and Lewes embarking on a trip to Egypt to gather material for the novel (Haight 473–74). Strangford recommended spending six or seven weeks in the autumn of 1874 on the Nile, preferable in a dahabieh instead of on a steamer, followed by wintering in a rental house at Cairo, Ramleh, or Thebes (474). But ill health prevented Eliot and Lewes from taking such a long trip, and they instead went to Surrey, where Eliot immersed herself in writing the novel and Lewes focused on finishing Volume 2 of *Problems of Life and Mind* (474). Eliot's "longing to go to the East" remained, but in December 1876, after the serialization of *Daniel Deronda* was complete, Eliot wrote to the American writer Elizabeth Stuart Phelps that this longing would remain unfulfilled, due to Lewes's continuing ill health (Eliot, *Letters* 6:319).

Unlike Florence Nightingale, who had seen visual representations of ancient Egyptian women during her travel, Eliot did not have the experience of visiting Egyptian temples and viewing the powerful images of Osiris and Isis or of Ramesses II and Nefertari. She had traveled widely on the Continent (particularly to France, Germany, and Italy) and incorporated the visual representations of women she saw in Continental museums into her fiction.[1] Unable to travel beyond the Continent and see the East firsthand, as contemporaries such as Strangford and Amelia Edwards were at this time, Eliot's knowledge of the other half of the world was developed by reading books and newspaper articles; she kept detailed records of her reading about Egypt, including notes about ancient Egyptian women, in her notebooks. As John Clark Pratt and Victor A. Neufeldt point out in the introduction to *George Eliot's Middlemarch Notebooks* (1979), Eliot read about the East from disciplines as diverse as linguistics, history, comparative religion, and mythology, and because her grasp of foreign languages was advanced, she read about this world from a variety of different national perspectives (xvii, xix). The breadth and depth of Eliot's reading was unusual for a woman of her time and confirms she did not have a superficial understanding of the East.

Still, many of the sources Eliot read were written from an imperialist perspective, and as I have shown in Chapter 1 of this book, by the time Eliot published *Daniel Deronda*, Britain's relationship to Egypt was strongly paternal. Egypt was bankrupt, and Britain and other European countries had stepped in to control the debt. While British imperialist views were not yet at their height, the view that Egypt needed Britain's help would have been widely disseminated and is evident in Lewes's letters, when he writes of England's "designs on Egypt" to Lord Robert Lytton, Viceroy of India from 1876 to 1880, in 1878 (122). Furthermore, as I have already discussed in Chapter 1, British interest in Egypt was shaped by its concern over control of the Middle East by other European countries and its awareness that countries such as France and Russia had taken up the causes of smaller groups perceived as oppressed by the Ottoman Empire (Meyer 748). France had taken up the cause of Catholics, and Russia the cause of Greek Christians, so Britain adopted the Jewish cause in order to justify an ongoing presence in the Middle East, including Egypt (748). Even before English Jews were invested seriously in establishment of a homeland in the Middle East, which became pressing after the 1881 Russian pogroms (750), Britain advocated a form of proto-Zionism that would allow it to justify involvement in the Egyptian political situation, since the British believed that supporting Jews would prevent Egyptian attacks on Syria (748). In Eliot's time, then, there was a significant Jewish context for British imperialism, even a slippage between Egyptian and Jewish identities, which was part of the larger discussion about the "Eastern question" in British imperialist discourse. Like the other women writers discussed in this study, Eliot was, to at least some degree, "bound by an English eye," and her understanding of the Eastern world was filtered through an imperialist lens.

In her reading, Eliot encountered numerous illustrations of Egyptian culture, in books such as Wilkinson's *Manners and Customs of the Ancient Egyptians* and Lane's *An Account of the Manners and Customs of the Modern Egyptians*, which Joseph Wiesenfarth indicates were sources for her comments about Egyptian culture in her Commonplace Book (141–42). Wilkinson's book included over 400 illustrations across three volumes, which depicted everything from key ancient monuments to the religious rituals performed by ancient Egyptians to the weapons used in battle to clothing worn and items used in everyday life. Though Lane's book had fewer illustrations (about 100 across two volumes), it also amply represented *modern* Egyptian life, with images of homes in Cairo, people of different classes, mosque rituals, special events such as weddings and funerals, and jewelry worn by modern Egyptians.

Eliot also read Amelia Edwards's *A Thousand Miles Up the Nile* (1876), from which she copied information into her *Daniel Deronda* notebooks (486–89), and she may have read Joseph Bonomi's *Nineveh and Its Palaces* (1857) and George Gliddon's *Ancient Egypt* (1843), which were part of George Henry Lewes's library (Baker, *George Eliot-George Henry Lewes* 24, 73). Edwards's book included about 80 illustrations, some of which were wood engravings and, more so than Wilkinson's and Lane's books, depicted the ancient sites Nightingale had seen in person as she traveled along the Nile. For example, in the chapter about Philae, Edwards included images of the Grand Colonnade, painted columns in the Portico of the Large Temple, and smaller shrines (both Christian and to ancient Egyptian gods such as Osiris). In the chapter about Abu Simbel, which was the temple Nightingale particularly liked for its representation of Ramesses II and Nefertari as the ideal husband and wife, Edwards included a full-page profile of Ramesses II from the "Southernmost Colossus" (419), and at the front of Edwards's book, there is an image of the "Great Rock-Cut Temple," which has four very large (65-foot) statues of Ramesses II. In the chapter about Medinet Habu, which Nightingale did not like because she believed Ramesses III's reign was guilty of corruption of power and made conditions for women difficult, Edwards included an image of the Palace Entrance and wrote more favorably of the temple than Nightingale had, stating that "the Temple and Pavilion at Medinet Habu . . . are to the life of Ramesses III precisely what Aboo Simbel . . . [is] to the life of Ramesses II. . . . [I]n Ramesses III we have . . . a king as brilliant, as valorous, and as successful as Ramesses II" (620–21).

Bonomi's book included close to 300 illustrations, which included people, places, and items, many of which show the influence of Assyrian culture, but also images of important ancient Egyptian gods and kings, including Amun-Ra and Ramesses IV (87, 159). In Gliddon's book, Eliot would have seen mostly hieroglyphs, including those for important ancient Egyptian figures such as Cleopatra, Ramesses III, and Amun (24, 28, 32). Although the illustrations in the books Eliot read were numerous, most were pen-and-ink drawings, which often flattened the effect of the images and certainly would not have compared to Nightingale's experience seeing images of Egyptian gods, goddesses, kings, and queens firsthand in the temples. Still, the drawings in Edwards's book were more three-dimensional, and even in Lane's and Wilkinson's books, the more two-dimensional drawings would have given Eliot the detail needed to envision the daily lives of ancient and contemporary Egyptians. Eliot noted the images of ancient Egyptian women's work from Wilkinson's book in her Commonplace Book, writing at one point, "Egyptian sculptures showing women weaving & using the distaff" (Wiesenfarth, *A Writer's Notebook* 6; see Figure 3.1). Eliot also may have seen images of ancient Egyptian women during her visits to the British Museum, where she viewed Greek and Roman antiquities (Eliot, *Letters* 5:359, 408), which would have reflected the influence of Egyptian culture on representations of women from more familiar ancient cultures.

While Eliot's exposure to visual representations of Egyptian women was limited, especially compared to that of Nightingale, her reading about Egyptian culture provided substantial information about ancient Egyptian women, which I discuss in more detail in the next section of this chapter. This reading is important to understanding her representation of Western women's emancipation in her later novels, *Romola* (1862) and *Daniel Deronda* (1876), both of which engage the East more fully than Eliot's earlier work does, offering readers a new look not only at Judaism but also Egyptian culture, via the description of Daniel as "an accomplished Egyptian" (563). Still, Eliot refers to ancient Egyptian women only once and in negative terms in building

Gwendolen Harleth's character, when the German Vandernoodt tells Daniel he doesn't "care a straw about the *faux pas* of the mummies" but believes Daniel is "one of the historical men," who is "more interested in a lady when she's got a rag face and skeleton toes peeping out" (372). Eliot also does not refer to ancient Egyptian women in building the title character in *Romola*, who provides the model for womanhood Daniel recommends to Gwendolen when he says she will be "among the best of women" (658). Although Eliot clearly understood the power of ancient Egyptian women, she avoided associating Romola and Gwendolen with these powerful women, since to do so would have been perilous in a culture that still sought more familiar models for women's emancipation.

Cheryl Baker Price, in "Poison, Sensation, and Secrets in *The Lifted Veil*" (2010), recognizes the danger of making such a link, arguing that when Eliot linked women characters to Egypt—as she did in *The Lifted Veil* (1859) by associating Bertha, a wife who plots to poison her husband, with an image of "a dying Cleopatra" and adorning her with a "great emerald brooch" featuring a "studded serpent with diamond eyes" (Eliot qtd. in Price 209–10)—she did so with the recognition that women such as Bertha threatened the domestic tranquility of traditional Victorian culture and suggested more independent lives for women, an emerging reality as women gained more social and legal power (206). Price also argues that closest to Bertha in Eliot's gallery of women characters is Gwendolen Harleth, since Gwendolen's "troubled marriage and ambiguous role in her husband's drowning invite censure and sympathy" (213). Price's argument confirms that critics who have considered Gwendolen as dangerously transgressive because of her independence, as Bonnie Zimmerman and Natalie Rose have done, are right to do so,[2] and the nineteenth-century reviewers of *Daniel Deronda* who express dislike for Daniel's character also characterize Gwendolen as "dangerous." The anonymous reviewer for the *Academy*, writing about the first installment of the novel in *Blackwood's*, states: "Gwendolen is already cast for the *rôle* of demon, but we do not know whether virtue is to be martyred or triumphant—in Rex or in Deronda" (Anonymous, Rev. of *Daniel*, *Academy* 362). Further, Saintsbury, writing for the *Academy*, sees Gwendolen as "an overwhelming success" but characterizes her as a woman who "hates" her husband; Saintsbury sympathizes with Grandcourt, who is in the "difficult" situation of "being hated by his wife" (372). Finally, the very hostile reviewer for the *Saturday Review* argues that while Gwendolen is the heroine of the novel (as opposed to the "ideal" Mirah, who is "monotonous in speech and same in attitude"), she is the least appealing heroine the reviewer has ever seen, both in terms of his "interest" in her and his "sympathy" with her (390). If she were not beautiful, he would only feel "repulsion," since she is "so selfish, so dead to duty and tenderness, so confident and unscrupulous" (390–91).

Eliot did not anticipate the criticism of Gwendolen's character as fully as she did that of Daniel, perhaps because Blackwood consistently confirmed her development of Gwendolen as a "witch" who is nevertheless "true to nature" and because Eliot had promised Blackwood that Gwendolen would be "spiritually saved, but so as by fire" (6:144, 182, 188). Still, while Eliot clearly had a transgressive woman in mind as she was building Gwendolen's character, she did not use her knowledge of ancient Egyptian women to build this character, building her instead through references to Western mythologies, especially Christian and Greek mythologies, which would have been more palatable to an English audience. In doing this, Eliot continued the pattern she had established with *Romola*, where she more thoroughly engaged the position of women in the East by placing women in relationships with men who have ties to the East but stopped short of directly showing how Eastern attributes might provide a direction for Western women as they contemplated their own opportunities for emancipation from a marriage system that still placed women in inferior positions to their husbands. While Eliot does include the mummy reference and uses open-ended symbolism that allows readers to infer an Egyptian context for interpreting Gwendolen's character, she avoids directly associating Gwendolen with Egyptian goddesses, a narrative representation that points to the perceived "danger" of the "deep East" felt by Victorians, particularly when women from this region of the world might have provided a model for Western women's emancipation. The result is an equivocal emancipation for Gwendolen, in which her future is unclear, a contrast to the more unequivocal emancipation for Gwendolen's model, Romola, whose character is also developed through Christian and Greek mythologies and whose future becomes clear after she is converted from paganism to Christianity by the friar Girolamo Savonarola, a form of emancipation similar to that advocated by Nightingale.

* * *

Before discussing Eliot's representation of Gwendolen's equivocal emancipation in *Daniel Deronda*, we should turn to an account of Eliot's reading about Egyptian women, which was part of a larger process of reading about the relationships between various cultures, especially the role mythology played in connecting cultures. In part a reaction to her own loss of faith in the early 1840s, Eliot came to embrace the idea that Western civilization should be understood in relation to Eastern civilization, that the origins of Western culture came from the East. Many critics have discussed this development in Eliot's thinking, in ways specific to their own research interests.[3] For my purposes, Eliot's reading about the relationships between British, Greek, and Egyptian mythologies is important because it displays Eliot's understanding that British mythologies about women could not exist without their Eastern counterparts. Further, Eliot's engagement with the debate about women's place in nineteenth-century British culture through her reading of the major texts used in this debate—including Mary Wollstonecraft's *A Vindication of the Rights of Woman* (1796), Sarah Lewis's *Woman's Mission* (1839), and John Stuart Mill's *The Subjection of Women* (1869)—indicate she understood the parallels between Western and Eastern women's cultural status common in even the most progressive nineteenth-century minds, since these texts paralleled Western and Eastern women's oppression. Through her reading, Eliot developed a view similar to that of Florence Nightingale, in that she could see parallels between the oppression of Western and Eastern women yet did not look for the specifically "Christian" qualities Nightingale found in the representations of women in ancient Egyptian temples. Further, she did not emphasize a solution to the problem of Western women's oppression as clearly as Nightingale did. Eliot remained more equivocal about how women might overcome this oppression, though she did much to expose women's oppression by acknowledging how both Western and Eastern women were dependent on masculine authority.

Eliot's reading about the Eastern origins of Western mythology appears in her published work as early as the mid-1850s, when she was writing articles about literature, art, and culture for periodicals such as the *Leader* and the *Westminster Review*. In "The *Antigone* and Its Moral," published in the *Leader* in March 1856, Eliot examines the Greek origins of British mythology by arguing that the primary theme of Sophocles's play—family loyalty versus loyalty to the government—is not unique to ancient Greece culture but is the same conflict faced by modern Britons as well. While Eliot writes that Britons "no longer believe that a brother, if left unburied, is condemned to wander a hundred years without repose on the banks of the Styx" (363), there were contemporary examples parallel to those of Antigone and Creon, and Eliot concludes that "[w]herever the strength of a man's intellect, or moral sense, or affection brings him into opposition with the rules which society has sanctioned, *there* is renewed the conflict between Antigone and Creon" (366).[4]

Eliot's understanding of the connection between Greek and Egyptian culture is seen in another article written for the *Leader*, "The Art of the Ancients" (1855), a review of Adolph Stahr's 1854 book about Greek culture and art, *Torso: Kunst, Künstler und Kunstwerk der Alten*. Here, Eliot shows the connection by detailing how ancient Greek art retained attributes of ancient Egyptian art. Laying out earlier critics' debate over whether Greek art was "indigenous" or "a higher development of oriental art," Eliot indicates that the well-known German art critic Johann Winckelmann held the former view while Ludwig Ross, a more popular "tourist" and critic, figured out that Greek art had descended from oriental art, based on artifacts he examined in his travels to the Levant (modern-day Syria, Lebanon, Jordan, Israel) and surrounding countries (modern-day Turkey and Egypt) (245). To support Ross's view, Eliot cites specific Greek sculptures from Stahr's book showing the Egyptian influence on Greek art: for example, the "reliefs at Samothrace representing Agamemnon seated on a throne . . . bear strong traces of the abstract Egyptian manner," especially the "repetition" of the "heralds" on either side of Agamemnon (245). Continuing her discussion of the Greek art in Stahr's book, Eliot mentions that Praxiteles, one of the well-known Attic sculptors of the fourth century BCE, inaugurated the "Venus ideal" that would culminate with his *Aphrodite of Knidos* (247), and an examination of Stahr's book reveals he devoted more than 20 pages to discussion of the various Greek and Roman Venuses (328–57), suggesting Eliot was well versed in representations of this particular goddess. There is no evidence that Stahr recognized the Egyptian equivalent of Venus, Hathor, but Eliot did. In her *Middlemarch* notebooks, Eliot notes the various Egyptian gods and goddesses and, in some cases, lists their Greek equivalents: "[H]*Athor*(=Venus)" is among those listed (229). Further, in her *Daniel Deronda* notebooks, Eliot quotes phrases from an appendix about "The Egyptian Pantheon" in Amelia Edwards's *A Thousand Miles Up the Nile*, listing once again the Egyptian gods and goddesses worshipped at Memphis and Thebes. Among these deities, she notes that Hathor is "Cow-headed, & crowned with the disk & plumes / Deity of Amenti, or the Egyptian Hades. [Worshipped at] Denderah" and Isis is "A woman crowned with the sun-disk surmounted by a throne, & sometimes enclosed between horns" (489).

Eliot clearly understood the connection between Greek and Egyptian mythologies, and her *Daniel Deronda* notebooks not only confirm this understanding but extend it to encompass the relationships between British, Greek, and Egyptian mythologies, since the notebooks indicate that the connections between these mythologies informed her development of Gwendolen Harleth's name. As Natalie Rose has argued, Eliot's notes about Gwendolen's name provide evidence Eliot recognized the "multiple origins for English culture" (121). Rose argues Eliot's notes recognize the Celtic elements in English culture that facilitate Eliot's presentation, in *Daniel Deronda*, of Daniel as a "lone knight" who tries to rescue Gwendolen and Gwendolen as akin to Malory's Guinevere, judged by the "punitive ideologies of Victorian womanhood" for her "resistant subjectivity" (126). But, Eliot's notes also reveal her recognition that Egyptian culture was one of the many Eastern cultures contributing to the development of English culture. Drawing on Charlotte Yonge's *History of Christian Names* (1863), Eliot writes in her notebook: "Gwen is considered as the British Venus. The planet is Seren-Wener as a morning star, Gweno as an evening star; nay, it is probable that Venus herself may be but a Cymric Gwen. Gwendolen, or the Lady of the bow, or perhaps from Gwendal, white browed, was, it seems, an ancient British goddess, probably the moon" (446). Having established Gwendolen as Cymric, or Welsh, Eliot notes that Yonge describes how the Welsh tradition merged with the English tradition in the Sir Arthur tales, where Gwendolen "is a beauty of Arthur's Court, & in the bardic enumeration of the thirteen wonders of Britain appears the gold chess board of Gwendolen" (446). Though the emphasis put on the Welsh origins of Gwendolen suggests Eliot was drawing on a Western model for thinking about Gwendolen's character, Eliot's notebooks indicate that Yonge traced Celtic people, of which the Welsh were one, to the East. Eliot makes two separate notes about this. The first note indicates that while the "isle of Erin," or Ireland, "has been supposed to be named from Eri, the West," philologists now believe its name can be traced to Boeotia, or modern-day central Greece (450), which suggests the potential for Eastern origins of the Irish. The second note indicates that the Scots' emigration path could be traced to Spain and then to Thrace (modern-day Greece, Bulgaria, and Turkey) (450). According to Yonge, Niul, son of Phenius and the King of Thrace, migrated to Egypt and named the Nile after himself before emigrating to Spain (450), an emigration path that, like the path of the Irish, suggests Eastern roots for the Celts. As I demonstrate later in this chapter, Eliot ultimately associates Gwendolen more fully with the British Venus than an Egyptian goddess such as Hathor, but it is clear that she understood the emigration and linguistic patterns that established the basis for the Eastern origins of Western cultures.

Eliot's notes in her Commonplace Book, which I discuss below, confirm her understanding of the influence of Eastern culture on Western culture. They do not, however, directly indicate how the connections between Western and Eastern mythologies relate to the position of women in nineteenth-century British culture. For that connection, we should turn to Eliot's reading of major eighteenth- and nineteenth-century texts about women's oppression. Though critics have rightly resisted the idea that Eliot makes a "feminist statement" in her novels, since her work seems less explicitly feminist than the late-Victorian novels written after the term "feminist" enters discourse about the social progress of women, Eliot did understand the difficult position of women in Victorian Britain. Not only did her own situation with George Henry Lewes, which resulted in an initial ostracization from society after she went to live with him in 1854 (McCormack 1), give her real-life experience with the struggles independent women faced, but over the course of her career, she read the key texts used in debates surrounding the "Woman Question," including Wollstonecraft's *A Vindication of the Rights of Woman* (1796), Lewis's *Woman's Mission* (1839), and Mill's *The Subjection of Women* (1869).[5] These texts equate the oppression of English women to that of Eastern women, while still privileging the position of Western women over Eastern women because of their Christianity.

In *Woman's Mission*, for example, Lewis argues that Christianity was the "one source of regeneration" for securing "woman's influence" in the private sphere and directly contrasts what Christianity provides women, as opposed to what Eastern religions offers them. While Christianity recognizes the qualities "proper to their sex . . . gentleness, lowliness, and humility" (141), Eastern religions ensure that women remained enslaved. "Can women be anything but Christians," writes Lewis, "when they hear the scornful thanksgiving of the Jew, that he was not born a woman—when they read in the creed of Mahomet that their highest destiny in the next world, (even if they enter it,) is to minister to the passions of which they were slaves in this" (142). While Wollstonecraft does not directly state that Western women have the advantage of Christianity to emancipate them in *Vindication of the Rights of Woman*, she suggests that when Englishwomen are treated in a non-Christian manner, they are oppressed. Using references to the Eastern woman's supposed oppression by Islam to support her point that Western women's education made them "alluring mistresses" rather than "affectionate wives and rational mothers" (71), Wollstonecraft writes. "[T]he books of instruction [for European women's education], written by men of genius, have had the same tendency as more frivolous productions; and that, in the true style of Mahometanism [which was erroneously thought to deny women souls], they are treated as a kind of subordinate beings, and not as a part of the human species" (71). Further, Wollstonecraft argues, those who write about women's education assume they are fit only for marriage and bearing children, privileging "libertine notions of beauty" over "strength of body and mind" (74). The result is that women enter marriage as "mere animals," behaving as "children may be expected to act. . . . Surely these weak beings are only fit for a seraglio [harem]!" (74).

Even in Mill's *The Subjection of Women*—which casts doubt on the view that Eastern women are oppressed, since Mill refutes the argument that races can be characterized according to "nature" (21)—Mill sometimes relies on stereotypes about Eastern women to make his point that English society should bring an end to the "legal subordination of one sex to the other" (1). Discussing the difference between a woman's power in marriage (i.e., through her beauty, affection for her husband, and even shared interests with her husband) and freedom (which he says gives a woman the ability to choose how to live her life and, therefore, is more important than power), Mill writes, "neither in the affairs of families nor in those of states is power a compensation for the loss of freedom. [A woman's] power often gives her what she has no right to, but does not enable her to assert her own rights. A Sultan's favorite slave has slaves under her, over whom she tyrannizes; but the desirable thing would be that she should neither have slaves nor be a slave" (70). By placing a reference to the Sultan's slave in the midst of an example about Englishwomen and marriage, Mill implies that Englishwomen are in no better position than Eastern women because they are treated as poorly as Eastern women are.

Eliot, then, would have been familiar with the parallel between the oppression of Western and Eastern women found in British texts concerned with women's emancipation, texts that reflect the influence of imperialism on even the most progressive British minds. Still, Eliot did recognize that Eastern women, particularly ancient Egyptian women, held powerful positions in their own societies. In *A Writer's Notebook*, a transcription of Eliot's Commonplace Book, Joseph Wiesenfarth indicates that Eliot's "interest in the condition of women" was based in part on her understanding of Egyptian women, about whom she had read in Wilkinson's *Manners and Customs of the Ancient Egyptians* (xix). I have already indicated that Eliot noted illustrations of ancient Egyptian women's activities in her Commonplace Book and copied statements by Wilkinson about Egyptian women, including one about the privileges they enjoyed: "The Egyptian women . . . appear to have enjoyed greater privilege & to have been treated with more courtesy on all occasions than in other ancient communities" (6). Following this statement, she makes notes about their access to wine, a privilege not extended to ancient Greek women; their control over their husbands, especially with regard to household matters; and their access to Royal power (6). These notes indicate that even as Eliot might have absorbed the imperialist attitudes expressed by Wilkinson, which I discussed in Chapter 1, she also understood the privilege accorded ancient Egyptian women, information that could be used to make comparative judgments about the position of women in nineteenth-century British society.

Eliot also copied into her Commonplace Book Wilkinson's comments about Egyptian marriage, which he drew from Diodorus, the first-century BCE Greek historian. "Diodorus informs us the Egyptians were not restricted to any number of wives, but that everyone married as many as he chose. . . . It does not however appear that they generally took advantage of this privilege; & Herodotus affirms that throughout Egypt it was customary to marry only one wife. . . . [I]f the Egyptians were allowed to take more than one wife we may conclude from the numerous scenes illustrative of their domestic life, that it was an event of rare occurrence" (6). Still, Eliot did not overlook the fact that some Egyptian men had multiple partners through harems. She copied Wilkinson's explanation that harems included both white and black women slaves, who typically would have been foreigners won in war or imported to be sold as slaves (6). Nevertheless, the children of these women would have had the same "rights of inheritance" as did the children of legitimate wives (7), a custom Wiesenfarth believes informed Eliot's writing of Lydia Glasher's situation as Grandcourt's mistress in *Daniel Deronda* (142) and a theme I believe Eliot develops in *Romola*, where Romola cares for the children of her husband's mistress.

*   *   *

Still, it is unlikely Eliot specifically intended that readers interpret Lydia Glasher's situation or Romola's care of Tessa's children in direct relation to Egyptian culture, since Eliot had some of the same concerns about *Romola* that she did about *Daniel Deronda*—that it would be too "foreign" for British readers, who were accustomed to her "Stories of English Life," a concern echoed in reviews of *Romola* (Eliot, *Letters* 3:339–40; Anonymous, Rev. of *Romola* 213–15). Further, as Felicia Bonaparte has shown, Eliot tends to use one specific type of mythological reference at a time rather than referring to multiple mythologies together. In *The Triptych and the Cross: The Central Myths of George Eliot's Poetic Imagination* (1979), Bonaparte argues that, in *Romola*, Eliot comments on the status of nineteenth-century British women's status through Greek but not Egyptian mythology, effectively showing how Eliot does not characterize Romola as Cleopatra in the scene in which Romola is betrothed to Tito. Bonaparte notes that the betrothal scene is "one of the most pictorial in the book" because of the contrast of Romola's and Tito's physical appearances: Romola is depicted as "light" and similar to Renaissance images of the Virgin Mary, while Tito is depicted as "darker" and similar to the pagan figure Dionysus (95–96). Bonaparte indicates Eliot went to great lengths to ensure Romola would look Florentine rather than Eastern by suggesting that Frederic Leighton, who illustrated the novel, mirror his depiction after the Florentine Ginerva Rinuccini's dress, including details such as the pearls she wore in her cap (97–99). According to Bonaparte, there is a similar pearl headdress in a portrait of Simonetta Vespuccia (c. 1480) by the artist Piero di Cosimo, and Eliot likely knew this portrait, since her descriptions of Romola in the novel are similar to those of Vespuccia (99). Yet, this portrait, explains Bonaparte, had been incorrectly identified as Cleopatra by Giorgio Vasari because of the snake around Vespuccia's neck, so Eliot urged Leighton to copy Rinuccini's trousseau because she wanted to show that Romola was becoming more Christian across the course of the novel (99). To suggest that Leighton follow the portrait of Vespuccia as a model would have associated Romola with Cleopatra and worked against the plot of Romola's conversion to Christianity. Clearly, Eliot did not want to directly link Romola to Cleopatra, since as I will discuss in more detail in my chapter about Glyn, Cleopatra increasingly represented Egyptian culture in a negative manner over the course of the nineteenth century.

Eliot also avoids creating a positive association between Romola and St. Catherine of Egypt when in the novel, Piero di Cosimo, observing the burning of so-called "pagan" books by the Church, sarcastically remarks that Romola is "fit to be a model for a wise Saint Catherine of Egypt," even though di Cosimo is sure Romola has read some of the books being burned (426). We know Eliot understood the Egyptian origins of women saints because she made notes in her Commonplace Book about St. Catherine and St. Barbara, who is referenced in *Middlemarch* without recognition of her Egyptian origins (Eliot, *Middlemarch* 114). These notes were based on Eliot's reading of Anna Jameson's methodical discussion of artistic representations of saints, *Sacred and Legendary Art* (1848), where Jameson acknowledges the Egyptian origins of these women but ultimately emphasizes their Western attributes over their Eastern qualities. Eliot includes in her Commonplace Book notes the detail that St. Catherine "was granddaughter of Constantine Chlorus, father of Constantine the Great, & her mother inherited the throne of Egypt" and that St. Barbara "was the daughter of a rich noble in [Heliopolis], who, fearful, of her great beauty . . . shut her up in a tower" (Wiesenfarth 63). And, though not included in her notes, Eliot would have read in Jameson's book that St. Barbara's father was a "turbaned Turk" (Jameson 2:498), confirming that St. Barbara's ethnicity, according to mythology if not accurate historical accounts, was not entirely Western European.[6] By presenting Romola's tie to St. Catherine sarcastically, Eliot avoids associating Romola with the Eastern world, an association that might have been seen as "dangerous" to British readers of the novel, who already felt a lack of connection with the novel because of its historical and geographical context.

One also must wonder whether Eliot specifically avoided directly characterizing Romola as Hathor, whom I have already described as the Egyptian equivalent of Venus and who was also known for her ability to nourish others with her milk, since she takes the form of a cow. Late in the novel, after Romola's husband has died and Romola has fully embraced the life of a Christian nun, Romola cares for Tito's mistress, Tessa, and her children. Further, Romola leaves Florence and travels by sea to a village that has been devastated by the Plague, caring for its children because many of the adults in the village have died. Bonaparte argues that Romola takes Tessa's children "under her protection" in her capacity as Antigone transformed into the Virgin Mary (207, 244), a reading that focuses on Eliot's use of Greek and Christian mythology rather than Egyptian mythology to characterize Romola. Still, while Romola is referred to in overtly Western terms, with Tessa and the residents of the village calling her the "Holy Madonna" and the "Holy Mother" (468, 562), Eliot would have known that the Egyptian goddesses Hathor and Isis had regenerative, life-giving powers. The qualities Romola exhibits with Tessa's children, nursing Lillo even though he is not her biological child (469) and then nourishing the children whose village has been devastated (562), are akin to the qualities possessed by these goddesses. Especially given that the village Romola visits neglects its corn crops and has lost many of its cows (559–60, 562), symbols associated with the primary Egyptian goddesses, Eliot would have known these associations with ancient Egyptian culture but did not incorporate these associations into the novel, instead privileging Christian and Greek mythologies as methods for building Romola's character.

Eliot's tendency to represent one myth rather than another, instead of stacking mythologies, is also evident in *Daniel Deronda*, where the character of Gwendolen Harleth serves to expose the problem of Western women's oppression. Told that she will be "among the best of women" by Daniel before he departs for the East to do his own good work on the behalf of Jewish people (658), emancipation via good work seems to be one solution to the "Woman Question" in the novel. Yet, Gwendolen's inability to embrace this model, as Romola does, suggests that Western women's emancipation is not so simple. Eliot exposes this problem but offers no unequivocal solution to it, in part because she emphasizes certain mythologies in building the central characters in the novel. While she directly refers to Egyptian culture in a positive manner when building Daniel's character, she does not directly link Gwendolen to powerful Egyptian goddesses in a positive manner. The initial characterization of Gwendolen through symbols such as the *serpent* (which serves to bring attention to Gwendolen as a fascinating woman at the beginning of the novel) and the *turquoise necklace* (which is central to the marriage plot pitting Daniel and Grandcourt against each other) could be associated with Egyptian goddesses, but these symbols are presented in connection with Western mythologies instead, suggesting that while Eliot more fully engages the East in *Daniel Deronda*, she remained "bound by an English eye," unable to fully use ancient Egyptian women as a model for Western women seeking emancipation.

Before showing how Eliot builds Gwendolen's character primarily through Western mythologies, it is worth detailing her development of Daniel's character. Of course, Daniel's discovery of his Jewish identity is central to the novel's plot and has been well discussed by recent scholars, including Patrick Brantlinger, William Baker, Bernard Semmel, and Mikhal Dekel, who cover the cultural contexts most relevant to my argument. Brantlinger, in "Nations and Novels: Disraeli, George Eliot, and Orientalism," (1992) argues that, with *Daniel Deronda*, Eliot was specifically responding to Benjamin Disraeli's more "racially pure" definitions of ethnicity in his "Young England" novels, providing a definition of ethnicity that was more open to "mongrelization" and suggesting that "racial unity," which was increasingly important to the Jewish community, could be found through the mixture of different ethnic groups (271–72). In particular, we know that Eliot was responding not only to Disraeli's *Coningsby* but also to *Tancred* (1847), the last in his "Young England" trilogy and a novel Eliot thought presented Jews in an "over-idealized" fashion when she read it. Writing to friend Mary Sibree in May 1847, Eliot characterized the novel as "more detestable stuff than ever came from a French pen" (Eliot, *Letters* 1:234–35), and in February 1848, writing to Mary's brother John, Eliot provided more detailed comments about Disraeli's "theory of 'races'" as portrayed in the novel (1:246). "As to his theory of 'races' it has not a leg to stand on, and can only be buoyed up by such windy eloquence as 'You chitty-faced squabby-nosed Europeans owe your commerce, your arts, your religion to the Hebrews'. . . . Extermination up to a certain point seems to be the law for the inferior races—for the rest, fusion both for physical and moral ends. . . . My Gentile nature kicks most resolutely against any assumption of superiority in the Jews" (1:246).

As William Baker explains in *George Eliot and Judaism* (1975), theologians such as Charles Hennell (*Inquiry Concerning the Origin of Christianity*, 1841) and David Friedrich Struss (*The Life of Jesus, Critically Examined*, translated into English by Eliot, 1846) had used sources from the Jewish tradition to "explain Christianity" and had placed emphasis on the superiority of Jews (29). According to Baker, when Eliot "rejected the religion of her youth, Christianity, by leaving the Church of England in the 1840s, "so she rejected the Jewish [tradition]" (29). Still Bernard Semmel has argued, in *George Eliot and the Politics of National Inheritance* (1994), that by the time Eliot wrote *Daniel Deronda*, she had mostly accepted Disraeli's theory that races could fuse, a major plot point in *Tancred*, since the title character, an Englishman, falls in love with a Jewish woman, Eva, who is "proud" of her heritage rather than ashamed of it (120).

As I already have shown, the Jewish community in England also had changed its position on the need for racial pride by the time Eliot published *Daniel Deronda*, and Mikhal Dekel, in "'Who Taught This Foreign Woman About the Ways and Live of the Jews?': George Eliot and the Hebrew Renaissance" (2007), further contextualizes Eliot's position on racial unity in the

Jewish community in England by detailing the reception of *Daniel Deronda* in that community. As Dekel explains, the Zionist movement would not emerge fully until the late 1890s, with the first Zionist Congress held in 1897, but there was a Hebrew Renaissance at the time Eliot wrote *Daniel Deronda* (785). As part of this Renaissance, the British Jew Hayyim Guedella planned to buy Palestinian land from the Turks in exchange for debt relief from Britain, and Guedella had portions of *Daniel Deronda* translated into Hebrew and published in the *Jewish Chronicle*, with a fuller translation by David Frishman published in book form in 1893 (785). Not surprisingly, this fuller translation left out much of the "English" portion of the novel (Gwendolen's story) and focused on Daniel's discovery of his Jewish heritage instead (793), an approach appropriate to the translation's target audience: young, Jewish men who would have been increasingly interested in an emerging Zionist movement and would have been able to read the Hebrew translation of Eliot's novel (most women in the Jewish community in England at this time would not have been able to read Hebrew) (787).

While the Jewish context of *Daniel Deronda* is significant, in part because Britain's interest in controlling the Egyptian political situation was discussed in terms of advocating for a Jewish homeland in the Middle East, no critic has discussed in detail how Eliot presented Daniel's Jewish identity through references to ancient Egypt, a presentation that contributed to a positive portrayal of Judaism at a time when the Jewish community sought such a representation. Eliot first uses Egyptian culture to develop Daniel's character when Mordecai (who recognizes Daniel's Jewish identity well before Daniel does), takes Daniel to the Philosophers Club and introduces him to a group of men who, despite their diverse ethnic backgrounds, all have some connection to Judaism. Engaged in discourse with these men about the future of Judaism, Mordecai draws on Egypt's cultural history to argue for a nationalist movement that will give Jews a chance to flourish, a vision Daniel ultimately embraces and uses when he travels East at the end of the novel. Mordecai envisions a "sacred land" for Jews, which will function "not as a place in loathsome idleness, but as a republic where the Jewish spirit manifests itself in a new order founded on the old, purified, enriched by the experience our greatest sons have gathered from the life of ages" (458). Here, Mordecai draws on an Egyptian model to articulate his vision for this sacred land, saying that "wise and wealthy" Jews can become "heroes," by using their "memories of the East and West" to create a "new Persia with a purified religion" (458–59). A "new Judea, poised between East and West," will be "a covenant of reconciliation" (459), Mordecai says, and Jews will achieve what the ancient Egyptians achieved, a nation that became productive because Egyptians took advantage of the larger forces available to them: "The Nile overflowed and rushed onward: the Egyptian could not choose the overflow, but he chose to work and make channels for the fructifying waters, and Egypt became the land of corn" (459). Jews can do the same, Mordecai argues, if they accept the opportunity. "Shall man . . . deny his rank and say, I am an onlooker, ask no choice or purpose of me? That is the blasphemy of this time. The divine principle of our race is action, choice, resolved memory. Let us contradict the blasphemy, and help to will our own better future and the better future of the world" (459).

Although Daniel cannot immediately see himself fulfilling the role Mordecai has articulated, since he does not yet know of his Jewish heritage, he does pledge to help Mordecai however he can, saying, "Everything I can in conscience do to make your life effective I will do" (461). And, once Daniel knows of his Jewish heritage, he embraces the vision Mordecai had for himself in his youth—"to behold the lands and people of the East"—which went unfulfilled when Mordecai could not embark on his journey because his mother needed his help, after losing Mordecai's sister Mirah to her degenerate husband (462). As Daniel prepares to go East with Mirah at the end of the novel, Daniel articulates his commitment to doing the work Mordecai could not do, telling Gwendolen, "I am going to the East to become better acquainted with the condition of my race in various countries there . . . The idea that I am possessed with is that of restoring a political existence to my people, making them a nation again. . . . I am resolved to devote my life to it" (688). Although Mirah doubts Daniel's commitment to fulfilling his mission at one point, saying to Mordecai, "does it ever hurt your love for Mr Deronda that so much of his life was all hidden away from you,—that he is amongst persons and cares about persons who are all so unlike us . . . ?" (563), Mordecai never doubts Daniel's commitment. "No, assuredly no," he says in response to Mirah's question, "Rather, it is a precious thought to me that he has the preparation which I lacked, and is an accomplished Egyptian" (563).

This reference to Daniel as "an accomplished Egyptian" can be interpreted as a reference to Moses, who was saved from death as an infant when an Egyptian pharaoh's daughter Bithiah pulled him from the Nile and raised him. Better known as the Jewish prophet who led the Israelites out of Egypt, Moses functions as a model for Daniel, the kind of hero Mordecai believes can take advantage of the overflow of the Nile and cultivate the crops that made ancient Egypt a productive nation. By journeying East with Mirah, Daniel will ensure that Jews build their own productive state. As Semmel notes, Moses's and Daniel's journeys are similar: Moses, "deprived of his family and national inheritance" as Jew, "had been raised an Egyptian prince. Made aware he was Hebrew, he relinquished his superior for an inferior status, and determined to lead his people to freedom and their own land. . . .

Deronda, abandoned by his mother, has his mission revealed to him by Mordecai. That mission is a terrestrial one, like that of Moses, as well as one of redemption—a national not an individual one" (123). Further, Terence Caves suggests, in his introduction to the 1995 Penguin edition of *Daniel Deronda*, that Eliot's linking of Daniel and Moses was intentional, since the notebooks she kept while working on the novel not only include quotes from *Tancred* and a description of Byron's grandniece gambling in Homburg (the inspiration for the opening scene of the novel) but also notes about "the exodus of the Israelites from Egypt" and "the meaning of the name 'Moses' in Egyptian" (xi–xii).

Daniel's character, then, is built around a direct reference to Egypt, but it is important to note that this reference to Egypt is through the Judeo-Christian tradition, and critics have linked Daniel's journey not only to that of Moses but also to that of Christ. In fact, Semmel continues his analysis of Moses's and Daniel's journeys by writing: "The myth and political program . . . of Daniel, one might suggest, mirror those of the disinherited Moses, and a disinherited Jesus. . . . Of uncertain paternity and awaiting an obscure mission . . . Jesus, disinherited so that he might redeem men from their sins, asked, in his dying words, why his father had abandoned him" (123). Eliot's understanding of Egypt as she builds Daniel's character, then, is within a Judeo-Christian context, in line with the larger cultural trend in Britain in the 1870s to view Britain's involvement in Egypt as linked to the Jewish cause. Further, Eliot comes to see Moses as an important Egyptian figure only later in life, since along with her comments against the superiority of Jews in her 1848 letter to John Sibree, she also comments on the problem Moses had, that he was "impregnated with Egyptian philosophy" (Eliot, *Letters* 1:247). Even when using positive representations of Egypt in the novel, such as the "accomplished Egyptian" reference, Eliot makes imperialist assumptions about the East.

Only once does Eliot directly suggest that Gwendolen might be linked to Egyptian culture in a positive manner, when she characterizes Gwendolen as an *English*woman, not an *Egyptian* woman, who fantasizes about travel to other parts of the world. When Mallinger Grandcourt, one of Gwendolen's suitors and her eventual husband, asks her where she might like to live when she is old enough to leave her mother, Gwendolen suggests she likely will always live with her mother, since the opportunities for Englishwomen to leave home are limited. "We women can't go in search of adventures—to find out the North-West passage or the source of the Nile, or to hunt tigers in the East" (113), she says to Grandcourt. Some readers may see Gwendolen's vision of herself as adventurer in the East as naïve, an example of Saidian Orientalism, in which the English characterize the East in a romantic manner in order to envision their own escape from Western conventions.[7] But Gwendolen's identification with women who travel to Egypt, as Emily Strangford and Amelia Edwards had at the time Eliot was writing *Daniel Deronda*, also establishes her character as a woman who seeks emancipation, and Gwendolen goes on to comment on the constraints placed on Englishwomen, characterizing them as flowers who become poisonous because society expects them to marry and remain at home: "We must stay where we grow, or where the gardeners like to transplant us. We are brought up like flowers, to look as pretty as we can, and be dull without complaining. That is my notion about the plants: they are often bored, and that is the reason why some of them have got poisonous" (113).

Still, this characterization of Gwendolen as a woman who wants to travel to Egypt includes no reference to powerful ancient Egyptian women themselves, and those symbols Eliot might have used to link Gwendolen to Egyptian goddesses are more explicitly linked to Western mythologies. The opening scene of the novel, in which the men who observe Gwendolen at Leubronn characterize her as a serpent, can be tied to the Egyptian goddesses Wadjet and Hathor but is more explicitly tied to the Christian Eve and Greek Nereids. Eliot would have been familiar with the key characteristics of Egyptian goddesses, including their associations with serpents. Wadjet, the serpent goddess who protected pregnant women and children, was aligned with Hathor, who is sometimes seen as "a snake who laughs with Wadjet" (Hart 77), and Hathor's association with the snake can be seen in Wilkinson's discussion of ancient Egyptian musical instruments, which includes an image of a sistrum at the British Museum featuring the "double face of Athor, wearing an 'asp-formed crown'" (325; see Figure 3.2). Both goddesses were associated with the Milky Way, or the "Nile in the Sky": Hathor's four cow legs were seen as "pillars" that supported the sky (Hart 76), while Wadjet was likely associated with the sky through her conflation with the goddess Renenutet, a cobra-shaped harvest goddess whose body was thought to mimic the shape of the Milky Way (Silverman 41). Unlike Western traditions, in which the serpent image often has negative connotations, the image carries more positive connotations in Egyptian mythology, such as serpents leading and protecting elephants in a "mutual," rather than "hostile," relationship (Lesko 69). Further, the Egyptian serpent is strongly associated with fertility and rebirth because of its ability to shed its skin and regenerate; Egyptians "honored" rather than "feared" snakes, as is more common in the West (69–70).

Still, despite knowledge of the serpent's positive symbolism in Egyptian culture, Eliot does not explicitly link the serpent to Egyptian mythology in the opening scene of the novel, linking it instead to Western mythologies. The men who characterize Gwendolen as a serpent seem to fear her, since they describe her as "a sort of serpent," all "green and silver," who "winds her neck about a little more than usual," and they joke that "A man might risk hanging for her," or at least "a fool might" (7). One of the men who observes Gwendolen even remarks, "Woman was tempted by a serpent: why not man?" (7), a clear reference to Eve of Christian mythology and her "fault" for Adam's fall. The narrator links another man's characterization of Gwendolen as a green-and-silver serpent who winds her neck about to the Greek tradition, by stating that she is a "Nereid in sea-green robe and silver ornaments" (7).[8] The narrator's association between the serpent and the Nereid has a more positive connotation than that of the Christian Eve, since Nereids often help sailors drowning at sea, but overall the characterization of Gwendolen as a serpent is a negative, Western interpretation of the symbol. Nevertheless, contradictory connotations evident in the men's characterizations of Gwendolen are appropriate, given that Eliot uses the serpent image to present Daniel's initial confusion over Gwendolen's character. "Was she beautiful or not beautiful?," thinks Daniel, the moment he sees her. "And what was the secret of form or expression which gave the dynamic quality to her glance? Was the good or the evil genius dominant in those beams? Probably the evil; else why was the effect that of unrest rather than of undisturbed charm?" (3). Here, Eliot's characterization of Gwendolen is not linked to any particular mythological tradition, leaving room for the reader to interpret Daniel's reaction to Gwendolen more freely. Certainly, Western ideals about women, such as the beauty and power of the Greek Venus, are implied here. According to William Smith's *Dictionary of Greek and Roman Biography and Mythology* (1844), a dictionary Eliot used in her study of ancient cultures (Pratt and Neufeldt xxvi), Venus "struck" the other gods with "admiration and love" but also "punished those who neglected her worship or despised her power" (Smith 228). Thus, Daniel might be seen as an admirer who is struck by Gwendolen's Greek beauty but fears the consequences of her wrath if he does not respect her power.

But Daniel's awareness of the power of Gwendolen's glance also has been linked to the transgressive power of Celtic women by Natalie Rose (126) and might be linked to the transgressive power of Egyptian goddesses as well. As Geraldine Pinch points out in *Magic in Ancient Egypt* (1995), ancient Egyptians did not distinguish power as good or evil in the way other cultures have. "Heka," the word for any unusual power, was possessed by all supernatural creatures in ancient Egypt, not just evil demons, and "akhu," the word for specifically magical power, was "neither good or bad in itself" (12). In fact, Pinch writes, "Both were powers that could be channelled toward creation or destruction" (12), and often, what might have been perceived as a negative power, such as the scorpion goddess Serqet's poison, became positive through the key concept of ancient Egyptian magic, "fighting like with like" (37). Hathor was among those goddesses who could "expel evil" (84); as a player in the well-known feud between Seth (the god most thoroughly associated with evil because he killed his brother Osiris) and Horus (Osiris's son), Hathor "shows her genitals to the sun god to drive out his bad humour" (84), expelling the evil of Seth to support Horus. In addition, Isis, whom I have already mentioned as the Egyptian goddess most thoroughly incorporated into Greek culture, lent a positive connotation to the power of Egyptian goddesses. Thomas Keightly's *The Mythology of Ancient Greece and Italy* (1831), which is part of Lewes's library (Baker, *George Eliot-George Henry Lewes* 108), shows the positive associations of Isis's power: Keightly links Isis to the Greek goddess of the harvest, Demeter, characterizing them both as "personifications of nature, or of the productive power of the earth" (227). Further, he relates the story of Demeter whom, disguised as Dôs, asks the daughters of Prince Keleos for the opportunity to serve their families. She ends up suckling the child of Metaneira, Demophoôn, who "throve like a god" under her care, a story that is parallel to one about Isis in Egyptian mythology (173), that of Isis suckling the god Horus, an image of which Keightly includes in his book (plate IX, image 6). The Egyptian context for understanding women's power, then, sheds a different light on Daniel's questions about Gwendolen's beauty and its relationship to good or evil, suggesting that it may be a mixture of both or that it transcends the Western binary of good and evil. Gwendolen's confusing effect on Daniel, who recognizes the power of Gwendolen's beauty and is unsure about what kind of power her glance signifies, may very well be connected to multiple mythologies, including Egyptian mythology. Without a specific cue from Eliot, twenty-first-century readers with postcolonial awareness can build an interpretation of Gwendolen's character that recognizes an Egyptian context for her relationships with Grandcourt and Daniel, including Daniel's role in guiding Gwendolen as she struggles with her emancipation from an unhappy marriage with Grandcourt, even if Eliot remained "bound by an English eye" as she wrote the novel.

After Gwendolen's encounter with Daniel in Leubronn, readers are returned to England, where they learn the details of Gwendolen's experience with the English courtship system before her flight to Leubronn. As I have already indicated, Gwendolen establishes herself as a woman seeking emancipation through her comment to Grandcourt that it is difficult for Englishwomen to travel to Egypt or other places outside England, a sentiment she also expresses to her first suitor, Rex Gascoigne, when she says she would like to "go to the North Pole, or ride steeplechases, or go be a queen in the East like Lady Hester Stanhope" (57).[9] Though Gwendolen later warns Grandcourt that she may become one of those women who will be poisoned by the constraints of English society, he seems to believe Gwendolen can be absorbed into the marriage system and therefore follows her to Leubronn after she, having learned about his affair with Lydia Glasher, retreats there. Daniel, on the other hand, seems to recognize that Gwendolen's independence will prevent her from being absorbed into such a system; when he discusses Gwendolen with his uncle, Sir Hugo, who thinks Gwendolen "a perfect Diana" and "worth running after" (136, 138), Daniel states: "I should rather be inclined to run away from her" (138). Although Eliot again uses Greek rather than Egyptian mythology by characterizing Gwendolen as Diana, readers familiar with Eliot's knowledge of Egypt will recognize that Daniel understands Gwendolen's inability to fit into the English marriage system and her desire for emancipation, emancipation she sees as possible through travel to the East, where ancient Egyptian women had been powerful.

Daniel understands this in part because of his own Eastern roots. As already discussed, Mordecai characterizes Daniel as an "accomplished Egyptian" in the scene at the Philosophers Club, but even as early as Chapter 16, the chapter following Daniel's statement that he would prefer to avoid an intimate connection with Gwendolen, Eliot begins to reveal Daniel's Eastern roots to the reader. Via narratorial commentary, readers are told that Daniel's reaction to Gwendolen should be seen in light of his own history—as someone who has known since age 13, when he mistakenly came to believe that Sir Hugo was not his uncle but his father, that he really does not know his roots and will have to discover them himself. Unsure of his origins, Daniel feels inclined to "study abroad" rather than remain in England after his education at Eton and Cambridge, and the various ways in which Daniel is characterized in Chapter 16—as an Ishmaelite (148), Moses or Mahomet (154), and Prince Camaralzaman (156)—all suggest he might have Eastern roots. Once Daniel discovers his Jewish identity, this identity becomes his primary link to the East, reflecting Eliot's awareness of the Egyptian context of Judaism. In addition to her notes about *Tancred*, the Israelite exodus from Egypt, and Moses's Egyptian name in her *Daniel Deronda* notebooks, she notes the presence of Hebrews in Egypt during the reign of Rameses II (287), and she likely read John Baker Green's *The Hebrew Migration from Egypt* (1879), a historical account of Jews in Egypt during Moses's time. Green's book is part of the Lewes library and includes a review by Green about another book, which Eliot pasted into the book and marked in the margins (Baker, *George Eliot-George Henry Lewes* 81). Further, in her *Middlemarch* notebooks, Eliot notes the influence of Hebrew on Egyptian language, stating that in addition to the Phoenician, Carthaginian, and Arabic languages being part of the "Semitic family," the Egyptian, Babylonian, Assyrian, and Berber "dialects are now considered to have a semitic character" (54), an understanding of the Semitic language family she gained from Ernest Rènan's *Histoire Général et Système Comparé des Langues Sémitiques* (1855) (140).

Eliot's understanding of the Eastern context for Judaism also can be seen in her characterization of Daniel as a "seraphic" boy in Chapter 17 (157), which illustrates Daniel's ability to understand Gwendolen's "dangerous" qualities. A term meaning both "angel" and "serpent" in the Hebrew tradition, "seraphic" suggests that Daniel has some of the same transgressive qualities that Gwendolen has, which need not be interpreted as strictly good or bad but as blurring this binary. In fact, Gwendolen seems to recognize these qualities in Daniel, since the narrator says that she sees "traces of the seraphic boy" when she perceives his "gaze" as "dreadful" (157). But the narrator also makes it clear that Daniel's seraphic qualities have been moderated in adulthood, characterizing his seraphic qualities as "disguised" (157) and noting that Daniel has the face and hands of someone in a Titian painting: "[n]ot seraphic any longer; thoroughly terrestrial and manly" (158). While Daniel has outgrown his "seraphic" qualities and wants to avoid association with the deep East via an intimate connection with Gwendolen, he does not diminish her power, even encouraging it by retrieving from the pawnbroker her turquoise necklace, a sign of this power and another symbol used by Eliot that might be linked to Egyptian mythology.

The narrator immediately identifies the necklace Gwendolen leaves with the pawnbroker as Etruscan, or Italian, but also states that the "three central turquoises" in the necklace were owned by Gwendolen's father, whom "she had never known" (11–13). Certainly, readers do not believe Gwendolen's father is Egyptian, but the narrator's characterization of the stones in the necklace as having unclear origins open the space to consider the object's link to other cultural traditions. There were Egyptian influences on Etruscan jewelry, most likely through the presence of Phoenician traders in Etruria (Guadalupi 146; Brendel 47), and the ancient Egyptian goddesses Hathor and Wadjet were associated with the menat necklace, a beaded necklace that is sometimes made of turquoise and protects the wearer from harm. Evidence that Hathor was called "nebet mef ket," or "mistress of turquoise," can be found in writings on the rocks at Wadi Maghara, an area of Egypt filled with turquoise mines (Hart 82). Yet, the narrator's direct identification of the necklace as Etruscan signifies again the danger of directly associating Gwendolen with ancient Egyptian women, especially since considering the turquoise necklace as a link between Western and Eastern cultures might influence readers' interpretation later in the novel, when Daniel learns Gwendolen has married Grandcourt and immediately thinks of "rescuing" her from the marriage (273). Daniel recognizes that his decision to retrieve Gwendolen's turquoise necklace marks the beginning of his involvement in her life, and his impulse to do this is directly linked to her femininity: "[I]n the movement which had led him to redeem Gwendolen's necklace for her, and which was at work in him still, there was something beyond his habitual compassionate fervor— something due to *the fascination of her womanhood*" (273, emphasis mine). In other words, it is her serpent nature, signified by her possession of the turquoise necklace, that has attracted Daniel to Gwendolen.

Grandcourt, on the other hand, cannot understand Gwendolen's independence, and the turquoise necklace is always threatening to him. Readers learn that, for the New Year's Eve ball, Gwendolen "longed . . . to put on the old turquoise necklace for her sole ornament; but she dared not offend her husband by appearing in that shabby way on an occasion when he would demand her utmost splendor" (377). Instead, she wears the necklace as a hidden bracelet, winding it around her wrist, an action that recalls the serpent-like winding of her neck at the beginning of the novel. When Grandcourt catches sight of the necklace/bracelet, he says nothing but later reprimands Gwendolen for wearing it, saying that she must "behave as becomes my wife. And not make a spectacle of yourself" (384). When Gwendolen challenges Grandcourt, by suggesting that his comments about the necklace stem from jealousy over her encounter at the ball with Daniel, who knows Gwendolen has worn the necklace as a way of "drawing his attention" (381), Grandcourt replies, "I don't care two straws about Deronda . . . You are my wife. And you will either fill your place properly—to the world and to me—or you will go to the devil" (384). Grandcourt's rigidity about how Gwendolen should behave points to his inability to understand her independence, which might not only allow her to talk to Daniel more freely than Grandcourt wishes but also would require him to acknowledge Lydia Glasher's children as legitimate heirs. Grandcourt is thoroughly attached to a Western standard for women, in which a wife must be subject to her husband and in which mistresses such as Lydia Glasher cannot be acknowledged.

While Daniel better appreciates Gwendolen's independence, and is more open to the emancipation her turquoise necklace represents, he too imposes an English standard for womanhood on her. When Gwendolen confronts Daniel about his judgments about her gambling—saying to him, "Oh, you cast an evil eye on my play," and exhibiting serpentlike attributes by "wheel[ing] her neck round" (279)—Daniel admits he was disturbed by her gambling in Leubronn in part because she is a woman (284). While he believes men should abstain from gambling as well, he says that he "regretted it the more because you were a woman," since men "need that you [women] should be better than we are" (284–85). In the midst of imposing this English standard on Gwendolen, which she rejects by replying, "You see, I needed you to be better than I was," Daniel realizes they have an understanding that "it was he who sent the necklace" (284–85). Even as Daniel appreciates Gwendolen's independence in a way Grandcourt cannot, he still tries to control Gwendolen's behavior, not necessarily rejecting her independence but trying to make her more palatable to Western culture by suggesting ways in which she might conform to English expectations about women.

Daniel's imposition of an English standard on Gwendolen is furthered by his suggestion that Mirah, whom Daniel "saved" by pulling her from the river as she tried to drown herself, can provide a model for Gwendolen to follow. Daniel's perception of Mirah as an "ideal" is important, since as I will show momentarily, Mirah is recast in Western terms over the course of the novel, making her more like Romola, whom Eliot confirmed was an "ideal" when her friend Sara Hennell characterized Romola as "pure idealism . . . a goddess and not a woman" (Eliot, *Letters* 4:103–04).[10] In the same chapter in which Vandernoodt characterizes Gwendolen as an Egyptian mummy with a rag face and skeleton toes, Daniel ponders Gwendolen's marriage situation, particularly whether she knows about Grandcourt's relationship with Lydia Glasher and is affected by that knowledge, "gnawed by a double, a treble-headed grief—self-reproach, disappointment, jealousy" (372). In his typically negative fashion, Vandernoodt characterizes the triangle between Grandcourt, Gwendolen, and Lydia as similar to that of Jason, Medea, and Glauce, but Daniel, thinking in more positive terms, suggests that Gwendolen follow Mirah's model when he encounters Gwendolen, wearing her turquoise necklace as a bracelet, at the party. Discussing Mirah's budding singing career with Gwendolen, he tells her about Mirah's loss of faith in herself by the river, saying "Some ray or other" prevented her from drowning herself and "made her feel that she ought to live. . . . She is full of piety and seems capable of submitting to anything when it takes the form of duty" (376). Still, Gwendolen rejects the idea that Mirah can provide a model, saying to Daniel, "Those people are not to be pitied. . . . I have no sympathy with women who are always doing right" (376).

Although Mirah is perceived as at least somewhat Eastern by characters in the novel because of her Jewish identity—an issue Alicia Carroll discusses in *Dark Smiles: Race and Desire in George Eliot* (2003)—Mirah becomes increasingly Western over the course of the novel. After her near-drowning, she adjusts to life with Daniel's friends, the Meyricks, and is described as exhibiting a "dainty neatness" in her dress and having a "glow of tranquil happiness" on her face, an image she herself acknowledges as completely different than how she appeared when Daniel found her drowning in the river (312). By the time her father reappears in the story, to beg for her financial help, she is described as wearing the "dress of an English lady," while he is "shabby, foreign-looking" (632), a phrase that recalls Gwendolen's recognition that

Grandcourt will see her as "shabby" (and perhaps foreign?) if she wears her "old turquoise necklace" (377). Mirah *is* characterized as possessing qualities that could be linked Egyptian women—she has the "fervid quality of emotion sometimes rashly supposed to require the bulk of a Cleopatra" (628), and a "little biting snake . . . stirred" in her "gentle bosom" when she realizes Gwendolen still has a "hold" on Daniel (645)—but, in keeping with the English standard that women will behave with decorum, she always keeps her jealousy over Daniel's friendship with Gwendolen in check and does not display it publicly, even if she feels it privately.

The contrast between Mirah and Gwendolen is developed further in Chapter 37, where the epigraph to the chapter suggests Gwendolen is part of "Circe's herd" while Mirah is a "fair ward Cecilia," and in Chapter 45, where Mirah is "demure as a nun" while Gwendolen is a "Van dyke duchess of a beauty," a characterization that usually would be interpreted positively but is less so next to the characterization of Mirah as a nun. These two examples also suggest that while Gwendolen retains ties to pagan culture through the reference to "Circe's herd," Mirah is increasingly distanced from pagan associations and linked to Christian ones, such as the "demure nun," a model that again recalls Romola as the ideal for womanhood Daniel advocates for Gwendolen. Mirah's disassociation from paganism is especially apparent in Chapter 37, where Daniel argues Mirah cannot be used as a model for Hans Meyrick's depiction of Berenice, the mistress of the Roman emperor Titus, since Daniel doesn't think Mirah would want to be associated with a "heroine of this sort" if she knew Berenice's full story (394). This distancing of Mirah from a pagan model suggests that she is more English than foreign, while Gwendolen is more foreign than English. Mirah herself characterizes Gwendolen as having "something foreign" in her that "would be a disturbance in [Daniel's] life instead of blending with it" (627), highlighting the danger of challenging the British imperialist view that foreigners, even those who were subjects of the British empire, should remain outside England.

Although Gwendolen never is linked directly to Cleopatra, as Mirah is, William Baker, in *George Eliot and Judaism* (1975), has linked them indirectly, via the epigraph that appears at the beginning of Chapter 35: "My desolation does begin to make / A better life," a line spoken by Cleopatra at the beginning of Act 5, Scene 2 of Shakespeare's *Antony and Cleopatra*, when Cleopatra goes to flatter Caesar after Antony's death. Baker first clearly identifies Daniel's mother, Leonora, with Cleopatra, since she truly is "desolate" because she is completely alone in the world. "She admits to not being 'a loving woman,' confesses that she 'might have been glad of' the enrichment of Daniel's company 'now,'" writes Baker (219). "Her husbands 'have been subject to' her will but her life has been a failure" (219). Baker also believes that Cleopatra's line applies to Gwendolen, who "has acted as if the rest of the world did not require consideration and admits when writing to Daniel that 'I only thought of myself, and I made you grieve'" (218). Though Susan Meyer does not discuss Leonora's or Gwendolen's link to Cleopatra via the Chapter 25 epigraph, nor does she discuss Leonora's or Gwendolen's desolation directly, she does provide a helpful explanation about why Leonora is desolate, detailing how Leonora, like other women in the novel, must be isolated, even "dead" in a metaphorical sense, in order to support Eliot's "solution" to the problem of gender and race transgression in British culture. Eliot, Meyer argues, sees an "idealized alternative culture," in which feminized Jewish men practice "self abnegation," as the solution to this problem (737–38), and Daniel represents this ideal of self abnegation, while Leonora resists this ideal by telling Daniel, in Chapter 51, how her father "only thought of fettering [her] into obedience" (qtd. in Meyer 742). In other words, Eliot's "idealized alternative community" includes Jewish men but excludes Jewish women, who become "desolate" or "dead," so that Jewish men can excel, as Daniel does. Still, of all the women in the novel, Meyer argues, Leonora puts up the most resistance to the ideal of self abnegation through "her refusal to submit to male domination" (743), calling into question Eliot's "solution" to the problem of gender and racial transgression.

My own reading of the chapters in which Leonora discusses her struggle with Daniel confirms Meyer's argument that Leonora is the only woman in the novel who fully resists a subordinate position, though I believe Gwendolen desires to do this but cannot, and Baker is right in drawing attention to the ways in which Eliot uses the quote from *Antony and Cleopatra* to develop Leonora's and Gwendolen's characters, though his reading of their characters emphasizes the more callous side of Cleopatra. This is perhaps because Eliot draws on a more callous depiction of Cleopatra, describing Leonora as a Cleopatra-like figure at the beginning of Chapter 53: "The Princess . . . entered, dressed in a loose wrap of some soft silk, in colour a dusky orange, her head again with black lace floating about it, her arms showing themselves bare from under her wide sleeves. . . . You might have imagined her a sorceress who would stretch forth her wonderful hand and arm to mix youth-potions for others, but scorned to mix them for herself, having had enough of youth" (565). In addition, Leonora is described as having "the manner of a queen rather than of a mother," as Daniel sits with her and listens to her frustration at having been forced into submission by her father (565). Like Leonora, Gwendolen also is described as a queen numerous times (33, 44, 66, 93, 245, 519), and Lydia Glasher, whom I already have shown is connected to Egyptian culture in Wiesenfarth's commentary about Eliot's references to inheritance rights in her Commonplace Book, is referred to as a "sorceress" by Gwendolen when she reflects upon her encounter with Lydia at Whispering Stones: "Gwendolen had never referred the interview at the Whispering Stones to Lush's agency; her disposition to vague terror investing with shadowy omnipresence any threat of fatal power over her, and so hindering her from imagining plans and channels by which news had been conveyed to the women who had the poisoning skill of a sorceress" (474). Though different critics have identified different women in the novel as closest to Cleopatra, Mirah, Leonora, Gwendolen, and Lydia all can be associated with her, and with the exception of Mirah, who comes to fulfill the expectations for ideal womanhood, none of these women can fulfill the gender expectations placed upon them.

The climax of Gwendolen's inability to meet Daniel's standards for English womanhood, despite his more nuanced understanding of her via his own Eastern roots, comes when Daniel, after two failed attempts to tell Gwendolen he has proposed to Mirah, is prompted by Hans Meyrick to finally tell her about the proposal, his Jewish identity, and his plan to travel east to begin fulfilling Mordecai's vision for a productive Jewish state.[11] This information "dislodges" Gwendolen from "[h]er supremacy in her own world," but it also helps her realize Daniel cannot be her savior. Though he assures her he will be closer to her—"more with you," he says—once he marries Mirah, Gwendolen seems to understand she cannot rely on Daniel anymore, saying to him, "You have been very good to me. I deserve nothing. I will try—try to live" (691). Free of his responsibility to Gwendolen, Daniel marries Mirah, who is described as the ideal English wife on their marriage day: she is "protected" from Gwendolen's (and Meyrick's) disappointment over the marriage and believes Daniel has been "a rescuing angel to many besides herself" (693).

Gwendolen also seems to think Daniel has been her angel, since her letter to him on his wedding day indicates she still plans to follow his advice and "live to be one of the best of women" (694). But, as Bonnie Zimmerman has pointed out, it is unclear how exactly Gwendolen will go about achieving this. "Gwendolen's end is open and uncertain," Zimmerman writes, arguing that the end of the novel does not definitively indicate whether Gwendolen herself will become an independent woman or remain more traditional, perhaps by marrying Rex Gascoigne (213–14). With this context in mind, Gwendolen's letter to Daniel on his wedding day should not be read as evidence Gwendolen will necessarily follow Daniel's ideal for English women. It is possible she will become more independent, anticipating the more explicitly feminist characters of late-Victorian New Woman novels. As Zimmerman states: "Gwendolen Harleth [is] a profound example of the unsexed Girl of the Period, and her open future thus symbolise[s] a turning point in history: the transformation of the long tradition of Female Influence and

Women's Mission into the feminism that would soon shatter the calm surface of domestic England" (215).

Still, as Meyer has argued, the novel clearly upholds national boundaries, suggesting that even Jewish women such as Mirah and Leonora must conform to British imperialist notions of acceptable roles for women, and according to Meyer ancient Greek women, whom I have established as less transgressive than ancient Egyptian women, help uphold these boundaries. Citing Daniel's recollection of Plutarch's story about Delphic women "guarding" the more transgressive Dionysian Maenads, "wild women . . . bearing the marks of foreign culture," Meyer asserts that this story "encapsulates the novel's strategy with regard to the forces that loom behind [Mirah's] 'refinement'" (753). But Meyer also believes that story is "inappropriate to delicate, diminished Mirah unless one thinks of her as standing in for other significations" (753). In fact, the story better applies to Leonora, as Meyer shows, and to Gwendolen, as I have shown. Zimmerman argues that Gwendolen at least has the potential to transgress, and the notion that Gwendolen will marry Rex Gascoigne should be viewed with at least as much skepticism as Zimmerman's reading that Gwendolen will transgress, since it seems unlikely that a marriage between Gwendolen and Rex could be successful.

Further, the entire relationship between Daniel and Gwendolen might be viewed with skepticism. Critics interested in the characterization of Daniel as Gwendolen's "priest" (Eliot, *Daniel Deronda* 369) have rightly recognized the ways in which Daniel's role of confessor (whether religious confessor or psychoanalytic guide) is problematic (and even a cause of Gwendolen's inability to emancipate herself), yet no critic has used the West/East context of their relationship to explain the problematic aspects of their relationship.[12] If Daniel is, indeed, a Judeo-Christian priest and Gwendolen's character can be linked to multiple mythologies, including Egyptian mythology, then Daniel's attempt to convert Gwendolen, to translate her transgressive Egyptian qualities into something more palatable to Western culture (as Savonarola does with Romola), is unsuccessful. Still, I would agree with Judith Wilt's comment that Daniel seems to be "reluctantly playing priest" (313), since the narrator explicitly tells us Daniel "dreads" Gwendolen's "confession" after the death of Grandcourt and thinks: "He was not a priest" (Eliot, *Daniel Deronda* 591). Perhaps because of his own connection to Eastern culture via Judaism, Daniel recognizes he cannot play this role in Gwendolen's life, unlike the male guides for Romola, who never express any doubt about their ability to direct the women whom they believe need their guidance. The unequivocal ending of *Romola*, in which Romola has been thoroughly converted to Christianity by Savonarola, sends the message that "pagan" women can be successfully converted, and that their emancipation depends on this conversion, a message very similar to that expressed by Nightingale in *Suggestions for Thought*.

The ending of *Daniel Deronda* is much more equivocal, but, with Eliot's knowledge of Egyptian culture in mind, I am inclined to see the ending—with Gwendolen's declaration "I shall live. I shall be better!"—as a rejection of Daniel's model for Victorian womanhood and an embrace of a new way of thinking about her place in the world. Zimmerman's argument that Gwendolen might be seen as a transitional figure between traditional mid-Victorian roles for women and more feminist, late-Victorian roles for them resonates with me, yet Meyer's argument that the novel's plot upholds boundaries Gwendolen cannot cross resonates as well. Eliot clearly stops short of showing how Eastern models of powerful women might provide a direction for Western women as they contemplated their own opportunities for emancipation, and Eliot still seems to be "bound by an English eye," though her perspective differs significantly from that of Nightingale. While Nightingale looked to Eastern culture as a way to understand and reinforce a Christian form of emancipation for women, Eliot presents Eastern culture as an integral part of Western culture, helpful to Jewish men seeking to establish heroic identities, yet this link between East and West remains unavailable to women seeking emancipation from Victorian gender constraints. Gwendolen's cry of "I shall live" at the end of the novel shows her desire for, if not the actualization of, emancipation. Eliot presents this desire for emancipation in a palatable form, not fully identifying Gwendolen with powerful Egyptian goddesses, since a more radical form of emancipation would have been completely "foreign" to Daniel—and completely "foreign" to Eliot's British audience. As it was, Eliot's novel was criticized for its attention to Judaism, another "foreign" element in British society, and Eliot's anxiety over the Gentile community's reaction to the novel, her worry that "The Jewish element seems to me likely to satisfy nobody" (Eliot, *Letters* 6:238), provides some explanation as to why Eliot associates Gwendolen primarily with Western mythologies. The risk of associating her with deeply Eastern ones would have been too great, since her audience was scarcely prepared to accept the other "foreign" elements in the novel.

Figure 1.1 Cleopatra wearing headdress that incorporates aspects of Maat, Hathor, Isis. Dendera Temple, Dendera, Egypt.

Source: Peter Horree/Alamy.

Figure 1.2   Isis, with sistrum, as she was sometimes incorporated into Greek sculpture. Musei Capitolini, Rome, Italy.

Source: MARKA/Alamy.

Figure 2.1 Ramesses II and Nefertari. Abu Simbel Temple, Abu Simbel, Egypt.
Source: Salsa/Alamy.

Figure 3.1 Ancient Egyptian women weaving and using distaff.

Source: John Gardner Wilkinson. *Manners and Customs of the Ancient Egyptians.* 1837. Vol. 2. London: John Murray, 1841. Molly Youngkin.

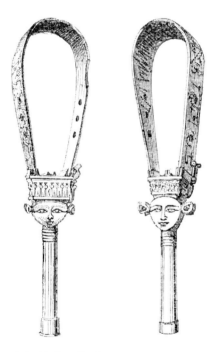

Figure 3.2 Sistrum with double face of Hathor.

Source: John Gardner Wilkinson. *Manners and Customs of the Ancient Egyptians.* 1837. Vol. 2. London: John Murray, 1841. Molly Youngkin.

CHAPTER 4

"[W]e had never chosen a Byzantine subject . . . or one from Alexandria": Emancipation Through Desire and the Eastern Limits of Beauty in Michael Field's Verse Dramas

In June 1894, writing in the collaborative journal kept by Katherine Bradley and Edith Cooper to record their working lives as the poet and playwright "Michael Field," Cooper recounted a discussion with two new friends, the aesthete designers and publishers Charles Ricketts and Charles Shannon, about the subject matter of their plays. "When we were talking with Ricketts and Shannon about *Stephania* [a play published by Field in 1892,] they said that naturally and inevitably they saw [the main characters] Otho and Stephania in the dresses of Byzantine mosaics—they appeared to them like some of the great figures at Ravenna. It was impossible to see them in the garb of the 10th century. Our new friends wondered we had never chosen a Byzantine subject . . . or one from Alexandria. The moment when the world was [Chris]tian and the few were still Pagan and still clung to the grape-god—was a moment of such tragedy" (Ms. 46782). Although Ricketts and Shannon questioned why Field had never published a play about Byzantium or Alexandria, in fact Bradley and Cooper had just completed *Equal Love*, a play about the Byzantine empress Theodora. They relayed their "joy" at finishing the play to Ricketts and Shannon and also talked about their recent letter to the actress Ellen Terry, expressing their interest in having her take the lead role (Ms. 46782). Though the play was never staged, Ricketts and Shannon published it in their magazine *The Pageant* in 1896, alongside poems by Algernon Swinburne, Paul Verlaine, and John Gray and paintings by Dante Gabriel Rossetti, John Millais, and Edward Burne-Jones.

The placement of *Equal Love* next to the works of some of the most important aesthetes of the period led Cooper to comment in the journal that the
play looked "very Preraphaelite . . . beautiful poetry rather than acute drama"
(Ms. 46784).

In tackling subject matter about the Byzantine empire, Bradley and Cooper engaged the East more fully than they ever had before, yet they would
not thoroughly tackle an Alexandrian subject for another ten years, and even
then, it likely was not in the manner Ricketts and Shannon had in mind—as
engaging Alexandria as it was in the third century BCE, when it was dominated by Hellenistic culture.[1] Still, thinking about Alexandrine culture more
broadly, in the sense that there were multiple cultures (including Egyptian
culture) associated with this city, Field had already engaged Alexandrine culture at the time of their conversation with Ricketts and Shannon, though
it had been in a limited fashion. In their dramatic work, they had made
passing references to Egypt as the site of the Old Testament Joseph's work
as vizier in *William Rufus* (1885) and as a place where Theodora lost her
first child Zuhair in *Equal Love* (1896), and they would include an Egyptian
character, Eclectus, in *The World at Auction* (1898). Further, though not published until 1908 as part of *Wild Honey from Various Thyme*, they had written
five Egyptian sonnets: "The Mummy Invokes Its Soul" in 1892 (Schaffer
108) and "Come to Me!," "Tafnûit," "Inevitable Death," and "The Beauty of
Gratitude" in 1897 (Ms. 46786). Also in 1908, they published the play
Queen Mariamne, composed in 1905 and the first of two completed plays in
their planned trilogy about King Herod (Sturgeon 198).

With the publication of the Egyptian sonnets and *Queen Mariamne* in
1908, Bradley and Cooper certainly engaged ancient Egypt, and particularly
ancient Egyptian women, more thoroughly. Two of the five Egyptian sonnets
feature ancient Egyptian women—Tafnûit (or Tefnut), the daughter of Atum
and sister and wife of Shu, and Nebta, a seventeenth-dynasty princess. Identified as "the lion-goddess of the sky" in the second sonnet, Tafnûit clearly has
power in ancient culture, since she is described as ruling with Shu, much like
Nefertari ruled with Ramesses II: "Royally / With him I rule; each morning form the East / Receive with him the sun" (Field, "Tafnûit" 8–10). Yet,
Tafnûit also is discussed as a helpmate to Shu, since she "was created that my
god might mate," and "Without him there is nothing, fame or sanctuary" (2,
14). Likewise, Nebta, featured in the fifth sonnet, is described as possessing
special powers, since she holds a piece of the healing gem malachite in her
hand (Field, "The Beauty of Gratitude" 12–14), a symbol that also is associated with Hathor. Still, Nebta also is discussed primarily in relationship to
male figures, since she is "a fairer sight" than 20 virgin maidens and through
her beauty serves to "lighten" the "sick heart" of a king, whose feelings are

the main focus of the sonnet (1, 10–11). These representations of ancient Egyptian women are neither clearly positive nor negative, but primarily descriptive, and the role the Egyptian sonnets play in the collection seems to de-emphasize ancient Egyptian culture and emphasize the Judeo-Christian tradition instead. Marion Thain, in *"Michael Field": Poetry, Aestheticism and the Fin de Siècle* (2007), has argued that the Egyptian sonnets recall "the historical orientation" found in Field's 1889 volume of poetry *Long Ago*, but the emphasis on "ancient history" found in these sonnets is balanced by other poems in *Wild Honey*, such as the "Royal Sonnets," which use "biblical references" to "counterpos[e] the ancient world of other gods with a growing Christian significance" (137), suggesting that although Field was engaging the East more fully, they continued to privilege Western traditions over Eastern ones.[2] Likewise, *Queen Mariamne* follows the Judeo-Christian tradition, using the Roman-Jewish historian Flavius Josephus's account in *Antiquities of the Jews* (c. AD 93) of Herod's interactions with other Roman rulers, including Antony and Cleopatra, to articulate a dramatic narrative about the relationships between powerful figures in ancient culture. As this chapter will show, although Cleopatra is characterized in relation to the Egyptian goddess Isis in the play, she is a thoroughly unsympathetic character, and it is Mariamne, referred to as the Greek goddess Venus in the play, who is the real heroine.

Like Nightingale and Eliot, Bradley and Cooper were unable to fully embrace the positive qualities of ancient Egyptian women, and their attachment to all things Greek contributed to their negative representation of women from the deep East. Although Bradley and Cooper certainly recognized the Egyptian presence in art and literature, they were so fully attached to a Greek ideal—which they had spent much of their career developing especially through their poetry—that they remained true to this ideal, even when they engaged the deep East in their later verse dramas. Although many critics have discussed Bradley and Cooper's attachment to a Greek ideal, this chapter details the development of a more specific *Graeco-Italian* ideal, which brought together the sexual desire evoked by Greek beauty and the softer, more familiar qualities of Italian beauty. The development of this ideal began in the early 1890s with Bradley and Cooper's conversations with the well-known art critic Bernhard Berenson, who took Bradley and Cooper into museums and galleries across Europe. Drawing on Bradley and Cooper's collaborative journal, in which they discuss in detail the paintings they saw, I argue they often followed Berenson's principles for critical analysis of art, which held that Italian Renaissance art best expressed beauty because it drew on Greek ideals about the body. Yet, they also developed their own ideas about beauty, which more fully acknowledged the physical attributes of women of diverse nationalities and ethnicities. Still, they struggled to embrace art that featured Egyptian subjects, unless these subjects were recast in Greek or Christian terms.

As a result of their hierarchical approach to beauty, they used a Graeco-Italian ideal in their 1892 ekphrastic collection of poetry *Sight and Song*, which featured poems about Venus based on paintings by Italian Renaissance artists. These poems suggested that certain forms of sexual desire, such as autoeroticism, offered women emancipation from unsatisfactory love situations and the ability to establish more satisfying relationships. In *Sight and Song*, Bradley and Cooper moved from representing Venus as unable to control love situations because she is not "fully Greek," to Venus as powerful, able to control these situations precisely because she has the ideal combination of Greek and Italian attributes. Bradley and Cooper then applied the Graeco-Italian ideal developed in *Sight and Song* in their later verse dramas, including *Queen Mariamne*, where they more fully engaged Eastern culture but were unable to present Eastern women in a favorable light, since they had fully absorbed the Graeco-Italian ideal and suppressed their earlier recognition that women of diverse nationalities and ethnicities were beautiful. Ultimately, their attachment to all things Greek shaped their vision for women's emancipation and excluded Egyptian women and other women of color from that vision.

*   *   *

The importance of ancient Greek culture to Bradley and Cooper has been well established by other critics. Most recently, Stephano Evangelista, in *British Aestheticism and Ancient Greece: Hellenism, Reception, Gods in Exile* (2009), and T. D. Olverson, in *Women Writers and the Dark Side of Late-Victorian Hellenism* (2010), have shown how Bradley and Cooper used references to ancient Greece in their work to establish their own form of aestheticism, which allowed them to embrace "modernity" (Evangelista 3–4) and emphasize same-sex desire as the result of "intense *eros*" rather than "aberrant" sexual feelings (Olverson 118). Also discussed by critics has been the centrality of Berenson, and his partner, Mary Costelloe, in Bradley and Cooper's embrace of ancient Greek culture in their personal lives. In "Faun Love: Michael Field and Bernard Berenson" (2009), Martha Vicinus recounts their Dionysian role-playing with Berenson and indicates that, not only did Berenson earn the nicknames "Faun" and "Dionysus" for his "youthful, otherworldly appearance," but Bradley and Cooper also referred to him as "Doctrine, gently mocking his pedagogical manner and utter conviction that he alone knew the fine arts as they should be known" (754). Critics interested in Field's *Sight and Song*, the ekphrastic collection of poetry based on artistic masterpieces Bradley and Cooper viewed with Berenson, have discussed Berenson's role as instructor to Bradley and Cooper and how the visual "gaze" they employ in this collection both reflected and resisted his instruction.[3]

While I fully agree that Bradley and Cooper often resisted Berenson's instruction, it is clear from their journal that this instruction gave them a venue for dialogue about ideals for women's beauty, particularly a Graeco-Italian ideal that developed out of their shared interest in Italian Renaissance art. In 1895, shortly after the publication of Berenson's second book, *Lorenzo Lotto: an Essay on Constructive Art Criticism* (1894), Cooper recorded conversations that she and Bradley had with Berenson about women's beauty, including discussions in which they reject Cleopatra as an example of ideal beauty and confirm that a Graeco-Italian ideal is preferable. Transcribing a discussion in which one of their female friends resists Berenson's belief that sexual desirability is part of a woman's beauty, Bradley argues for a definition of beauty that focuses more fully on a woman's intellect and her power over men through this intellect (Ms. 46783). Their female friend cites courtesans as women who are sexually desirable but have no intellect and, therefore, cannot be termed beautiful, and Bradley adds to this category of sexually desirable but unintellectual women Shakespeare's Cleopatra, stating, "she was simply disgustingly sexual and nothing else—show me a simple trace of intellect in her!" (Ms. 46783). This discussion precedes one in which the Graeco-Italian ideal of beauty is confirmed, with Berenson and Cooper agreeing on the importance of "see[ing] beauty as the Greeks saw it, as the Renaissance saw it," rather than falling into the trap of viewing beauty according to fashion, "in lines or colours that have been found desirable at different periods and by many different schools" (Ms. 46783). While they agree that "Beauty—as a type, as a diagram—is relative," with the "quantity of beauty . . . variable according to the types or types enjoyed," they also agree that "Beauty as a vital organizer is qualitative, invariable, absolute" (Ms. 46783).

A more Western ideal of beauty is privileged by Bradley and Cooper then, and while they did not always agree with Berenson about what constituted beauty, Cooper, in particular, found that she and Berenson were often "thinking on the same lines" about these matters (Ms. 46783). Furthermore, Bradley declared in January 1895 that Berenson's book on Lotto was to be a "Bible to us this year, at least" (Ms. 46783), and Bradley and Cooper certainly were influenced by the other books Berenson published in the 1890s—*The Venetian Painters of the Renaissance with an Index to Their Works* (1894), *The Florentine Painters of the Renaissance with an Index to Their Works* (1896), and *The Central Italian Painters of the Renaissance* (1897). All of these books contain ideas Berenson had worked out through the instruction he gave Bradley and Cooper in museums and galleries as they looked at paintings together, and these materials reveal that although Berenson acknowledged that beauty was relative, he had specific principles by which he judged beauty, principles he passed on to Bradley and Cooper. For example, during his lecture on the Lombard school in Paris in July 1892, which Cooper describes in the journal, Berenson comments on the difference between "picturesque" beauty and "real" beauty by comparing Cooper and Costelloe. Cooper recounts this incident in the journal, writing, "Sim [Bradley] has the misfortune to remark, as she looks at Mary and me, how she would like these two faces painted. He answers 'Field [Cooper] would paint well; but Mary has far too much beauty to be painted.' He then makes us the text of a discourse on the difference between mere picturesqueness and real beauty. I do not mind the truth being said about me, but my heart blenches a little at the personal comparison he draws" (Ms. 46780).

This distinction between picturesque and real beauty is contextualized in *Florentine Painters*, where Berenson makes it clear that although real beauty perhaps cannot be painted, there are certain principles for representing the human body, found in the work of ancient Greek and Italian Renaissance artists. Berenson's explanation of these principles in *Florentine Painters* is part of a larger discussion about aesthetic experience, in which Berenson lays out his belief that aesthetic experience centers around the "stimulation" of the viewer's "tactile imagination," or the experience of feeling a "sensation of pleasure" from the "form" of the painting, which should occur as soon as the viewer sees the painting (9, 13).[4] According to Berenson, the tactile imagination is most immediately stimulated when looking at the work of the fourteenth-century painter Giotto because he uses specific artistic elements to make the figures seem real to the viewer. Writing about Giotto's *Madonna Enthroned with Angels and Saints* (1355), Berenson says, "Our eyes scarcely have had time to light on it before we realise it completely—the throne occupying a real space, the Virgin satisfactorily seated upon it, the angels grouped in rows about it" (13–14). Although Berenson believes Giotto's work does have "faults," including the fact that "the types represented do not correspond to my ideal of beauty" because the figures are "too massive," he is able to "forgive" these faults because of Giotto's use of light, shadow, and line (15). Giotto's "functional" use of line, in particular, allows the viewer to "see how it outlines and models, how it enables you to realise the head, the torso, the hips, the legs, the feet" (16), and Berenson understands why Giotto focuses on such types, which "both in face and figure are simple, large-boned, and massive,—types, that is to say, which in actual life would furnish the most powerful stimulus to the tactile imagination" (15).

Berenson, then, had a set of principles about beauty he applied when viewing art: the figures should not be too massive, the lines should be functional to mitigate figures that did not fit the ideal, and the parts of the body should be well defined and natural looking. With these principles in mind, Berenson goes on to explain that this understanding of the body comes from the Greeks and would be achieved again only by the Italian Renaissance painters Masaccio, Botticelli, Leonardo, and Michelangelo. After Giotto, Berenson argues, Italian painters only imitated his work, and the result was simply "pretty faces" (20), what I suspect Berenson means when he refers to Cooper's beauty as picturesque. While Berenson believes Fra Angelico improved the depiction of facial beauty with paintings such as *Coronation of the Virgin* (1434–1435), it was Masaccio who returned Florentine painting to the ideals of the Greeks. Writes Berenson,

> Types, in themselves of the manliest, he presents with a sense for the materially significant which makes us realise to the utmost their power and dignity. . . . what strength to his young men, and what gravity and power to his old! How quickly a race like this would possess itself of the earth, and brook no rivals but the forces of nature! (28–30)

Later, Leonardo and Botticelli would achieve the same "tactile" quality seen in Giotto's painting, in which "every line, every indentation, every boss appeals so vividly to the sense of touch . . . our fingers feel as if they had everywhere been in contact with [the] body" (66, 72). And, Michelangelo probably understood the body best; according to Berenson, "Nowhere outside of the best Greek art shall we find, as in Michelangelo's works, forms whose tactile values so increase our sense of capacity, whose movements are so directly communicated and inspiring" (88).

The body as it had been portrayed by the Greeks, then, determined Berenson's ideal, and since the Italian Renaissance painters strove to achieve this ideal, the Greek and the Italian bodies are fused in the ideal Berenson presented to Bradley and Cooper. Of course, that does not mean Bradley and Cooper blindly followed Berenson's Graeco-Italian ideal when viewing art. In calling Berenson "Doctrine," they identified him with a "critical," more academic view of art, and they distinguished their view from his by presenting themselves as "artists" rather than "critics," reflecting the late-Victorian aesthetic view expressed by contemporaries such as Oscar Wilde.[5] They were particularly resistant to Berenson's suggestion that Cooper take up critical writing about art, and they commented that studying the "Old Masters" could make one "stringently academic" (Ms. 46783). Instead, they tried to maintain a more "creative" perspective, which allowed them a more flexible definition of beauty, but they could not escape Berenson's influence entirely. Two specific examples of their assessment of women's beauty in painting—their viewing of Eduoard Manet's *Olympia* (1863) with Berenson at the Luxembourg Museum in Paris in 1892 and their viewing of Dante Gabriel Rossetti's *The Beloved* (1855–1856), which they saw on their own in August 1890 at Guildhall in London—are helpful in seeing how they absorbed Berenson's European influence but also articulated their own ideas about women's beauty.

Their experience seeing Manet's painting is a clear example of British women's indifference to women of color, and one in which references to ancient Greek and Egyptian cultures turn out to be central. In June 1892, Bradley and Cooper visited the Luxembourg Museum in Paris with Berenson and saw for the first time Manet's well-known image of a nude, white woman lying on a red couch, with her black servant and a black cat in the background. As was typical in their visits to museums and galleries, Berenson led Cooper and Bradley to the painting, commented on it briefly, and then left Cooper and Bradley to study it on their own, while he visited other galleries with Costelloe, an approach that continually irritated Cooper and Bradley and finally led them to pay Berenson for lessons so they would receive his full attention (Ms. 46780). As recorded in the journal, Berenson's reaction to the painting is one in which he overlooks the black servant holding the bouquet of flowers, commenting only on the nude, white woman. Still, Berenson complicates the relationship between white and black, European and African, West and East, by referring to Olympia as both Venus and Cleopatra. Cooper describes his reaction as they approach the painting: "He takes us straight to the much-discussed Manet—'Olympe[.]' [He says,] 'It is Cleopatra, who has just unrolled herself from mummy clothes, and the cat knows it'[.] He pauses—'C'est la prostitution eternelle'. Before this picture he and Mary leave us to go on to the Louvre. . . . We sit down for an hour before Manet's *Venus*, as Bernhard will call it" (Ms. 46780).

Berenson's reference to the painting as "Manet's *Venus*" shows his awareness that Manet was drawing on the Graeco-Italian ideal of beauty in his representation of the white woman, particularly Titian's *Venus of Urbino* (1538) and Giorgione's *Sleeping Venus* (1510), both of which depict Venus in a reclining pose, with Titian's Venus wearing jewelry similar to that worn by Manet's figure. But, his lack of commentary about the black servant in the background is also telling, since it reinforces the notion that European women set the standard for beauty, while women of color were simply accessories, included in the painting to create a contrast to the central figure. Still, Berenson's comments also reveal that even as Western art ignored women of color, it relied on Eastern influences for its ideal of beauty. The fact that Berenson identifies Olympia, clearly a European woman, with Cleopatra highlights his awareness of the Eastern influence on Western culture. Though

Berenson attaches a negative connotation to this influence by associating this Cleopatra-like figure with prostitution (anticipating the conversation he, Cooper, and Bradley will have about courtesans and Shakespeare's Cleopatra as purely sexual women), he reinfuses Olympia with a positive association by referring to her as Venus, a Greek ideal so perfect it would become the standard for Italian Renaissance painting. Thus, Berenson's commentary on the painting provides a complicated view of beauty, in which Western and Eastern ideals are intertwined.

With Berenson's comments about Olympia in mind, Cooper and Bradley contemplated the painting and recorded their thoughts, which follow Berenson's emphasis on the central European figure in the painting and give less attention to figures of other nationalities and ethnicities. The reaction of Bradley to the painting is strong. "I can only stare at the firm, alert features, the simple directness of the face," Bradley writes of the nude figure in the journal. "[N]o stain of scruple is on the brow or mouth; the deep eyes have made terms, they have not smiled meretriciously, they have not wept hypocritically" (Ms. 46780). This description captures the detached attitude Olympia projects, and Bradley goes on to describe Olympia in more detail, characterizing her eyes as "deaf," since "they have never listened to love," a comment suggesting Olympia's experiences with love are not pleasurable (Ms. 46780). This notion that Olympia and other "Venuses" do not experience pleasure in their sexual encounters with men is a key point that Cooper emphasizes in her reaction to Olympia as well and a point found in the poems from *Sight and Song* I discuss later in this chapter. While Bradley has much to say about Olympia, she does not mention the black servant in the background of the painting, except to acknowledge in rather abstract terms that the servant stands ready to hand a bouquet of flowers to her mistress. "Art is brought to allure her in the coloured bouquet," Bradley comments, but then returns quickly to the nude figure: "she herself simply dominates in her nude verity" (Ms. 46780).

Cooper's thoughts about the painting, also recorded in the journal, do more to recognize the servant's presence, but do so without acknowledging her individuality. Cooper focuses primarily on Olympia, noting that although "her proportions are too small—almost stunted," she is striking, possessing "the queenship of sterile passion, an attractive majesty, complete in itself" (Ms. 46780). Cooper continues to describe the couch on which Olympia reclines, and then focuses on her body, stating, "Her body has the colour of very old marble; the outlines and shadows are dark. . . . In her hair is an old-rose bow, narrow black-velvet round the throat, a bracelet on the arm. This union of nudity and ornament marks the self-consciousness of the body—that it exists to fascinate" (Ms. 46780). Cooper had already observed the presence of ornamentation in Titian's representation of Venus as a distraction from the lines of the body, stating in 1890 about his *Venus and Cupid with Partridge* (c. 1532–1533) that it was a "pity that [Venus's] bracelet and ring sever the perfect lines of nakedness" (Ms. 46778). There is the sense she feels the same way here, where the ornamentation is what signals that Olympia is meant to fascinate men rather than experience pleasure herself, an important marker of women's emancipation in the *Sight and Song* poems. Cooper goes on to state that Olympia's "dark eyes" are "assured of receiving homage and ennui from everything on which they look," and that gives viewers the impression that what Olympia experiences is "not pleasure" (Ms. 46780). Cooper focuses on this lack of pleasure in great detail but, like Bradley, sums up the servant and cat in two simple, purely descriptive sentences: "A negress in faint pink, chocolate and grey turban (her head of the intensest brown) brings a bouquet, ostentatious, flattering. A black cat stands at Olympia's feet" (Ms. 46780). This description acknowledges the servant's presence more fully, since she is described as an actual person rather than the abstract holder of flowers, yet it reinforces the idea that the servant has only a peripheral place in the painting. For both Bradley and Cooper, the black servant is irrelevant, and Olympia is the central figure, similar to the many Venuses they will describe in *Sight and Song* as resisting love in some fashion—either by engaging in something other than love (sex for sex's sake, as is the case with Olympia), by remaining innocent of heterosexual love (as in Botticelli's *Spring*), or by returning the male gaze to control the love situation (as in Botticelli's *Venus and Mars*). As their comments about *Olympia* indicate, they, like many of their contemporaries, responded to paintings without resisting hierarchies based on nationality or ethnicity. They focus on the beauty possessed by white, European women rather than that possessed by women of color, just as the great masters did.

Still, there are moments in the journal where Bradley and Cooper recognize the beauty of non-European nationalities and ethnicities, and their viewing of Rossetti's *Beloved*, which features the bride from Song of Solomon wearing a Japanese dress and surrounded by women of diverse ethnicities, illustrates this. Of the painting, Cooper writes, "Rossetti's *Beloved* is most lovely in colour and grouping. The chief half-length figure is in sunny yellow green with pine-green scarf—on her gown is vermillion and pine-green embroidery. Within her golden hair are vermillion fanlike ornaments. Her eyes are light blue and her complexion soft as softest roses" (Ms. 46778). While Cooper follows the painting's composition by focusing on the central European figure first, her commentary about women of other ethnicities is more detailed than in *Olympia*. "To her left is a dark girl, holding a tiger-lily, with intense eyes and features of lovely, amorous fierceness. To the right an arch, Irish-eyed girl, with clear rose in her cheeks, hold[s] a pomegranate branch in scarlet flower. Behind are two other heads—in front of the Beloved a negro-girl, with vivid, wistful eyes, who holds a pot of roses which gather together the tints and beauties of the clustered complexions" (Ms. 46778). While it certainly can be argued that Rossetti's contrast of the light blue eyes of the central figure to the darker features of the surrounding figures illustrates a hierarchy of beauty based on nationality and ethnicity (and Cooper follows this hierarchy in her description of the painting), Cooper's comment that the pot of roses brings together the various complexions of the women suggests all the peripheral women support the central figure's beauty. Further, Cooper goes on to say, "The picture is gem-like with eyes—blue and light, yellow and black, all clear with youth and due value is given to their brilliance" (Ms. 46778). This comment in particular suggests Cooper recognized beauty in all the women in the painting, even if the European figure remained central and women of other ethnicities were resigned to support roles.

Given the emphasis on European figures in Western painting, and Bradley and Cooper's tendency to confirm this emphasis in their commentary, it is not surprising that Bradley and Cooper rarely comment on Egyptian art in their journal, though the journal does show they recognized the presence of Egyptian culture in Western art beyond references to Cleopatra. For example, while gathering material for *Sight and Song* in the Dresden Gallery in August 1891, Bradley and Cooper saw the Italian Renaissance painter Battista Dossi's painting *Der Traum*, or *The Dream* (1544), which features a large central woman figure—possibly the Greek queen Hecuba—put into a sleeping state by an old man, Somnus. As Hecuba lies alongside the river Lethe, she experiences the nightmares depicted in Statius's *Thebaid* and Ovid's *Metamorphosis* (Humfrey and Lucco 261–62). In describing this painting in the journal, Cooper first focuses on the central figure, writing, "A woman lies (from right to left) on a black rock. . . . Her arms, great as those of a daughter of the Titans, are heavily folded; her face has no charm of youth in the healthful features. She sleeps on a white pillow—she sleeps and dreams" (Ms. 46779). After focusing on the central European figure, Cooper goes on to describe the various animals that comprise her "nightmare"—a "vigilant cock," a "grey moon-eyed owl," a "dog-fish drag[ging] along the head of a sword-fish," and a "white bird its eyes gouged out"—as well as two heads emerging from a basket, "one like Sesotris in his boyhood (could there be anything more terrible than an ancient Egyptian King *im Werden* [being made]?), the other a negro's with a tongue that hangs like a hot dog's" (Ms. 46779).

Cooper's description of the two human heads emerging from the basket as African (and one specifically Egyptian) reveals the race hierarchies European painters and viewers assumed, based on Western fear of encountering the

"Other," a concept well established through British imperialism and thoroughly deconstructed in recent years by postcolonial critics. This description follows, for the most part, that of Berenson, who commented on the painting in an article about Correggio Cooper read before viewing the painting (Thain and Vadillo, *Michael Field, the Poet* 315). Cooper transcribed Berenson's comments into the journal after her own entry:

> There is a picture in the Dresden Gallery, which although executed by Battista, the brother of Dosso and somewhat cold in colour, is as good an example of Dosso's fancy as one need ask for. One sees a woman asleep, extended somewhat in the pose of the Ariadne of the Vatican. . . . A procession of unheard of monsters . . . strides stealthily . . . toward the water's edge. . . . To the left-hand corner in a wicker basket . . . sit two creatures with human faces, one with long loose teeth, the other with his tongue thrust out of his cheek. The part of the town across the river from them is even more phantastic. (Ms. 46779)

Berenson's description, like Cooper's, plays into the Western fear of the Other, since he identifies the central figure as the Greek Ariadne, a figure more Western than Eastern, and emphasizes the fantastical experience of the dream, both for the Ariadne figure and for the viewer, by characterizing the procession of animals as "monsters" and the humans in the basket as "creatures." Still, he does not identify the humans in the basket according to nationality or ethnicity, as Cooper has, and he puts these "creatures" into a comic framework, by comparing Ariadne's dream to Shakespeare's *Midsummer Night's Dream*. "How like the vision to the Midsummer Night's Dream. It is a trifle more spectral, but it is no less fantastic and quite as humorous" (Ms. 46779). This suggests that Berenson is able to contain the Western fear of the unknown within a comic structure, perhaps an even more Orientalist sentiment, in the Saidian sense, since it protects Westerners from their own terror.

Yet Bradley's thoughts about the painting, which Cooper also copied into the journal, reinforce Cooper's emphasis on the terror felt by Europeans when encountering the Other, since Bradley focuses even more closely on the nightmare experienced by the central figure. Bradley expresses this in verse form, writing: "Spectries watching spectral things / Sluggish underneath the night, / And half-cumbered in affright. / What o'clock? / Say the cock. / And she shudders at the shock; / For the vision has no hours" (Ms. 46779). Bradley's characterization of the woman as "shudder[ing] at the shock" of dreaming about the creatures described in more detail by Cooper and Berenson confirms the imperialist stance from which many Europeans would have viewed Eastern images in art. Although Cooper, Berenson, and Bradley are not in complete agreement about the meaning of the painting, they all work within a similar, European framework that places the Egyptian figure in the painting at the bottom of a racial hierarchy.

Negative associations with Egyptian figures are also seen in Bradley and Cooper's journal in April 1891, when they go to see the British Museum's Keeper of Roman and Greek Antiquities, Alexander Stuart Murray, and find him "set down among the mummies" (Ms. 46779). Murray—whom Bradley and Cooper had met in 1889 through a letter of introduction from John Miller Gray, Curator of the Scottish National Portrait Gallery (Ms. 45853)— is not in his office when they arrive. While they wait for him, they "sniff the mummies—we see their gaudy cases—the gaudiness of fashion turned monumental—their pitiful, bony dust," and they look at photographs of Egyptian rulers, which are hanging outside Murray's office door. "By Murray's door are photos of Ramesis II and III with a few other folk of their ages. The sun at last has reached them in their monstrous secrecy—it has seen their faces with its manifesting truthfulness. There is horror, brute calm, an immemorial [indecipherable word] about the expressions" (Ms. 46779). Expressing a view that assumes British superiority to (or at least British ignorance of) ancient Egyptian culture, Cooper continues, contrasting the images to those of dead people in the morgue: "The portraits of the Morgue are less shocking—they are printed from transient models: these from incorruptible (or perhaps I should say long-suffering) clay. In one case of the Graeco-Egyptian time—when the eternal [indecipherable word] of the Greeks for the body in life gives us pictures of the departed as they were seen among men—is the head of a child, a little pomegranate of a child. . . . Poor little One, that once lay so soft in the Embalmer's hands!" (Ms. 46779).[6]

Despite these negative depictions of ancient Egyptians in the journal, there are some positive references, but only when Egyptian figures are recast in a Greek or Christian context. On an earlier visit to see Murray in May 1889 with Robert Browning, Bradley and Cooper view "an Egyptian Sappho,—a fine, inspired figure with lyre," which produces in Browning a "poetic reverie" (Ms. 45853). As Yopie Prins argues in *Victorian Sappho* (1999), the celebrated first woman poet from Lesbos "became a name with multiple significations in the course of the nineteenth century" and "an artifact of Victorian poetics," since the appropriation of her work by Victorian poets "influenced the gendering of the lyric as a feminine genre" (3). Bradley and Cooper, writing as Field, adopted Sappho's form in order to "enter[ ] into a domain often coded as masculine, and, by the end of the nineteenth century, increasingly homosexual," and through their entry into this masculine domain, they revisioned ancient Greece as "inhabited not only by the [male] pupils of Socrates, but also by young women" (77). According to Prins, Browning recognized the "erotic subtext of their poetry" but believed it might take 50 years before they would "make their mark" on the literary world with their poetry (76, 79). Prins's discussion of Field's work clearly shows the importance of ancient Greece in aestheticist literature in the late Victorian period, but while Prins refers to Egypt in her description of Sappho's lyrics, the fragments of which were found in Egypt in the early twentieth century (23, 129), she does not trace fully the Egyptian context for Sappho as she appeared to Bradley and Cooper in the British Museum.

Though the exact object viewed by them cannot be identified definitively, it likely was the bas-relief of Sappho and Alcaeus pictured in Victor Duruy's *History of Greece and of the Greek People* (1892), which shows Sappho and Alcaeus holding a lyre between them as Alcaeus admires Sappho (180). John Miller Gray describes a bas-relief of Sappho and Alcaeus in a January 30, 1889, letter to Bradley and Cooper and recommends they ask Murray to show it to them, since it might be suitable for the cover of their 1889 collection of Sappho-inspired poems *Long Ago* (Ms. 45853). Furthermore, the bas-relief that Gray recommended is also discussed by George Ebers (a German Egyptologist who wrote historical romances with elaborate footnotes based on his research) in his novel *An Egyptian Princess*. First published in English in 1864 but revised multiple times to reflect new archaeological finds, a new edition of this novel was advertised in spring 1888 in periodicals such as the *Athenaeum* and the *Bookseller*, where it was listed in the same column as an edition of Field's plays *Canute the Great* and *The Cup of Water*. Ebers opens *An Egyptian Princess* with two Greek men visiting the garden of Rhodopis, a Thracian "slave and courtesan" who became a "queen" when Sappho's brother Charaxus fell in love with her and freed her from the Egyptian pharaoh Amasis (8). In Ebers's telling of the story, which is based on Herodotus's account, Sappho first writes "biting verses" about Charaxus and Rhodopis but later becomes "an enthusiastic admirer" of the courtesan-cum-queen (14–15), and in telling this story, Ebers includes a footnote about a "bas-relief in the British Museum," which "was found at Melos and represents Sappho, with Alcaeus [the other famous Lesbos poet and admirer of Rhodopis] grasping at her lute" (13). Though there is nothing overtly Egyptian about these depictions of Sappho, both Duruy and Ebers emphasize the Egyptian roots of ancient Greek culture in their references to the bas-relief, with Duruy stating that "all Greek art and religion came from Egypt" (180) and Ebers stating that though the Egyptians were "hateful" toward non-Egyptians, they "had been compelled to admit foreigners into their land," with the "Greeks follow[ing] the Phoenicians in Egypt" (15).

While Bradley and Cooper chose different representations of Sappho for the book, they clearly saw an image of Sappho at the British Museum they perceived to be "Egyptian." In addition, they also referred to "a beautiful, nude figure of a girl with a lyre" as "an Egyptian Sappho" when they attended an exhibit at the Academy in Kensington in April 1889 (Lysack 942). This additional characterization of Sappho as Egyptian indicates a pattern in their recognition of Egyptian contexts but also their tendency to engage Egyptian culture more fully when it was presented in more familiar Greek or Christian contexts. In fact, some of the Christianized depictions of Egypt that Bradley and Cooper note in their journal were so appealing they purchased photographs of them to display at home. For example, while in Frankfurt in 1891, they saw Bartolomeo Veneto's *St. Catherine of Egypt* (c. 1520–1530), which Cooper describes as having "Gold hair that has grown straight from the sweat of suffering—a head full, imaginatively, of the martyr's doom, in the mystery of wh[ich] she is looking, as the angels look into the mystery of the Cross" (Ms. 46779). This depiction is not unlike those Westernized depictions of St. Catherine in Anna Jameson's *Sacred and Legendary Art* that I discussed in my chapter about Eliot, and the National Inventory of Continental European Paintings describes Veneto's St. Catherine as reflecting "fashionable" portraits painted in the sixteenth century (n. pag.), indicating Veneto was following an Italian model for beauty rather than an Eastern one. This painting was among the photographic reproductions Cooper purchased for Bradley's birthday in 1891, and in 1892, they also purchased a photograph of Correggio's *Rest on the Flight to Egypt* (c. 1515–1517), which Cooper describes as picturing the Madonna "holding . . . a babe on her weary knee, her face full of maternal patience" (Ms. 46780). In 1893, they would see this painting firsthand with Berenson in the Uffizi (Ms. 46781), and it, like that of St. Catherine, is a fully Christianized view of Egypt, with no acknowledgment of ancient Egyptian religion or the other world religions (Judaism or Islam) that developed in Egypt after ancient times.

*   *   *

Given Bradley and Cooper's mediated encounters with ancient Egypt, it is not surprising that as their career developed, they adopted an ideal of beauty more familiar to their Western audience. Furthermore, for two women looking for ways to express their same-sex love, ancient Greek and Renaissance Italian cultures offered stronger contexts for their expression than did ancient Egyptian culture. Building off the Graeco-Italian ideal they had learned from Berenson, Bradley and Cooper used their 1892 ekphrastic collection of poetry, *Sight and Song*, to show how this ideal might be used to resist heterosexual love and offer alternatives such as same-sex love and autoeroticism. Their efforts to offer such alternatives in *Sight and Song* have been well discussed by critics.[7] However, these critics have not shown how Bradley and

Cooper established a Graeco-Italian model for beauty by distinguishing certain Venuses as "not Greek" because they did not possess the Italian qualities that made them familiar to European viewers and other Venuses as "fully Greek" because they did possess these Italian qualities. This distinction is important when we consider how Bradley and Cooper approached the heroines of their plays, where they attributed Graeco-Italian qualities to women characters of many different nationalities but continued to represent Egyptian women in a negative light and rejected more Eastern ideals of beauty in representing European women who sought emancipation from difficult circumstances.

Bradley and Cooper's use of Venus in *Sight and Song* was influenced, of course, by the ancient sculptures of her, which were variants on Praxiteles's *Aphrodite of Knidos*. Bradley first saw these variants while traveling on the Continent in 1880 and wrote about them in some detail in her letters to Cooper, who remained in England. Writing of her admiration for the most famous of these variants, the *Venus de Milo*, Bradley says that the *Venus de Milo* is "the perfect woman—perfect in and of herself—with no thought of man, no entreaty for his love: yet with breasts so sweet one longs to drink from them. . . . A lovely creature, not Cupid's mother, not Adonis' bride; 'das ewig weibliche' the eternal womanhood is what she expresses! I am so glad to have seen her" (Evangelista 100). Bradley also writes of the *Venus de Medici* and the *Capitoline Venus*, two other well-known variants, which cannot compare to the *Venus de Milo*. Bradley is "disappointed" by the *Venus de Medici*, who is "entirely self-conscious," and although the *Capitoline Venus* is admirable because her clothes are "beside her, not on her," so that "the lovely form from throat to foot is unmutilated," her "bosom" is nothing close to that of the *Venus de Milo* (100). Bradley recounts how her traveling companion, Jane Scott, sums up the difference between the three Venuses, saying, "the Venus de Medici courts, the Venus of the Capitol tolerates, and the Venus de Milo disdains the love of man," and Bradley goes on to say she prefers Titian's *Venus of Urbino* to the *Venus de Medici* because Titian's version "looked like a ripe peach in the sun" (Field, *The Fowl and the Pussycat* 22). Although this comment does not directly refer to Italy, the phrase "looked like a ripe peach in the sun" resonates with many of the comments Bradley and Cooper make about Venus as depicted by Italian Renaissance painters (especially Giorgione), comments I will discuss in more detail later in this chapter.

Bradley and Cooper's interest in Venus, then, comes from a penchant for a Graeco-Italian ideal of beauty, and all of the poems about Venus in *Sight and Song* are based on paintings by Italian Renaissance painters—Correggio's *Venus, Mercury and Cupid* (c. 1525); Botticelli's *Birth of Venus* (c. 1486), *Spring* (c. 1482), and *Venus and Mars* (c. 1483); and Giorgione's *Sleeping*

Venus (c. 1510). Still, not all of these Venuses possess the qualities Bradley and Cooper believed was the right combination of Greek and Italian qualities to be considered fully Greek. Bradley and Cooper's journal is helpful in understanding their unique representation of Venus in *Sight and Song*, since it contains descriptions of the paintings the poems were based on, as well as a wider range of Venus paintings Bradley and Cooper saw in museums and galleries as they were composing the poems. I discuss Bradley and Cooper's comments about the paintings they viewed, along with the poems themselves, as a way to clarify which Venuses were fully Greek in their minds and why they chose a Graeco-Italian ideal over an Egyptian ideal to express their belief that emancipation was possible through sexual desire.

The first poem about Venus in *Sight and Song*, "Venus, Mercury and Cupid," is based on Correggio's painting by the same name and depicts Venus asking Mercury for his help in educating their son Cupid. While there is no obvious reference to Venus possessing the ideal Greek body in the poem, analysis of this painting by art historians indicate that although Venus looks directly at the viewer (rather than turning her head in profile or partial profile to the left, as was the case with the *Aphrodite of Knidos* and its many variants), she holds the contrapposto pose of the *Aphrodite of Knidos*, with her weight on her right foot and her right hand covering her genitals (Ekserdjian 270). Cooper's journal comments about the painting, which she viewed at the National Gallery in August 1890, do not address Venus's pose, but they do indicate that Cooper saw this Venus as possessing some Greek qualities, via the sylvan setting of the painting, which was the location of Greek Dionysian activity. "[W]hat a delightful picture it is!," Cooper writes. "Venus is a sylvan Queen, with eyes as wonderously shy as a doe's, with smirking undecided lips, forehead on which are fugative [*sic*] lights, and womanly white body shaded green with the forest's verdure" (Ms. 46778). The reference to Venus as a "sylvan Queen" is captured in the early lines of the poem, "Of a Venus, in the braid / Of bright oak-boughs," which refers to the forest setting, a setting Field uses to evoke a Greek atmosphere in subsequent poems as well.

With the Greek contrapposto pose of Venus and Cooper's commentary in mind, "Venus, Mercury, and Cupid" seems a relatively safe way to open a collection of poetry that addresses controversial issues surrounding love and sexual desire, issues so controversial Cooper believed Field's publisher Elkin Mathews was worried about publishing at least one of the Venus poems in the collection. "He seems anxious, disquieted," she wrote in February 1892. "I believe the *Venus* and the Crivelli *Pietà* are in his mind—he is 'a man forbid'—he cannot speak, even if the offending poems should keep the 400 [copies of] Sight and Songs on his shelf" (Ms. 46780). Although Cooper seems unsure why Mathews was hesitant, Bradley seems to understand better the controversy that might surround even the safest poem in the collection. Her journal comments about Correggio's painting contrasts Cooper's description of this Venus as a "sylvan Queen." Recorded in her own hand at the end of August 1890, Bradley writes, "There is infinite dreaminess in the eyes of Venus—that look of shadowy pain, that delicious pathos we see in the eyes of wild creatures—she is apart from learning—she does not hold her power by the tenure of knowledge. . . . She is resigning her boy to learn art and trickery from Mercury—she who is simple love, shy and uninstructed" (Ms. 46778). Bradley's characterization of Venus as more serious because she lacks power over Cupid's education raises a related, but slightly different, issue that runs throughout the *Sight and Song* collection—that Venus often is sad or depressed because she cannot control the love situations in which she is involved—and the issues of power suggested by Bradley's comments about Correggio's painting is the sort of thing that might have worried Mathews.[8]

Power issues between women and men are even more pronounced in the Botticelli-inspired poems in *Sight and Song*: "Birth of Venus," "Spring," and "The Figure of Venus in 'Spring.'" Jill Ehnenn, who discusses the Botticelli-inspired poems in some detail, argues that Venus is sad because she knows that heterosexual love will keep her from Flora, who moves to cover Venus's nakedness in "Birth of Venus" and who considers leaving Venus for heterosexual love in "Spring" (225). Marion Thain furthers Ehnenn's argument that Field resisted the notion of heterosexual love through the use of the "sad" Venus; in "Spring" particularly, Field repeats the line about Venus's sadness to challenge normative concepts about time (85–86). While Thain does not directly state that this use of synchronic time is connected to representing the lesbian desire of Venus and Flora, her larger argument—that Field uses a more cyclical concept of time to transport themselves into the character of Venus in a way male writers such as Dante Gabriel Rossetti, who had also written about Botticelli's painting in his 1881 "For Spring by Sandro Botticelli," could not (83–84)—suggests Field resists heterosexual love through this more cyclical representation of time.

Still, Ehnenn and Thain do not fully explore how the Greek context for the Botticelli-inspired poems might contribute to Field's resistance to heterosexual love. In *Birth of Venus*, Botticelli replicates the pose of the *Venus de Medici*, which he studied in preparation for creating this painting (Mack 116), yet Bradley's journal comments about the painting specifically characterize Botticelli's version as *not* Greek. Written in Cooper's hand, her commentary runs:

> But what is this cool, cool sea, sprinkled with blown rose-leaves and the shy, recoiling girl-form that seeks to veil itself in its coiled wrappings of lucent hair?

Not the Greek Venus, joyous and unabashed: she will glide gratefully into the great, outspread, rosy cloak the figure on the right is wanting to lay over her—not the Greek Venus—she does not even by amorous bend of the head indicate her knowledge of that lusty swelling male-force on the left. (Ms. 46778)

At first glance, Bradley appears to think that to be Greek is to know heterosexual love—to know the "male-force" of the figure to the left, Zephyrus. But, given the aesthetes' association of Greek love with homosexual love, her commentary also suggests that to be Greek is to know homosexual love—the "unabashed" love that is true to one's desire.

Further, Bradley assumes that the body, which in Botticelli's painting is only a copy of a Greek statue rather than a representation of the body true to the "unabashed" Greek spirit, will reflect sexual desire, since she goes on to say, "This then, if we must have nudity, is how a Christian artist draws it: the soft guardian eyes of almost tearful shadow, the whole body timid, full of the instinct of flight" (Ms. 46778). It is the non-Greek, Christian body that possesses the "tearful shadow" that Bradley referenced earlier as "shadowy pain" in her description of the Correggio painting, and Bradley even more explicitly recognizes that Greek culture offers an alternative to heterosexual, Christian love by anticipating Lord Alfred Douglas's famous line about homosexual desire as "Love that dare not speak its name" when she writes: "That the things of Love are unspeakable, that the sorrow of it cannot be told, that shadow face expresses to us. There is strong covert in the great orange-trees, and underneath them somberest earthly shade, exquisitely contrasting with the lovely little lucent frilly pucker of the nipples under the shell" (Ms. 46778). According to Bradley's commentary, homosexual Greek love is "covert," found in the orange-trees, a comment that echoes the presence of "oak-boughs" in Field's poem about Correggio's painting, while heterosexual, Christian love is associated with the "lovely little lucent frilly pucker of the nipples under the shell," or the tame, "not Greek" representation of Venus by Botticelli. In characterizing Botticelli's Venus as not Greek, then, Bradley's commentary reinforces Ehnenn's idea that heterosexual love will try to disrupt bonds between women, and this notion is reinforced when Bradley suggests in her commentary that Zephyrus and Flora are in direct competition for Venus's love. While Zephyrus appears to have the upper hand in competing for Venus's love, since his breeze ruffles the roses associated with Flora and the ends of Venus's hair, there still is an alternative open to Venus, since she will soon come to the land, to the sylvan setting of lemon-trees, rushes, and grass where Flora awaits her (Ms. 46778).

Rereading "Birth of Venus" with this context in mind, we note the absence of any reference to the Greek pose of Venus in the opening stanza, and Field's description of Venus as "a girl who seeks to find / New-born beauty with a tress / Gold about her nakedness" reads more like a depiction of Eve than of the *Venus de Medici* or the *Venus de Milo*. It is Flora, described in the second stanza as "corn-flower dressed," with a "wild-rose at her breast," who represents unabashed Greek love and offers Venus the opportunity for something other than the "timid" Christian love Bradley describes in the journal. Using phrases from Bradley's commentary, the poem presents Venus as a "Virgin stranger, come to seek / Covert of strong orange-boughs / By the sea-wind scarcely moved,— / She is Love that hath not loved" (37–40). The "strong orange-boughs" recall the "sylvan" setting seen in the Correggio-inspired poem discussed earlier, and the reference to the inability of the sea-wind to move the orange-boughs recalls Thain's analysis of Field's use of synchronic, cyclical time to resist a more diachronic, progressive concept of time. The diachronic, heterosexual love of Zephyrus (seen in the sea wind that pushes Venus toward land) cannot move the synchronic, homosexual love of Flora (which is found in the orange-boughs), and Venus's status as "Virgin stranger" who is "Love that hath not loved" no longer carries a negative connotation. It simply means Venus has not known lesbian love yet.

Clearly, Field chose the ancient Greek ideal of Venus because it offered a way to express lesbian love in a way ancient Egyptian ideals about women could not, and moving onto their poem "Spring," we can see the importance of the Greek ideal continuing across the *Sight and Song* collection, even as Field worked out what qualities constituted a fully Greek representation of Venus. As other critics have noted, there is practically no physical description of Venus in the poem. Instead, it begins with her emotion: "Venus is sad among the wanton powers" (1). Looking back at Botticelli's painting, we can immediately see this is not the Greek Venus, not even in terms of the Greek pose seen in the previous painting. This Venus is fully clothed and only barely holds the contrapposto pose. Although Christine Havelock has pointed out that a clothed Venus is not necessarily a more "conservative" Venus, since Greek artists emphasized the sensuality of the body even when draped (34), this Venus's sensuality does not appear through her drapery, and her clothing is more along the lines of dress used in medieval paintings of the Virgin Mary.[9] Moreover, she adopts a pose seen in religious paintings of Christ, her right hand raised to bless the people who surround her, a pose Cooper comments on in the journal and which is highlighted in "The Figure of Venus in 'Spring.'" This Venus is the "timid" Christian version Bradley describes in the journal, and Cooper's journal description of her as a "suffering Venus" because "she knows the anguish of the doom of love" (Ms. 46778) also suggests a Christian figure. Yet the promise of Greek life is present through the "wanton powers" that surround Venus, described as powers that "make delicious tempest in the hours / Of April or are reckless with their flowers" (2–3). The contrast between diachronic time/heterosexual love and synchronic time/homosexual love evident in "Birth of Venus" is even more pronounced here, captured in lines about the movement of the wind onto the land where Flora stands among the sylvan orange trees (4–8, 22–24). This representation suggests that Field wanted more powerful women than the Christian tradition offered but did not find this powerful type in ancient Egyptian culture, since ancient Egyptian culture did not offer the possibility for same-sex desire found in ancient Greek culture.

In their Greek context, then, the Botticelli-inspired poems take on new meaning. Certainly, they celebrate lesbian desire, as previous critical readings of the poems have emphasized, but they also show where Field located lesbian desire—in ancient Greek culture—and how this desire was connected to power, an aspect of Greek culture Havelock emphasizes when she argues that nudity in Greek art is not simply about sex. "We tend to see [nudity] rather narrowly—at least in women—as an outright, even immoral, offer of sex, whereas the Greeks, to whom sexuality was not so prescriptive, seem to have regarded nudity in a broader context as a display of power and liberty" (36). My reading of the poems—one that emphasizes the connection between the Greek body, lesbian desire, and power—reveals Field understood how important the overturning of gender hierarchies was to women's emancipation. Still, my reading also reveals that the concept of emancipation presented by Field did not overturn hierarchies based on nationality or ethnicity. It was European women, not Eastern women, who would gain emancipation by embracing Greek culture.

Such opportunities for European women's emancipation are even more evident in the poem based on Botticelli's *Venus and Mars*, where for the first time in *Sight and Song*, Venus is represented as taking control of a love situation, since she turns the gaze upon her male lover. This poem is rarely discussed in criticism about *Sight and Song*, yet it clearly was important to the collection, since Cooper double checked it against the painting in the National Gallery before its publication and was pleased to find it captured the "poetry of the picture" (Ms. 46779).[10] The lack of critical attention to this poem is surprising, since it provides a crucial transition between the "not Greek" representations of Venus by Botticelli and the fully Greek representation by Giorgione, which appears toward the end of the collection.

Cooper's commentary about the painting, recorded in the journal on July 27, 1891, builds off her earlier commentary about Botticelli's *Spring*, where heterosexual love is associated with a particular aspect of nature, the sea breeze. Here, heterosexual love comes as a storm that might do serious damage, yet, unlike in *Spring*, where it is doubtful Venus can weather the sea breeze of Zephryus, this Venus is able to respond to the "power and fury" that has possessed Mars (Ms. 46779). She even seems to flourish as a result of it, "like a shoot after thunder-rain" (Ms. 46779). While this clearly is a different Venus than the one Cooper saw in Botticelli's other paintings, Cooper still characterizes this Venus as a "tragic" figure, possessing the "sadness" seen in previous Venuses: "she is modern, cold, she is sad, she is awake" (Ms. 46779). This characterization suggests Venus still lacks the fully Greek spirit, which would unabashedly enjoy love instead of feeling sad or depressed about it. However, Cooper's addition of phrases such as "modern," "cold," and "awake" indicates this Venus has a new awareness previous Venuses did not possess, and this awareness is what should allow her to embrace a more fully Greek form of love in the future.

Rereading the poem in light of Cooper's commentary about Botticelli's painting, we find Field presenting this Venus as distinctly different from those in previous poems. The poem opens: "She is a fate, although / She lies upon the grass, / While satyrs shout *Ho, ho!* / At what she brings to pass" (1–4). The word "fate" recalls a disagreement between Cooper and Berenson over the three Graces in Botticelli's *Spring*, in which Cooper characterized the Graces as girls not yet marked by Eros's darts (Ms. 46778). By identifying this Venus as a "fate," we assume she is not a "Grace," has experienced hetero-sexual love, and knows that the struggle for power in romantic relationships is a reality of life. This Venus is also characterized as a Queen, recalling the "sylvan Queen" reference in the poem about Correggio's *Venus, Mercury, and Cupid*, since the poem continues, "And nature is as free / Before her strange, young face / As if it knew that she / Were in her *sovereign* place, / With shading trees above" (5–9, emphasis mine). The characterization of Venus as having a "strange, young face" may seem odd, but as my analysis of the poem based on Giorgione's *Sleeping Venus* will show, this characterization indicates this Venus does not have the ideal combination of Greek and Italian quali-ties Bradley and Cooper had learned from Berenson. Once the Greek ideal is inserted into the Italian landscape, Venus will feel more familiar to viewers, and her "strangeness" will disappear.

Nevertheless, this Venus does seem more comfortable in nature than pre-vious Venuses, since she does not need to combat the forces of nature rep-resenting the "storm" of heterosexual love. In fact, everything about Venus's pose suggests she is comfortable in nature and also with her relationship with Mars: "Her head, erect in pose / Against the laurel-leaves, / Is looped with citron hair. . . . She rears from off the ground / As if her body grew / Triumphant as a stem / That hath received the rains, / Hath softly sunk with them, / And in an hour regains / Its height and settledness" (17–19, 27–33). Field's description highlights Botticelli's anticipation of the reclining pose Giorgione would make famous with *Sleeping Venus*, which showed that although a woman might give up the contrapposto pose of the *Aphrodite of Knidos*, she could still exude the confidence of that statue. By using a different type of pose, Botticelli brings Venus closer to the "unabashed" Greek spirit that Bradley identified when discussing *Birth of Venus*. Although Venus is clothed, she possesses the confidence of the later, nude reclining Venus. This characterization of Venus as especially confident is an interesting contrast to the characterizations of the reclining Cleopatra by Lucy Snowe in Brontë's *Villette* and Nightingale's characterization of herself as resisting the "divan incumbent" pose as she sails down the Nile on her trip to Egypt. For Brontë and Nightingale, the reclining woman, especially when she is Egyptian, is prone to roles that involve a loss of agency, whereas for Field, the reclining woman, especially when she is fully Greek, represents confidence and the power to control love situations.

Still, the confidence exuded by Botticelli's Venus cannot overcome Field's feeling that as long as Venus is involved in heterosexual love, she is a tragic figure. After describing Mars and the satyrs that surround him, Field again draws on lines from Cooper's commentary to sum up the relationship between Mars and Venus. "O *tragic forms*, the man, / *The woman*—he asleep, / *She* lone and *sadder* than / The dawn, too wise to weep / *Illusion* that to her / Is empire, to the earth / Necessity and stir / Of sweet, predestined mirth! / *Ironical* she sees, / Without regret, the work her kiss has done / And lives a *cold* enchantress doomed to please / her victims one by one" (73–84, emphasis mine). Though the last line of the poem suggests Venus cannot escape heterosexual love once she has chosen it—she can only be the "cold enchantress doomed to please / her victims one by one"—she at least has the awareness about heterosexual love previous Venuses in the collection do not.

Field's poem about Giorgione's *Sleeping Venus*, the last of the Venus poems in *Sight and Song*, shows that, despite the ending of the poem about Botticelli's *Venus and Mars*, an alternative to heterosexual love does exist. As other critics have shown, Giorgione's Venus experiences the autoerotic alternative to heterosexual love not possible for the Venuses depicted in the other poems in the collection. Still, the Greek context of this representation should be more fully explored, since it confirms autoeroticism is part of the fully Greek spirit, which Cooper and Bradley understood as containing Italian elements and which no doubt contributed to their preference for ancient Greek culture over ancient Egyptian culture. The first evidence of their thoughts about Giorgione's painting comes in February 1891, when they go to the National Gallery with Berenson and see a photograph of the painting. Bradley exclaims in the journal, "But oh—that Venus of Giorgione's, the long undulating body repeated in the curves and fluctuation of the landscape" (Ms. 46779). There is further commentary about the painting later in February, when Cooper and Bradley go to Berenson's and Costelloe's rooms in London and again see the photograph, which Berenson had obviously purchased.[11] Cooper writes of the photograph, "The limbs repeat the feminine amplitude of the Earth—she lies under the great air, in the midst of a rich grave landscape and her arm round her head is of one line with her side" (Ms. 46779).

Already, Bradley and Cooper seem to recognize that Giorgione had fully Italianized Venus, making her more familiar to European viewers than his predecessors had. In *Venus of Urbino*, Titian had included ornamentation on Venus's body (breaking the natural lines that put women in harmony with the landscape) and placed Venus in an interior setting with the accoutrements of marriage surrounding her, but Giorgione places Venus in a more natural setting, with a natural body. Cooper's extensive comments about this aspect of Giorgione's painting appear in the journal in August 1891, when she and Bradley finally see the original in the Dresden Gallery. Cooper writes, "Her chestnut, braided hair" is "only a little brighter than the bank above," and "Her right arm is bent back over her head, and the curve from the elbow to the knee has the extensive softness of undulating land" (Ms. 46779), indicating the harmony between Venus's body and the landscape. During a second viewing of the painting a week later, Cooper adds description of Venus's facial features, which have both Grecian and Italian elements (she has "olive cheeks" and a "long, Grecian nose"), and Giorgione's integration of her body into the landscape makes her a Venus that Cooper feels comfortable with: "Here we have beauty with us, by our home-steads—no stranger from the sea, no apparition, no enchantress, but simple as our fields, as nobly-lighted as are our harvests, pure as the things man needs for his life that use cannot violate" (Ms. 46779).

In this description, not only does Venus have specific Grecian features to identify her nationality clearly, she now is fully Greek in spirit, since she has completed the journey from the sea, where, to recall my earlier analysis of the Botticelli-inspired poems in *Sight and Song*, heterosexual love reigns. Here, she is fully associated with the land, where, as we also have seen earlier, the potential for alternative forms of love (including homosexual love and autoeroticism) reside. Cooper's assertion that Venus is one with the land, to the degree that even "use cannot violate" her, suggests Venus can be restored to the ideal Greek love, homosexual love, even after she has experienced the more violating form of heterosexual love. Cooper's commentary about Venus and the land also is significant because it suggests Giorgione has placed the Greek body into a specifically contemporary European landscape with which the viewer is more familiar. This recalls my discussion, in Chapter 1 of this book, about the difficulty of integrating sky-oriented Egyptian goddesses into sea-oriented Greek culture. There was also the difficulty of integrating sea-oriented Greek goddesses into land-oriented Northern European culture, but Italian landscape provided the venue for such a transformation. Cooper's feeling that this Venus represents "beauty with us, by our home-steads" and is "no stranger from the sea but simple as our fields" indicates this Venus is closer to European women's attributes and emotions than previous Venuses, reflecting the imperialist attitude that caused Field to "other" people who still felt like "strangers" to them—the Egyptian figure in Dossi's *The Dream*, for example.

Bradley's commentary on Giorgione's *Sleeping Venus*, which is written in Cooper's hand, confirms this Venus is fully one with the land, and her commentary also emphasizes the *Italian* quality of the landscape. Briefly highlighting the specifics of Venus's body, Bradley quickly moves to commentary about Venus's relationship to the land. "She is a goddess of the Earth—the Earth is her temple, she is no foreigner, no visitant—but of long, quiet summer afternoons and sacred country-life. There is nothing rustic about this picture. It is only *Italian* landscape that could thus take flesh in a Venus. There is about her nothing bitter or barren—everything is of harvest—silent ripening, fulfilment" (Ms. 46779, emphasis mine). Bradley's use of the word "fulfilment" here is significant, since Cooper had previously used it to describe the "tragedy" of Botticelli's *Venus and Mars*, where the "fulfilment of love" they experience is "so like the fulfilment of life": "tragic" because Mars must "sleep in illusion," while Venus is "watchful lest it cheat her again" (Ms. 46779). Now "fulfilment" is wholly positive, and it is in Italy, not in another European country, where this fulfillment is possible. By saying "There is nothing rustic about this picture" and "It is only Italian landscape that could thus take flesh in a Venus," Bradley suggests there is something important about the combination of the Greek and Italian qualities Berenson emphasized in his ideas about the ideal body in art.

Rereading Field's poem about Giorgione's painting in this context, this Venus is immediately set apart from other Venuses in the collection by Field's association of her with the land rather than the sea in lines 4–6: "She has left her arched shell, / Has left the barren wave that foams, / Amid earth's fruitful tilths to dwell." Further, lines 1–3 and 9–14 echo Cooper's commentary about the painting and establish this Venus as one who has a unique familiarity with the land: "Here is Venus *by our homes* /And resting on the verdant swell / Of a soft country flanked with mountain domes: / . . . / *Pure as are the things that man / Needs for life* and using can / Never *violate* nor spot— / Thus she slumbers in no grot, / But on open ground, / With the great hill-sides around" (emphasis mine). Venus's familiarity with the land is made possible by the infusion of the Italian landscape with the Greek body. Though there is no direct reference to the Grecian nose Cooper identified in her commentary, there are other indicators this Venus is fully imbued with the "unabashed" Greek spirit, with five of the nine stanzas of the poem devoted to specific aspects of Venus's body. Some of these stanzas closely correspond to Cooper's journal commentary about the painting. The sixth stanza, for example, uses Cooper's commentary about Venus's face. "She lies asleep: her chestnut, braided hair only a little brighter than the bank above. . . . Her face is oval, the tint olive . . . the brows restfully crescent-shaped" (Ms. 46779) becomes "Cheek and eyebrow touch the fold / Of the raised arm that frames her hair, / Her braided hair in colour like to old / Copper glinting here and there: / While through her skin of olive-gold / The scarce carnations mount and share / Faultlessly the oval space / Of her temperate, grave face" (72–79). This attention to the details of Venus's face recalls the reference to her Grecian nose in the journal, and the emphasis on her olive skin and chestnut hair as similar to the colors of the landscape brings attention to the Italian qualities of her features.

The reclining pose of Venus is also central to the depiction of a different kind of Venus in the poem. Stanzas three, four, and five all address aspects of the reclining pose, with stanzas three and five again drawing heavily on Cooper's journal commentary. Sandwiched in between, the fourth stanza brings attention to the confidence of the reclining pose, with the opening lines: "With *bold freedom of incline,* / With an uttermost repose, / From hip to herbage-cushioned foot the line / Of her left leg stretching shows / Against the turf direct and fine" (43–47, emphasis mine). Next to the poem inspired by Botticelli's *Venus and Mars,* these lines read as an extension of the confidence that Venus can control love situations. This Venus retains the reclining pose seen in *Venus and Mars,* but she also is more relaxed, exuding an even greater level of confidence than her predecessor. The final stanza of the poem also emphasizes the reclining pose and uses this pose to characterize Venus as one who has remained the same across time, recalling Thain's argument about Field's use of time to resist normative concepts, including heterosexual love. The stanza opens: "And her resting is so strong / That while we gaze it seems as though / She had lain thus the solemn glebes among / In the ages far ago / And would continue, till the long, / Last evening of Earth's summer glow" (113–18). Venus's reclining pose, then, connects the past (ancient Greek culture), the present (Italian Renaissance culture), and the future (Field's culture of the 1890s), and the centrality of the Italian landscape in making this connection is iterated in the final lines of the poem: "We can never fear that she / From Italian fields will flee, / For she does not come from far, / She is of the things that are; / And she will not pass / While the sun strikes on the grass" (121–26). Though Field does not directly incorporate the lines from the journal commentary that this Venus is "no stranger from the sea, no apparition, no enchantress" (Cooper) or "no foreigner, no visitant" (Bradley), the lines in the poem "For she does not come from far, / She is of the things that are;" recall these characterizations and reinforce that this Venus is one with whom European women can identify.

The movement across *Sight and Song* from Correggio's and Botticelli's marginally Greek and powerless Venuses to the very powerful and fully Greek Venus by Giorgione shows the importance of the Graeco-Italian model for beauty in Field's writing. For Field, the Italianized Venus offered European women a way to control the love situations in which they were placed and offered emancipation through same-sex passion and autoeroticism. With this ideal in mind in the 1890s, Bradley and Cooper applied the idea of "Venus-as-inspiration-for-women's-emancipation" to the heroines in their verse dramas well into the early twentieth century, even when they more thoroughly engaged Eastern subject matter. Playwriting had been an integral part of Field's writing since the mid-1880s, when Bradley and Cooper published the verse dramas *Callirrhoë* and *Fair Rosamund* (1884) as their first work under the name "Michael Field."[12] For Bradley and Cooper, playwriting was an extension of their poetry writing, yet they were always anxious about their success with this genre. Their verse dramas typically met with mixed reception by their male critics (Moriarty 123–27), and when their only staged play *A Question of Memory* (1893) was poorly attended, they were sorely disappointed with their friends for not being more supportive of their work (Donoghue 82). Still, they continued to write plays, producing 27 of them, nearly one for every year of their career (Sturgeon 29). Outside Mary Sturgeon's assessment of the plays in *Michael Field* (1922) and a few more recent articles about them, very little has been written about the plays,[13] but a clear trend in the plays is Field's assignment of Greek qualities to the central women figures. Among the dramas Field wrote, about half include references to Venus or Aphrodite, and about a third include references to other Greek or Roman goddesses, including Artemis, Athena, Demeter, Diana, Flora, Hebe, Hecate, Hera, Minerva, and Persephone. Two plays, *The Tragic Mary* (1890) and *Stephania* (1892), provide particularly good examples of how Field used references to Venus to build women characters, often combining Greek and Italian qualities to present their heroines in a sympathetic manner. Still, the attention Bradley and Cooper gave to infusing their heroines with Greek and Italian attributes resulted in lack of attention to the Eastern qualities of beauty they recognized in at least some of their observations about art, such as the beauty possessed by women of diverse ethnicities in Rossetti's *Beloved*. To understand the limits of Bradley and Cooper's ideal of beauty, I turn first to *Tragic Mary* and *Stephania* and then to *Queen Mariamne* (1908), a play in which their privileging of Greek over Egyptian qualities is more explicit, to show how Bradley and Cooper infused many of their heroines, regardless of nationality or ethnicity, with Greek and Italian attributes but did not apply these attributes to Egyptian women.

For *The Tragic Mary*, Bradley and Cooper went to great lengths to research their Scottish subject, Mary Queen of Scots, who served as Queen Regnant of Scotland from 1542 to 1567 and Queen Consort of France from 1559 to 1560. They went to Holyrood, the palace where Mary resided from 1561 to 1567, to view relics related to Mary's life, and they collected as many portraits of Mary as they could find with the help of John Miller Gray (Ms. 46777, 45853). Mary already had been the focus of at least 19 other printed dramas and 14 stage productions in the nineteenth century (Taft 266), but in Field's play, she is presented as more admirable than the men who prosecute her because she has the qualities of the Greek Aphrodite. The play especially focuses on Mary's marriages after the death of her husband, King Francis II, marriages in which Mary's suitors had a vested interest in her royal position and were willing to kill in order to maintain that position. After returning to Scotland in 1561, Mary first married her cousin Lord Darnley (who killed his rival to the throne, the Italian David Riccio) and then married the 4th Earl of Bothwell (likely Darnley's murderer).

Field's use of Greek qualities to build Mary's character is evident in Act II, Scene 2, when Mary's secretary Lethington (the man most helpful to the Queen as she struggles to establish her authority with the men who try to control her) urges Mary to be patient in her quest for the English crown, stating, "My dearest queen, / Seek not the crown of England as a toy. / Be patient; set yourself to govern now / Sole as Semiramis and be remembered / Hereafter, 'mong adoring men, a goddess / And heavenly Aphrodite" (149–54). Field's reference to both Aphrodite and Semiramis, the Assyrian queen from 810 to 806 BCE who reportedly took charge of her husband's troops after his death by dressing as their son, shows that even as early as *The Tragic Mary*, Field was engaging Eastern ideals for women, but the more dominant reference in the play is clearly Aphrodite/Venus. Later, in Act 3, Scene 1, when Mary is angry with Darnley and wants to leave Scotland for France, Lethington again characterizes her as above the fray because of her likeness to the ancient Greek goddess. "Slip from your sphere! / Not so, my lady Venus; we will chase / The noisome meteor from the firmament, / And, spell-bound, guard our passion for the stars" (190–93). Lethington, who despite his support for Mary often works in consort with Bothwell, encourages Mary to remain in Scotland, so they can conspire to get rid of Darnley, and Mary agrees, ultimately marrying Bothwell because she believes she has no other choice.

Once married to Bothwell, though, she sees herself less as Aphrodite and more like Helen of Troy, whom Mary believes remained true to Menelaus after she was seduced by Paris. Mary says to Lethington, "I love the legend that she never swerved / From wifely faith, that Paris' capture was / A spectre that dislimned into thin air / When Proteus from his shadow in the rocks / Rose, and restored his guarded fugitive / Unblemished to her husband" (V.iii.102–07). When Bothwell finally frees Mary from her marriage to him, she again describes herself in Greek terms, but as Diana rather than Aphrodite, since she feels "free as air, / As Dian in the woods" (V.iv.232–33). While the play ends without further reference to Mary as Venus or Aphrodite, Field's use of references to the penultimate Greek goddess early in the play recasts Mary's image, an aim Bradley and Cooper articulate in the preface to the drama, where they argue that previous representations of Mary, especially portraits of her, do not adequately capture her character (vi). Still, they recognize the limits dramatists face in "delineating" Mary, since only a few facts about her life were known, and they close the preface by stating that the "real woman of magical nature must remain undiscovered and triumphant" (viii). Nevertheless, their delineation of Mary does much to make her a more sympathetic character. Even at the end of the play, when Mary raves about how she will be "queen / Again" (V.vii.446–47), readers feel compassion for Mary and recognize Mary as a heroine, in part because she has been presented as similar to Venus. Further, the fact that the Scottish and Catholic Mary could be recast as Venus suggests that women of many nationalities and religions were heroines for Field. Still, as I will demonstrate later, this model did not include women of all nationalities and religions, especially those associated with Egyptian culture.

Stephania (1892), another play with a sympathetic central woman character, is perhaps the best example of the Graeco-Italian ideal that Field had developed in the Venus poems in *Sight and Song*, since Stephania clearly possesses Greek and Italian qualities. Stephania is initially characterized as an Italian courtesan waiting to take revenge against the German Otho, who hanged Stephania's husband after conquering Rome, but by the end of the play, she succeeds in restoring dignity to Rome through a strategy that involves playing to Otho's weakness for Greek beauty. Interestingly, it is Otho who is first characterized as having Greek qualities in the play, since Otho's Italian friend Gerbert, who has helped him conquer Rome, strokes Otho's ego, asserting that Otho's mother "Gave you her purest Grecian blood" and thus the Grecian qualities of "eloquence," "courage," "learning," and "Great powers of meditation" (I.335–39). Otho returns this compliment, telling Gerbert he is the one who tamed his "Saxon rudeness" and "rescued / The Greek within me from rusticity" (I.390–91). Yet, Otho comes to believe Stephania also has

Greek qualities, telling her, even after she insists she is "From purest Roman stock," that she must have some pre-Roman roots: "But your brows / Are conscious and imperial, they belong / To ages of dominion and of pleasure / Unequalled in Olympus when the Gods / Were satisfied with sacrifice, and Hebe / Brought them the heavenly cup" (II.656–74). These qualities make her appealing to Otho, who says, "I see in you / All that I want" (II.679–80). Ultimately, Stephania's perceived Grecian qualities convince Otho to choose her over Gerbert (III.193–98, 390–93), and Otho is surprised when Stephania reveals she is his enemy's widow. The Roman rebels retake the city, Otho dies, and Stephania, an ideal combination of Greek and Italian qualities, restores dignity to Rome, as well as to herself and her husband's memory. In the final lines of the play, she says she will "bow my heart / In awe of the great triumph I have won / For Italy, my womanhood, and thee" (III.841–43).

While Field used the Graeco-Italian model to create what Bradley and Cooper thought would be sympathetic heroines, Victorians did not necessarily sympathize with these characters. The writer George Meredith preferred the character of Otho to Stephania, saying to Bradley and Cooper in an October 1893 letter, "For do you not mean that one should give one's heart to her case less than to Otho? But so it is with me. Her case cannot be pleaded in the abstract. To win sympathy with her to the end, her situation has to be pictured" (Field, *Works and Days* 88). Yet, the comments Bradley and Cooper made about Stephania in their journal make it clear they expected readers to sympathize with her. Despite negative comments about *Stephania* from Meredith and what seemed like a lack of enthusiasm from Elkin Mathews when he received the manuscript in June 1892 (Ms. 46780), Bradley and Cooper were happy with what they had produced (Ms. 46780). They delighted in their discussions about her with Selwyn Image, who was designing the cover for *Stephania* (Ms. 46780), and were surprised when he and friends such as Arthur Symons and George Moore gave them the cold shoulder after negative reviews of the play appeared (Ms. 46781). "What can it be!," wrote Cooper in the journal. "*Stephania* cannot be responsible for it all" (Ms. 46781).

Field, then, used the Graeco-Italian ideal developed in *Sight and Song* to urge a sympathetic understanding of women who do not follow societal conventions, but this attachment to the Graeco-Italian ideal prevented Field from representing Egyptian women in a sympathetic light when more actively engaging Eastern culture in the plays written after the turn of the century. In *Queen Mariamne*, the first in a planned trilogy about Herod, Field met with the limits of infusing women of all nationalities and religions with Greek and Italian qualities. Although Cleopatra, who represents Egypt in the play, is referred to once as a "dusky Venus," this reference has a negative connotation, since it is used in conjunction with a statement by Antony, who tells Herod that Cleopatra has no "faith or governance, this queen / Save that of a dusky Venus" (II.ii.35). Further, Cleopatra is strongly contrasted to Herod's wife, Mariamne, who represents the truer Greek ideal. From the beginning of the play, Mariamne, a member of the Hasmonean people who ruled Judea from 140 to 163 BCE, is associated with Greek beauty, via her likeness to her brother, Aristobulus, whom Herod characterizes as having a "lovely body" (I.i.45) and possessing the godlike powers of Apollo (I.i.34–35). Cleopatra, on the other hand, is initially described as having "eyes narrow as a crocodile's" in the stage directions in Act II, Scene 1, and these eyes "glitter" as she delights in "pilfering" statues of Isis in Alexandria (II.i.30–31). When her attendant Charmin objects to such activity, Cleopatra scoffs and declares, "I am Isis, / Soothing her jewels with my hands" (II.i.35–36), suggesting Cleopatra's claim to Isis's jewels is legitimate because she possesses the same divine authority the ancient goddess possessed.

Though other women writers of the early twentieth century, such as Elinor Glyn, would present Cleopatra in a more favorable light, Field's characterization of Cleopatra remains negative throughout the play and follows Bradley and Cooper's reaction to Cleopatra ten years earlier in their 1895 conversations with Berenson about beauty, in which they characterized her as "disgustingly sexual" (Ms. 46783). In *Queen Mariamne*, even Cleopatra's lover Antony characterizes Cleopatra negatively, describing her as "fast as Circe on her worshippers," and Antony's coruler, Octavius, calls her a "mighty idler" because she wants to rule Judea (II.ii.29, 49). While Herod tells his attendants to treat Cleopatra well, he refuses to participate in the "Idolatry of Isis" Cleopatra undertakes (III.i.37), and Mariamne's mother warns Mariamne about Cleopatra's power, saying she must "rise and rule" her husband, so "Egypt" (Cleopatra) doesn't (III.iii.80–81). Cleopatra is presented as thoroughly manipulative, much in the way Shakespeare represented her, a topic I will discuss in more detail in my chapter about Glyn. Though Cleopatra contemplates killing Mariamne, something she might do if she were in Egypt and had access to an "Engulfing crocodile or asp that sucks" (III.iv.13), she convinces Herod to kill her instead. When Herod comes to believe Mariamne has taken a lover, he puts her on trial, where she remains "silent / As trophies or cold statues," not defending herself against the charges (V.ii.16–17). After Mariamne is found guilty and executed, Herod's friend Nicholas assesses her embalmed body with a reference to Venus, saying, "Wonderful! / A mystery of Venus laid aside / To rest in the gold watches of the sea / And like a trophy, or a spoil of war" (V.iv.38–40). Herod goes a step further, telling his children that Mariamne is "as a goddess—but we must not be afraid of her" (V.iv.81–82), a comment that contrasts her to Cleopatra, who has been the kind of goddess Herod fears.

Although there are no direct references to Mariamne as possessing the Italian qualities of Giorgione's Venus, as we saw in some of Field's representations of Venus in *Sight and Song*, there is a softening of her Greek qualities at the end of the play. Herod "scans" Mariamne's dead face, looking for "folly," but he cannot find it (V.iv.44). Instead, he finds that her face is always changing: "she grows / And changes like a sunrise in its clouds; / She is not fading from me. And sometimes / She smiles; and there are moments she forgives me, / And moments of revenge" (V.iv.46–50). Still, while there is a softening of Mariamne's Greek qualities here, she may be "too Eastern" to possess the clearly Italian qualities that Field recognized as central to their ideal of beauty and its power to emancipate women. A 1909 review of the play in the London *Times*, which Bradley and Cooper learned of through John Gray, certainly emphasized the "Eastern atmosphere" of the play, arguing that the play had an "overpowering sensualness of the days of ancient splendor that assails the reader," and the characters in the play were "all tigers. . . . They all seem to move swiftly, silently, stealthily" (Ms. 46799). "Even Mariamne has something tigerish about her" (Ms. 46799), wrote the reviewer, suggesting even she was beyond the limits of Bradley and Cooper's (and Berenson's) Graeco-Italian ideal.

Still, Bradley and Cooper thought the reviewer had written "a beautiful estimate of Mariamne's character at the end of the Review" (Ms. 46799), so they perhaps believed they had engaged Eastern culture in writing *Queen Mariamne*, even if their representation of Cleopatra in the play suggests otherwise to twenty-first-century readers of the text. Like the other women writers discussed in this book, Bradley and Cooper remained "bound by an English eye" in their attempt to engage Egyptian culture more fully. Though they excelled at developing a Graeco-Italian ideal that could be applied to women of many different nationalities, their inability to cast Cleopatra, representative of Egyptian women, in positive terms shows the limits of their engagement with the East. Even after they had written about an Alexandrian subject, the kind of subject matter Ricketts and Shannon had inquired about in 1894, their own experiences as British subjects prevented them from representing Egypt in its most complex form.

CHAPTER 5

The "sweetness of the serpent of old Nile": Revisionist Cleopatra and Spiritual Union as Emancipation in Elinor Glyn's Cross-Cultural Romances

Just a year before Bradley and Cooper published *Queen Mariamne*, Elinor Glyn faced serious controversy when she published *Three Weeks* (1907)—a romance between the Englishman Paul Verdayne and an unnamed Eastern European "Lady," whose trademark is lounging on tiger-skin rugs as she seduces Paul in multiple countries, including Italy, Greece, and Egypt. In 1907, the British Empire was at its height and about to begin its descent, as its colonial subjects began to assert independence and claim the right to govern themselves. Although Egypt would remain under the British Protectorate until 1922, the tensions that led other colonies to assert independence in the twentieth century were already present in Egypt at this time. Glyn herself had traveled to Egypt in 1901 and 1902 (Glyn, *Romantic Adventure* 102), participating in the imperialist culture I have already characterized as separating British administrators from the Egyptian people, a culture that fueled the first serious nationalist demonstrations in 1919 (Thompson 274). Yet, despite this context for Glyn's novel, little of the criticism about *Three Weeks* focuses on the imperialist context for Glyn's use of the romance or the role of the romance in early twentieth-century representations of women's emancipation. Instead, critics have focused primarily on the attempts to censor Glyn's novel because of its attention to sexual relations outside of marriage: while Paul is not married, the "Lady" is.

Although over two million copies of the book were sold in the first decade of its publication, it was banned at Eton (Glyn, *Elinor Glyn* 126–27), and in Boston, the Boston Watch and Ward Society encouraged booksellers to

keep the novel off their shelves (Sova 248). Still, the controversy surrounding *Three Weeks* actually contributed to the book's sales (Sova 249) and made
Glyn famous—even infamous. Through popular references to Glyn, such as
the poem that begins, "Would you like to sin / with Elinor Glyn / on a tiger
skin?" (Horak 105), Glyn came to be known as the woman who made sex
outside marriage respectable, since she presented it as an inevitable part of
British society life and something that helped women survive unhappy marriages to men who were more interested in material wealth than in main-
taining emotional connections with their wives (Keating 443, 478; Glyn,
Romantic Adventure 52). Though many of Glyn's friends condemned Glyn
for her frank representation of extramarital relationships (Glyn, *Elinor Glyn*
127), others recognized her contribution to making wider society aware
of the problems of the upper classes, arguing that Glyn's representation of
extramarital relationships was mild compared to representations of this issue
by her contemporaries. For example, screenwriter Anita Loos, in her memoir *A Girl Like I* (1966), defended Glyn's representation, stating that Glyn
"handled the subject [of adultery] in so dainty a manner as to make D. H.
Lawrence's *Lady Chatterley's Lover*, with its identical plot, a sewer of clinical
realism" (118).

In addition to focusing on the controversy surrounding *Three Weeks*, critics have discussed how Glyn harnessed the fame she gained from the novel's
publication and translated this into success in the American film industry
in the 1920s, when studios recruited authors to transform the film industry's reputation from low brow to high brow (Glyn, *Elinor Glyn* 273–75).[1]
Glyn's work, both before and after she came to Hollywood, is best characterized as middle brow, since it walked a fine line between appealing to a mass
audience and making the audience feel as though it was engaging high art.[2]
Glyn achieved this in part through her use of the romance, a popular genre
that still had ties to the great literary tradition of the medieval romance. The
typical romantic plot—in which a man and a woman encounter obstacles to
their union but usually overcome these obstacles—dominates Glyn's work,
but as her memoir *Romantic Adventure* (1936) shows, her understanding of
romance was more complex than a simple plot device, since she defined it as
"a spiritual disguise, created by the imagination, with which to envelop material happenings and desires, and thus bring them into greater harmony with
the soul" (2). In this sense, Glyn was not unlike her late-Victorian predecessor Marie Corelli, whose romances (including *Ziska*, which I already have
discussed in Chapter 1) also were meant to present a spiritual alternative to
a materialist world. As Rita Felski writes of Corelli's romances in *The Gender
of Modernity* (1995), "Through the power of romantic love, individuals are
raised to a spiritual plane of ineffable plentitude beyond the trivial constraints

of human history" (126). Nevertheless, as Kirsten MacLeod points out in her edition of Corelli's *Wormwood: A Drama in Paris*, many readers turned to Glyn instead of Corelli after the turn of the century because Glyn's romances "were more exotic and lurid in their depiction of female sexuality and were free of the moralizing element that dominated even the most sensational of Corelli's romances" (20).

Still, Glyn herself resisted the characterization of her work as "lurid" and maintained that her goal was to represent a spiritual rather than physical form of romance. In defining the romance as a "spiritual disguise . . . with which to envelop material happenings," Glyn created a space for herself to merge the romance and the realistic novel, a strategy she used to distinguish her work from Corelli's, which Glyn believed did not use firsthand observation as thoroughly as it should have. Speaking of Corelli's novels in an interview with the *New York Times* in 1907, Glyn said: "In reading a book by Marie Corelli recently, I was greatly amused by her description of a butler with a powdered wig! And in another book, I read about a lady who went to supper at the Ritz in Paris wearing a diamond tiara! That showed me at once that the author had never been in Paris. One doesn't sup at the Ritz in a tiara. None of my characters would do such a thing" (Anonymous, "Elinor Glyn" n. pag.). While Glyn preferred romance to realism, she valued firsthand observation and often relied on her diaries, which detailed her travel to diverse countries, for inspiration for her fiction. During her travels in Egypt, for example, she wrote "pages and pages" of "rhapsodies of her first view of the country" (101). Unfortunately, these diaries were lost in a fire in 1959, according to her granddaughter Elspeth Chowdharay-Best (Chowdharay-Best n. pag.), so we only have the excerpts recorded by Glyn herself in *Romantic Adventure* or by Anthony Glyn in his biography of his grandmother. Still, these excerpts provide a good foundation for understanding Glyn's representation of Egypt in *Three Weeks* and its centrality to Glyn's concept of the romance as a spiritual union, which provided women with emancipation from unhappy marriages.

As I have already indicated, Glyn's understanding of the romance was more complex than the simple plot device of two people overcoming the obstacles to their love, and this more complex understanding of romance influenced the cross-cultural narratives she created. As David R. Shumway argues in "Romance in the Romance: Love and Marriage in Turn-of-the-Century Best Sellers" (1999), *Three Weeks* shows that the romance is not "a simple set of prescriptions" that "dictat[e] particular beliefs or behaviors," but one of "many variations" on the love and marriage narrative existing under the category of "romance" (113). *Three Weeks*, Shumway asserts, draws on the medieval conception of romance as something that "only comes into existence where love is fatal, frowned upon and doomed by life itself" (113), since the main characters' romance is the "cause of great pain" and death, rather than a narrative emphasizing the more formulaic plot device of the triangular relationship in which obstacles must be overcome (115). Although Shumway does not discuss Glyn's own conception of romance as "spiritual" rather than "material," her conception is implied in his analysis, since only a spiritual form of romance can exist once one of the main characters dies. Glyn's novels—particularly *Three Weeks* but also *His Hour* (1910) and *Halcyone* (1912)—deserve the type of serious analysis Shumway accords the romance not only because they fall under this genre but also because they reveal the qualities I have identified as so important in other British women's engagement with the East: their awareness that visions for Western women's emancipation might draw on Eastern models, especially powerful ancient Egyptian women, but to represent fully the power of Eastern women would alienate a Western audience.

Glyn especially would have been concerned about alienating a Western audience, not only because of her commitment to appealing to a mass audience with her literature, but also because her own politics were conservative, shaping what she thought about women's emancipation. Unlike her more liberal contemporaries—such as Elizabeth Robins, who saw suffrage as the key to women's emancipation[3]—Glyn rejected such solutions. In *Three Things* (1915), a collection of essays on topics such as marriage, divorce, and motherhood, Glyn writes that the natural balance of the world was out of sync in the early twentieth century, with "political demagogues shouting the untenable fallacy that all men are equal . . . and hooligan suffragists smashing windows" (Glyn, "The Old Order Changeth" 15).[4] For Glyn, women's emancipation was much more likely to emerge from more gradual change, produced by Nature herself, rather than forced by human desire for quick change. "Nature," writes Glyn, ". . . will not be hurried, or she produces the abnormal" (16). In a time where Nature is being hurried by human desire, Glyn argues, the best thing people can do is use "common sense" to "gather their forces together and seriously apply themselves to consider how they can better this condition of things. In their daily life they can do so by setting up a high standard of sanity and right behaviour, by the encouragement of fine aims and high ends, by the firm avoidance of hypocrisy and hysterical altruism, and by intelligent explanation to those under their care of the reason why individual responsibility is necessary for the welfare of the community at large" (23–24).

For Glyn, it was not just women's emancipation that was important; instead, both women and men were in need of emancipation from the distorted modern world, and the romance provided a return to the values that would allow Nature to determine the relationships between women and men and to progress at the slower pace Glyn believed was best for society as a whole. The spiritual union found in romance, then, becomes a form of emancipation for both sexes, and Glyn's engagement with ancient cultures supplements this aspect of the romance, since these cultures provided a setting in which women could act as imaginary Eastern goddesses, guiding Western men to a spiritual union without threatening them, as the more radical British suffragettes did. Still, Glyn's engagement with the East was shaped by her position as an aristocratic Englishwoman, whose informal education resulted in a commodified view of the East, condensed into objects, events, and experiences that appealed to women in the high society circles in which Glyn participated. Further, it was influenced by her experience encountering the "deep" East, including Egypt, through Greek and Italian cultures, which had absorbed and transformed Egyptian culture into something more palatable to Westerners, as I have shown in previous chapters of this book.

While Glyn used her commodified view of the East to show that romance could cross national and ethnic boundaries—that romance was a form of emancipation for women and men who valued a spiritual union—she often backed away from full acknowledgment of the Eastern influence on Western culture, since her novels typically begin with images of women as powerful entities because of their affiliation with Egyptian culture but shift to an intermingling of Egyptian and Greek images and ultimately end by privileging British ideals for women. In *Three Weeks*, the novel that most thoroughly illustrates Glyn's awareness of the intermingling of Greek and Egyptian culture, as well as the strongest privileging of British ideals for women at the end of the novel, Glyn initially uses her understanding of Greek and Egyptian culture to present romance as a genre in which understanding one's partner's national differences is vital—and possible through imaginative encounters with the "deep" East. The romance between Paul and the Lady occurs because Paul understands the East better through his spiritual union with the Lady, who is strongly identified with Egyptian culture in the first half of the novel. But the romance turns from emphasizing a spiritual union to focusing a more physical form of romance as the novel progresses, and the Lady is recast in terms more familiar to Westerners—first through images of Greek women that soften the power of Egyptian women and then by British ideals for women, which emphasize women's procreative and mothering qualities.

*   *   *

Before detailing Glyn's representation of women in *Three Weeks*, it is important to discuss how Glyn's knowledge of Greek and Egyptian culture was a commodified view of the East, meant to appeal to society women living at the height of British imperialism in the early twentieth century. As I have shown in Chapter 1 of this book, the relationship between British administrators in Egypt and the Egyptian people in the late nineteenth and early twentieth centuries was one in which the British treated Egyptians as though they were incapable of governing themselves. Society women such as Glyn knew these administrators directly and absorbed their attitude when they traveled to Egypt. The circle in which Glyn moved, both in England and abroad, was still holding onto traditional forms of enjoying their wealth, even though Britain was coming to realize the impossibility of continued colonial dominance. For women, in particular, nostalgia for "things past" manifested itself in objects, events, and experiences, since their lives were dominated by social activities with their female peers. Further, as I have shown in Chapter 1, women in Glyn's social circle received a more informal education (meant to support their participation in these social activities but not advance their careers) rather than the more formal education accorded to their male peers, and this distinction resulted in a commodified form of knowledge about the East among women.

From an early age, Glyn understood the expectations of upper-class women, since her grandmother, who had married a descendent of the French aristocracy, used the story of Marie Antoinette's fortitude during the French Revolution as a model for Elinor's conduct, telling Elinor that people of her class never allowed their "fear" to show (Glyn, *Elinor Glyn* 29). This attachment to "tradition" made Glyn conservative, in the sense that she valued principles and concepts that seemed out of date by the beginning of the twentieth century. Still, this model also made her appreciative of traditional arts, including classical literature. Occasionally instructed by tutors but more often educated through her own reading in the family library, since she and her sister Lucy rebelled against their tutors (37), Glyn developed an interest in ancient Greek and Roman culture. She read Edward Gibbon's *Decline and Fall of the Roman Empire*, spent time drawing "Greek profiles," and contemplated studying Greek language, though she came to realize that her interest was primarily Greek history and politics, which she could learn through English translations (Glyn, *Romantic Adventure* 37). Like many women of her generation, Glyn's informal education likely meant she was not encouraged to learn Greek, and even her reading in classical literature sometimes came in a commodified form. She was especially affected by Charles Kingsley's *The Heroes; or, Greek Fairy Tales for My Children* (1856), a children's book with illustrations by Kingsley himself that had been marketed as a Christmas gift book by Macmillan upon its initial publication (Glyn, *Elinor Glyn* 38; Klaver 413). Kingsley's book would become the primary source for Glyn's novel *Halcyone*, the story of a young English girl who turns to an Oxford professor (based on the real-life philosopher F. H. Bradley) to learn the classics and then falls in love with one of his former pupils, John Derringham (based on Lord Curzon, Viceroy of India from 1899 to 1905 and Glyn's lover from 1908 to 1916). Glyn's attachment to Kingsley's book, and her decision to base one of her novels on it, points to the commodified form of knowledge about Greek culture Glyn possessed, since Kingsley's book presented Greek mythology in a manner accessible to children.

As an adult, Glyn's informal method of educating herself about ancient cultures continued, primarily through rereading classical literature she had enjoyed as a child (Glyn, *Elinor Glyn* 321) and through conversations with men in her social circle. Both Curzon, whom Glyn met when he attended a performance of the stage version of *Three Weeks* in 1908 (Glyn, *Elinor Glyn* 169), and Bradley, whom she met while wintering in Saint-Raphaël in 1910–1911 (Wollheim 13), engaged her intellect with conversations about Greek culture, as did the British statesman Lord Alfred Milner and the high-ranking judge Sir Francis Jeune, both of whom Glyn met while on rest cure in Carlsbad in 1902 and 1903 (Glyn, *Elinor Glyn* 95, 103). The opportunities Glyn had to engage in conversations with these men was, no doubt, a privilege that came from her upper-class standing; women of lower classes would not have had access to these men. Still, it is important to recognize that Glyn's gender prevented her from gaining the formal education men of her class profited from. The fact that she never learned Greek, a clear signifier of the formal education men such as Curzon, Bradley, Milner, and Jeune received, shows the limits of her education.

While Glyn developed her knowledge of Greek culture as best she could, given the limitations imposed by gender, the emphasis on collecting objects that represented other cultures by members of Glyn's class also contributed to the commodified view of the East that Glyn draws on in her fiction. From Curzon, Glyn received a miniature bust of Girolamo della Robbia's *Venus*, which Curzon thought Glyn resembled (Glyn, *Elinor Glyn* 169). This statue takes on the role of a flesh-and-blood person in *Halcyone*, when the main character Halcyone asks the statue for advice, since her own mother has died and cannot provide guidance. In the novel, the statue is one of a number of objects Halcyone finds in a treasure chest from one of her ancestors, Sir Timothy La Sarthe (109–10, 521–22). Though Halcyone is too attached to the statue to contemplate selling it, she is happy to present the other items to her aunts, who sell the items in order to ensure a comfortable lifestyle in their old age (524, 527). Both the objects in Sir Timothy's chest and Curzon's miniature of *Venus*, which was one of a number of presents Curzon bought for Glyn (Gilmour 430), not only had sentimental value but cultural and commercial value. This value was produced and ensured through British imperialism, which sought to "protect" Greek relics such as the Elgin Marbles from rulers, especially the Turks, whom the British viewed as incapable of preserving ancient culture.

In addition to the miniature bust of *Venus* given to Glyn by Curzon, another of Glyn's possessions that made its way into her fiction was the tiger-skin rug, the object that most thoroughly came to represent Glyn to the public. Purchased with royalties from her first book at a fur shop close to the Hotel National in Lucerne, Switzerland (Glyn, *Elinor Glyn* 94), the rug is an obvious signifier of Britain's simplistic understanding of India as an exotic animal to be conquered and displayed. It not only represents the romance as spiritual union in *Three Weeks*, since Glyn saw the rug as an integral part of the seduction between a man and a woman, but it also is associated with the East in the novel, since the Lady writhes about on the rug like a serpent as she seduces Paul Verdayne (119–21). I have already linked the image of the serpent to the East, and especially to Egyptian culture, in my discussion of George Eliot's work, and as my analysis of *Three Weeks* will show, the serpent plays an important role in Glyn's representation of the East as well. The Lady's writhing about on the rug like a serpent is yet more evidence that Glyn's purchase of the tiger-skin rug, and the purchase of subsequent tiger-skin rugs for Glyn by Curzon and Milner (Glyn, *Elinor Glyn* 126), influenced Glyn's use of commodities in her fiction, and the purchase of these commodities was possible in part because of the wealth Europeans amassed as a result of British imperialism. As I have already mentioned, the relationship between British administrators in Egypt and the Egyptian people was distant, and Curzon's and Milner's presents to Glyn reflect this abstract view of other cultures, the feeling that other cultures could be summed up in miniature busts or exotic home accessories.

In addition to the commodity objects through which society women acquired knowledge of other cultures, fashion was another way in which women of a certain class engaged cultures other than their own, and fashion that imitated the dress of ancient cultures frequently appears in Glyn's fiction. Glyn's sister, Lucy Duff Gordon, who was related through marriage to the Egyptian traveler Lucie Duff-Gordon (Frank 114–15) but appears not to have traveled to Egypt herself, was a couture designer who incorporated Greek and Egyptian elements into her dresses, and through Lucy, Glyn understood the role ancient culture played in early twentieth-century women's fashion. Duff Gordon writes in her memoir, *Discretions and Indiscretions* (1932), about the Grecian influence on her designs: "I loosed upon a startled London, a London of flannel underclothes, woolen stockings and voluminous petticoats, a cascade of chiffons, of draperies as lovely as those of Ancient Greece" (66). She goes on to characterize as "goddesses" the models who wore the dresses she made for "mannequin parades," or fashion shows meant to encourage upper-class women to buy her dresses (Etherington-Smith and Pilcher 73). Each model received "a name in harmony with her personality," and among them were "Diana" and "Hebe," names that obviously came from Greek mythology (Duff Gordon 73, 78). According to Duff Gordon, "Dolores," though not possessing a Greek name, had a "Grecian profile" (79); "Gamela," whose name was Arabic for "Black Beauty," had features similar to the Egyptian goddess Isis (79); and Hebe was "sphinx-like" (80), combining both Greek and Egyptian elements.[5] Although Glyn's sense of fashion was more "classic" than Lucy's (20), Glyn certainly was familiar with Lucy's designs. Her wedding dress was designed by Lucy (Etherington-Smith and Pilcher 52), she sometimes attended Lucy's Parisian shows (202), and she asked Lucy to hold a charity fashion show to benefit World War I French refugees, whom Glyn was working to repatriate (Duff Gordon 266–68). Duff Gordon herself describes the designs for the show to benefit refugees as done "in wonderful colors and lines whose symmetry was, I felt, worthy of the old Greek ideals" (268).

The fashions Lucy designed and sold to society women influenced Glyn's fiction, where Glyn used fashion to show readers that her central women characters had a certain class status and were part of high society. In *Three Weeks*, Paul first notices the Lady while dining at a hotel in Switzerland, where the "rustle" of her silk dress passing his table alerts him to her presence (14–15). Dressed and accessorized as she is, with a "great sapphire gleaming from the folds of gauze on her neck" (20), the Lady certainly seems to have the wealth needed to acquire her dresses from a couture designer such as Duff Gordon, and later in the novel, once the Lady wears clothes that reflect the ancient cultures Glyn draws on to build her character, she also is presented as the type of client Duff Gordon might dress. As I will discuss in more detail later, when Paul and the Lady hold a "souls' wedding" in Venice, at which they sing Greek hymns and drink wine, the Lady wears a "pale green gauze" that "cling[s] in misty folds round [the Lady's] exquisite shape" (183), a garment one can imagine Duff Gordon's models wearing in a fashion show.

With the craze for Greek and Egyptian fashion came Greek- and Egyptian-themed social spaces, which society women would have frequented. Duff Gordon writes of a Grecian-themed restaurant in New York, which she and Gamela (along with Isadora Duncan's brother Raymond, who regularly wore Grecian dress) visited for dinner. The decorations included "stately pillars" and "couches in place of the ordinary chairs," and Gamela wore a "flowing robe of white chiffon with its stenciled border and with her lovely black hair dressed in a loose knot she looked like some goddess stepped out of the pages of mythology" (152–53). Similarly, the journalist Beverley Nichols, who describes Glyn as "Queenly" in his autobiography *The Sweet and Twenties* (1958), writes of such social spaces, describing a visit to Lady Bland-Sutton's house, which had an Egyptian-themed dining room "modelled on the discoveries of Tutankhamen" (136). Glyn certainly would have attended dinners and other social events in such spaces, and these experiences contributed to the commodified knowledge of Greek and Egyptian culture Glyn developed as a result of her class status and then used in her fiction. Paul's initial sighting of the Lady at a hotel in Switzerland immediately places readers in the type of venue members of high society would have patronized while traveling abroad, and as I discuss later, Paul and the Lady frequently visit places that reflect the ancient cultures Glyn had informally studied, such as a villa near Constantinople, designed in the "graceful Ionic style" of the classical Greek period (253).

Most notable among Glyn's socialite experiences were her trips to Egypt with her husband and children in 1901 and 1902, which had a strong impact on the storyline of *Three Weeks*. During these trips, the family engaged in many of the same activities they would have been a part of in England, showing that wealthy Britons maintained their expensive lifestyle when traveling abroad. In *Romantic Adventure*, Glyn describes how the family stayed at the Savoy Hotel, which was directly across from Prince Mahomet Ali's palace, so Elinor and her husband Clayton were at the "centre of gaiety and sociability" (102). The children also participated in society events, attending a ball to which they wore European gowns and powdered their hair in eighteenth-century style (103). Still, Glyn did take a nighttime trip to see the Sphinx, which, to hear her describe it, was her attempt to go beyond the typical activities of society life in Egypt.

> Only the Sphinx, and the vast desert, impressed themselves upon the consciousness of those who gazed, and the experience was unforgettable. New, deep thoughts and emotions surged up in me as I stared at the strange form. The full moon shed an unearthly light and the luminous sand appeared pink, the shadows indigo, and the sky unbelievably blue. . . . The enjoyment of this vision, undisturbed and unmolested, was, I realized, the unconscious object of my visit to Egypt. . . . I seemed to feel myself become a part of that Immortal Being whom these Ancient Egyptians sought to commemorate in this strange edifice of stone. (108)

The experience affected Glyn so deeply that, the following evening, she took her children back to see the Sphinx, even though other Englishwomen she knew disapproved of keeping children out so late at night (Glyn, *Elinor Glyn* 92).

While seeing the Sphinx served as an authentic cultural experience for Glyn during her trip and clearly affected her, since she incorporated this experience into *Three Weeks*, it also reflects the influence of imperialism on British women writers' highly romanticized perceptions of Egypt, which were completely ignorant of the everyday lives of Egyptians. As evidence of Glyn's inability to avoid an imperialist perspective, other aspects of her Egyptian experiences are described in her memoir with a strong Orientalist angle, indicating Glyn was still "bound by an English eye" as she traveled. She writes about the "Pink Palace of the Wicked old Princess" in Cairo, which she describes as "straight out of the Arabian Nights" (Glyn, *Romantic Adventure* 105).[6] Here, she again draws on a commodified form of knowledge about the East, since English translations of Scheherazade's tales were modified to appeal to a wide range of classes (Zipes 54). Though Glyn clearly had tried to move beyond her social circle and experience Eastern culture more directly than her friends had, she sometimes seems unable to escape an Orientalist view of Egypt, and she sums up her trip by emphasizing the British imperialist aspect of it. Writing about the trip in the context of the death of Queen Victoria in the same year, she says that, in Egypt, "we found that glorious Victorian tradition still existed in its purest perfection[: t]he fundamental good sense, good humour and good taste, and the wonderful courage and gallantry of the civil and military officials assembled in Cairo" (99–100). Although Glyn recognizes she overlooked the failures of the English government at home, particularly in terms of its treatment of the working classes, in Egypt she was so enamored with the British military officials she met she became "a rabid Conservative, and a passionate supporter of British Imperialism" (100–01). As much as Glyn tried to move away from a perspective influenced by her class standing, she could not escape the imperialist way of looking at Egypt she had learned at an early age and practiced in her adult life.

*   *   *

With Glyn's experience as a British society woman in mind, then, we can turn to analysis of *Three Weeks*, in which Glyn used a commodified view of the East to present her conception of romance as an union in which national and ethnic boundaries might be crossed, creating emancipation for both women and men interested in the spiritual rather than physical aspects of romance. As Laura Horak, in "'Would you like to sin with Elinor Glyn?': Film as a Vehicle of Sensual Education" (2010), has shown, Glyn was promoting in *Three Weeks* a "sexual ideology" of "spiritual communion" rather than "mere animal instinct" between a man and a woman (75–76), and Glyn herself says in *Romantic Adventure* that the "origin" for the novel was the "unsatisfied longings for a sympathetic companion" she felt with regard to her relationship with her husband Clayton as they traveled through Switzerland in

1902 (128).[7] For Glyn, the "sympathetic companion" she sought was a man who would engage in a "spiritual communion" with her, and Horak has convincingly shown that all the elements of a spiritual communion—"enhanced arousal through restricted physical contact, role plays of dominance and submission, and a eugenic progress through racial hybridity" (75)—can be found in *Three Weeks*.

Writing about these elements in the novel, Horak states:

> Step-by-step, the Queen awakens the young . . . boy through tales of romance and travel. . . . Once she arouses Paul's mind, she teaches him the agonizing pleasure of erotic spectatorship; he can look at but not touch her. . . . The Tiger Queen furthermore teaches Paul to play with positions of dominance and submission. . . . [T]heir love child embodies a harmonious hybridity between the spirit of the mother and the . . . looks of the father. . . . In contrast to advocates of racial purity, Glyn praised the vitality of these interracial unions—but only within the mannered confines of the upper classes. (78–80)

I would argue that the third element of the spiritual communion Horak identifies, "a eugenic progress through racial hybridity," is key to understanding Glyn's sexual ideology, but I believe Glyn more thoroughly presents this element than Horak suggests. Glyn does more than simply bestow Paul and the Lady with a "love child" that embodies both the Eastern European spirit of the Lady and the English looks of Paul. She specifically traces the development of this hybridity, showing how Paul must understand his partner's national differences through his Eastern adventures with the Lady. Using references to Egyptian culture to build the Lady's character, Glyn draws on the commodified form of knowledge about the East she learned as a British society woman in order to educate readers about national hybridity. Still, Glyn backs away from full acknowledgment of the Eastern influence on Western culture toward the end of the novel, replacing the Egyptian ideal with first a Greek ideal and then a British ideal, reducing the Lady to a procreative mother, a British ideal for women that emphasizes the more physical aspects of romance. Unlike ancient Egyptians, who placed women's procreative abilities in the broader context of creating and supporting the entire world, as the creation goddesses Maat and Nut did, British ideals put emphasis on women's procreative abilities primarily within their own families and as a means to advance the family's status within the nation. My reading of *Three Weeks*, then, differs from Horak's in that it fully acknowledges Glyn's understanding of British nationality through its relationship to ancient cultures; emphasizes how Glyn's understanding of British nationalism intersects with her view of the romance as the site for the emancipation of women and men; and highlights how Glyn backs away from her ideal of a spiritual rather than physical romance because she privileges Western nationalities over Eastern nationalities.

The first evidence of Glyn's commodified knowledge about the East comes early in the novel, after Paul has identified the Lady, whom he has seen at dinner, as possibly Eastern European (20–21). Paul is invited to the Lady's room, which is rich in décor and features a couch with a tiger-skin rug over it, showing Glyn's incorporation of her own experiences with commodity objects and spaces. Here, Paul realizes the Lady is not just an Eastern European woman but a "divine goddess," who makes him feel like he has "embarked upon an adventure which savoured of the Arabian Nights" (38), a comment that resonates with Glyn's use of *Arabian Nights* in *Romantic Adventure* to describe her experience seeing the Pink Palace in Egypt. The Lady, in taking Paul on such a journey, uses what Paul perceives as exotic Eastern charm to seduce him: "She leant back among the purple cushions, her figure so supple in its lines, it made him think of a snake. . . . Her eyes in their narrowed lids gleamed at him, seeming to penetrate into his soul" (42–43). Though there is no physical consummation of the relationship that night, showing the restraint from physical contact Horak identifies as a key element of spiritual communion, Paul is nevertheless "intoxicated with excitement" by his experience with the Lady, and one of the ways Glyn achieves this effect is by employing the *Arabian Nights* reference, which English readers would have recognized.

Glyn then becomes more specific about how the Lady might be associated with the "deep" East, identifying her directly with Egypt. When Paul receives a letter from the Lady inviting him to go sailing with her, the letter is written on "thin, un-English" stationery, which has "the most minute sphinx in the corner" (46). This immediately suggests the Lady has Egyptian qualities because the trademark symbol for communication from her is a major Egyptian landmark. Yet, research about stationery of this time reveals Glyn is drawing on a symbol that reflects British imperialist influence in Egypt, since a letter with a Sphinx design likely was inspired by stationery commissioned by the Egyptian Postal Administration but designed by the British printing company, Thomas De La Rue and Company, Limited. According to the Royal Philatelic Society, whose members staged a 2005 exhibition including stamps produced by De La Rue's company, the Egyptian Postal Administration hired De La Rue to produce stamps beginning in 1878, and the design agreed upon by the postal administration and De La Rue "consisted of a central vignette of the Sphinx and Great Pyramid, similar to the vignettes that had appeared on Egypt's Second and Third Issues in 1867–69 and 1872–75" (Royal Philatelic Society n. pag.). This design appeared on stamps and stationery from 1879 to 1909, constituting a "long and productive association between De La Rue and the Postal Administration that lasted for more than

40 years" (n. pag.). A combination of English and "un-English" influences, the stationery the Lady writes on is a consumer object that Glyn would have been familiar with through her encounters with the Egyptian postal system, and this object presents Egypt in its commodified form, as a country that can be summed up by one of its major landmarks, the Sphinx.

The Lady's association with Egypt is furthered when, well into the novel, she takes Paul to Egypt via their imaginations, functioning as an Eastern goddess who can influence Western men without threatening them. During one of their many meetings in which the Lady stretches out on the tiger-skin rug and "undulates" like a snake or "purrs" like a tigerish cat, the Lady says to Paul, "Fly with me to Egypt where the sun always shines," and she proceeds to describe key landmarks in the country readers would be familiar with: Cairo, the Nile, and finally the Sphinx (110–11). Paralleling Glyn's own memory of the "serenity of the East, with its slow-moving camels and . . . blue-clad natives" and the "intense, deep sapphire colour of the Egyptian sky" (Glyn, *Romantic Adventure* 101), the Lady paints the landscape surrounding the Sphinx for Paul: "Ah! it is a bright day again, and we have all the green world between us and the great vast brown track of sand. And those are the Pyramids clear-cut against the turquoise sky, and soon we shall be there" (111). Then, the Lady focuses on the Sphinx itself, saying, "Oh! the strange drug of the glorious East, flooding your senses with beauty and life. 'Tis the spell of the Sphinx, and now we are there, close in her presence. . . . [W]e are alone, the camels and guides afar off—we are alone, . . . you and I and the moon. . . . Look, there is the Sphinx! Do you see the strange mystery of her smile and the glamour of her eyes. She is a goddess, and she knows men's souls" (112). Glyn, having already identified the Lady as a goddess who can see into Paul's soul when she seduces Paul as a snake might (42–43), uses this characterization of the Sphinx as a goddess who also sees into men's souls and, thus, transforms the Lady even more fully into a deeply Eastern woman who can help Paul understand a culture different from his own, a key component to the growth of his soul.

Incidentally, women who can see into men's souls also are found in Glyn's later novels: *His Hour*, where the Sphinx assesses the soul of the heroine Tamara (1–2), and *Halcyone*, where Halcyone and the statue of Aphrodite possess this ability (51, 134). Women who help men understand cultures other than their own, then, are not always strictly Egyptian but sometimes a combination of Egyptian and Greek, continuing the trend seen in the works of some of the other women writers in this book, who also use this combination to make Egyptian women more palatable to a Western audience. Glyn, whose favorite line in Kingsley's *Heroes* was "I am Pallas Athene, and I know the thoughts of all men's hearts and discern their manhood or their baseness"

(Glyn, *Elinor Glyn* 103), understood the parallels between Egyptian and Greek culture, even if she had not studied these cultures as thoroughly as Eliot had or traveled in Egypt as extensively as Nightingale had. Part of the reason the Lady in *Three Weeks* is so enticing to Paul is because her Eastern aspects (i.e., her ability to see into his soul) are at least somewhat familiar to him through Greek culture, making her more palatable, and less threatening, to him than a purely Egyptian woman might be.

In addition to merging Greek and Egyptian cultures through her emphasis on women who can see into men's souls, Glyn merges these two cultures by repeatedly associating the Lady with Cleopatra. I have already discussed Cleopatra as a representative of Egyptian women in the work of the other women writers in this book, especially their use of the serpent image to make this connection, and Glyn uses the Cleopatra-as-serpent image extensively. Similar to the Sphinx, which functions to represent Egypt in the commodified form of the stationery design, the serpent also functions as a symbol of Egypt shaped by the commodified form of knowledge about Egypt held by upper-class British women in the early twentieth century. Upper-class women such as Glyn understood Cleopatra and the serpent primarily through the theatrical and film productions of Shakespeare's *Antony and Cleopatra* that emerged in the late nineteenth and early twentieth centuries, rather than through factual information about Cleopatra. As Joyce Tyldesley, in *Cleopatra: Last Queen of Egypt* (2008), points out, the image of Cleopatra as a serpent-figure has no grounding in visual images of Cleopatra from her own time. There is only one image, found on a Hellenistic coin from 50 to 49 BCE, that definitively can be said to represent Cleopatra, and this coin shows Cleopatra in profile, without a serpent (60). Further, recent art historians have shown that many of the ancient sculptures thought to have been Cleopatra because of the presence of a serpent around her neck or as part of a headdress are actually Greek Aphrodites, with the symbol of the serpent added to them by people trying to increase the value of the sculpture (59–60).

Still, the image of Cleopatra as serpent-like persists because late-nineteenth- and early-twentieth-century theatrical and film productions accepted these misrepresentations of Cleopatra as authentic, followed historical and literary representations of Cleopatra that also present her as serpent-like, and perpetuated the myth that Cleopatra killed herself with the poison of a serpent. According to Tyldesley, even the Graeco-Roman historians Cassius Dio and Plutarch, whose accounts of Cleopatra as the evil seducer of Antony have been influential in how she was remembered (150), present the serpent-poison theory as only one possibility about how she died (191–92). They also present the theory that she applied poison to a hair comb and pricked herself with it—a more likely possibility, Tyldesley says, given how difficult it would have been for Cleopatra to kill herself and the two other people who were with her with live serpents (192–93).

It is Shakespeare's *Antony and Cleopatra* (1606), particularly nineteenth-century theatrical productions of the play, which brought the myth about Cleopatra's death by serpent poison into widespread acceptance. Until the second half of the nineteenth century, theatre companies rarely performed the play, but after 1850, when the number of productions increased, this myth was perpetuated to theatregoers (Wyke 251; Bate and Rasmussen 157–59). Early-twentieth-century films followed suit in perpetuating this myth, particularly the 1908 American *Antony and Cleopatra*, which was directed by the Shakespearean actor Charles Kent (Wyke 248). While Glyn would not have known the 1908 film version at the time she was writing *Three Weeks*, she likely knew the late-nineteenth- and early-twentieth-century theatrical productions of the play, especially Victorien Sardou's 1890 production starring Sarah Bernhardt and Herbert Beerbohm Tree's 1906 production starring Constance Collier. We know Glyn saw Bernhardt in Sardou's *Theodora* in 1880 (Etherington-Smith and Pilcher 29) and used Bernhardt's performance in it as the inspiration for her own depiction of the Lady in the 1908 private stage production of *Three Weeks* (119), so it seems likely she knew Sardou's production of *Cleopatra*. Glyn probably knew Tree's production as well, since she participated in one of Tree's *tableaux vivants* in 1900, performed at the same theatre where his *Antony and Cleopatra* was staged (Glyn, *Elinor Glyn* 83).[8]

Accounts of Sardou's and Tree's productions indicate they were, like most late-nineteenth- and early-twentieth-century theatrical productions, lavish in set design and costuming that played up the Eastern aspect of Cleopatra's character. Jonathan Bate and Eric Rasmussen describe Tree's production as typical of those of the time, in that its "archaeological spectacle—elaborate scenic reconstruction of Egyptian antiquity—was the keynote and successfully upstaged individual performances" (159). Of Sardou's production, Carol Ockman and Kenneth Silver report it was "among the richest and most thoroughly researched in fin-de-siècle stage design" (9), and the jewelry worn by Bernhardt, including a spectacular pectoral made of pearls and turquoise-colored beads, still can be seen in prominent museums today (12, 188). Both productions seem to have mostly followed Shakespeare's presentation of Cleopatra as a powerful but negative force—as seducer of Antony, she represented the threat of Egypt to the Romans—and, as I have already shown, this is the representation of Cleopatra that Michael Field follows in *Queen Mariamne*. Yet, Shakespeare also presented Cleopatra as nevertheless a tragic figure because of her supposed death by serpent poison, and Sardou's and Tree's productions seem to emphasize this aspect of her character. Several accounts of Sardou's production indicate Bernhardt used a real snake in the dying scene, and her long, slow performance of Cleopatra's death compensated for other weaknesses in the script, such as Cleopatra hiding behind a curtain and listening to Antony for half an act and a scene in which, in a jealous rage, she kills a slave and destroys everything on the stage (Horville 56; Menefee 45; Verneuil 200; Skinner 247).

In the case of Tree's production, Tree's decision to cut nearly two-thirds of Shakespeare's text meant that, even with its "archaeological spectacle," the production "focused on the lovers" (Bate and Rasmussen 159). Some critics felt that at certain points, this was disappointing for audience members invested in seeing an accurate representation of Shakespeare's text, but it still made for compelling theatre. The London *Times* critic, for example, wrote,

> It is the passion-*motif* . . . that Mr Tree concentrates the whole force of his stage. . . . Hence the passionate duologues between Antony and Cleopatra is given all the advantage of scenic magnificence and orchestral illustration. . . . Weird nerve-thrilling Oriental strains are in the air. You hear those same strains even in Rome or Athens . . . whenever Antony's thoughts turn to the far-away Cleopatra. . . . Antony falls on his couch murmuring 'Cleopatra', and covering his eyes that he may shut out the present scene and dream of her, again to the faint sound of the Oriental music. You will search in vain for any indication of this 'business' in Shakespeare; but it is ingeniously, and quite legitimately, invented; it helps the unity of expression. (Brown 52–53)

The *Daily Telegraph* reviewer, too, liked the emphasis on the lovers, writing:

> [T]he piece is very well played. [As Cleopatra,] Miss Constance Collier, handsome, dark-skinned, barbaric, dominates the scene wherever she appears. Nor has she ever had a better chance, or more fully availed herself of it, than when in the second act she has to prove how close the tiger's cruelty lies under the sleek skin of cultivated woman. Mr Tree's Mark Antony was a fine, masculine, resolute rendering of a hero ruined by love. . . . Antony is the Samson caught by Delilah; a sort of primitive, elemental hero, whose degradation is all the more sure because his intellect is so inferior to his heart. (Brown 53)

Still, Tree's production, more so than Sardou's, seems to have drawn on Shakespeare's representation of Cleopatra as threateningly seductive, and Glyn incorporates this aspect of her character in *Three Weeks*. Glyn's use of the tiger-skin rug and her reference to the Lady as purring like a cat seem to echo the *Daily Telegraph* reviewer's characterization of Cleopatra as a woman with "the tiger's cruelty," and a picture from the performance shows that there was a tiger-skin rug on the floor during Cleopatra's dying scene (Glyn, *Three Weeks* 43, 78, 109, 138; Brown 53; Bate and Rasmussen 160).[9]

Further, Madeleine Bingham, in *"The Great Lover": The Life and Art of Herbert Beerbohm Tree* (1978), indicates that Constance Collier wanted to play up Cleopatra's seductive qualities, a view of Cleopatra relevant to Glyn's characterization of the Lady in *Three Weeks*. Collier rejected the idea that Cleopatra had a "domestic side," refusing to act when Tree insisted she appear onstage with five children after he learned Cleopatra herself had this many children (170). But, Collier embraced Tree's interest in representing Cleopatra's association with the Egyptian goddess Isis, which appears only briefly in Shakespeare's play (170). In Tree's production, the entry of Cleopatra, dressed as Isis, into Alexandria in front of a mixed crowd of supporters and detractors was "the richest scene" of the play: "Cleopatra robed in silver, crowned in silver, carrying a golden scepter, with the sacred golden calf in her hand went in procession through the streets of Alexandria while the populace screamed at her, half in hate and half in superstitious fear and joy" (170). Like Collier's Cleopatra, the Lady shows no interest in domesticity for the first half of the novel. She is waited on by the maître d'hôtel rather than waiting on a husband herself (16), and while she is sometimes characterized as having mother-like qualities when she interacts with Paul (58), he recognizes she is "not a bit like his mother" (60), whom he describes as "a perfectly domestic and beautiful woman, but somehow he felt sure she had never made his father's heart beat" (179–80). The Lady clearly rejects a traditional mother role as a powerful position for women, pointing out to Paul that it is mistresses rather than wives who have "ruled the hearts of men. Think of Pericles and Aspasia—Antony and Cleopatra—Justinian and Theodora—Belisarius and Antonina—and later, all the mistresses of the French kings—even, too, your English Nelson and Lady Hamilton! Not one of these was a man's ideal of what a wife and mother ought to be" (179).

Glyn's characterization of the Lady also seems to follow the *Times* reviewer's characterization of Collier's Cleopatra as "barbaric" when, about halfway through the novel, the Lady realizes she and Paul are pursued by her attendants, Dmitry and Vasili, while trying to enjoy Venice together. Writes Glyn, "Her cloak had fallen aside a little, disclosing a shimmer of purple garment and flashing emeralds. She looked barbaric, her raven brows knit. It might have been Cleopatra commanding the instant death of an offending slave" (158). While Dmitry and Vasili worry they will be whipped by the Lady for following her without permission, the Lady's barbaric look makes Paul's "pulses bound," an "extra note" in the "mad dream of exotic emotion" he experiences when he is with her (158), suggesting Paul is not frightened but aroused by the Lady's likeness to a vengeful Cleopatra. Still, once Dmitry and Vasili fall off, the narrator tells us that the Lady returns to her "sweeter" self, the "sweetness of the serpent of old Nile" (159), the form of the serpent Paul seems to prefer. The phrase "serpent of old Nile" comes directly from Shakespeare's play, but Shakespeare uses the term negatively, when Cleopatra wonders whether Antony is thinking of her, his "serpent of old Nile," while she "feed[s] myself / With most delicious poison" (I.v.25–27). Unlike Michael Field, who does not break from the negative aspects of Shakespeare's characterization of Cleopatra, Glyn clearly revises his characterization by infusing his phrase "serpent of old Nile" with a positive connotation.

Glyn further develops a more positive view of Cleopatra in a later scene, by referring to the American poet and sculptor William Wetmore Story's representations of her. While still in Venice, the Lady and Paul discuss how their love is different from the average person's. The Lady believes it is the sort of love that "happens perhaps once in a century" and likely "makes history of some sort—bad or good" (177), and Paul proclaims, "Let it! . . . I am like Antony in that poem you read me last night. I must have you for my own, 'Though death, dishonor, anything you will stand in the way'" (177). The Lady agrees, saying she prefers the poem's depiction of Antony and Cleopatra to that of Shakespeare, since the author of the poem "knew all about those wonderful lovers better far than your Shakespeare did, who leaves me quite cold when I read his view of them. Cleopatra was to me so subtle, so splendid a queen" (177). The poem Paul refers to is William Wetmore Story's "Marcus Antonius" (1868), in which Antony asks his messenger Fonteus to tell Cleopatra he will do anything, including giving up "honour, prudence, interest" (7), in order to experience "the wild strength of love" with her again (8). Antony admits he has lied to his legal wife Octavia with his "pretense / Of love" (27–28); prefers Cleopatra, or "One hour in Egypt's eyes," to Octavia, or "a score of Roman centuries" (48–49); and only wants to be with his "soul's wife," Cleopatra, whom he will see soon after Fonteus gives her Antony's message (9–10, 76–77). In the poem, we can see the more positive representation of Cleopatra that emerges from Antony's perspective of her; he defines Cleopatra primarily through the positive qualities she exhibits as his lover rather than as the evil seducer of men Shakespeare and some Graeco-Roman historians emphasize in their representations of her. Nowhere is Antony's Cleopatra "barbaric," and though Antony once refers to Cleopatra as a serpent in the poem, it is as a term of endearment: "Tell my dear serpent I must see her—fill / My eyes with the glad light of her great eyes, / Though death, dishonor, anything you will, / Stand in the way!" (38–41). One imagines Glyn knew the companion poem to "Marcus Antonius," "Cleopatra" (1868), in which Story also depicts Cleopatra according to qualities Antony might seek out as her lover,[10] and when the Lady makes the rather bold statement that she prefers Story's representation of Cleopatra to that of Shakespeare, one expects this is because, in both poems, Story more fully develops the feelings of the two lovers, particularly their love and passion for each other. Paul's response to the Lady's view that Story's representation is better than Shakespeare's confirms it is the development of Cleopatra's character as a lover that is appealing in Story's representations. "Of course she was just you, my heart," Paul says. "You are her soul living over again, and that poem you must give me to keep some day, because it says just what I shall want to say if ever I must be away from you for a time" (177–78).

Nevertheless, Glyn's revisionist Cleopatra is short lived, since Paul and the Lady are separated soon after this; the threat to the Lady's life from her husband becomes too great, and the Lady does not want to put Paul's life in danger as well. Still, before they separate, Paul suggests they return to Europe, specifically to Greece, to "see the temples and worship those old gods," who "knew about love" (178). This begins a process in which Glyn recharacterizes both Paul and the Lady as more Western, first Greek and then British, a process that shows how Glyn ultimately avoids full acknowledgment of Eastern influence on Western culture and also backs away from a clear message about the emancipation of women and men through spiritual communion. While Paul better understands the Lady's Eastern European culture as a result of his imaginative travels with her to Egypt, both he and the Lady return to "safer" roles in the last third of the novel. Returning to Venice, they celebrate their "souls' wedding," where they sing Greek hymns and drink wine (185–86), suggesting that at least for now, Paul and the Lady maintain the spiritual communion Glyn emphasizes so strongly in her romances. Whether their wedding is meant to parallel a specific one in Greek mythology (perhaps that of Dionysus and Ariadne or Psyche and Cupid) cannot be proven, but Glyn clearly does not use symbols from Egypt when describing it. The Lady appears as "the most radiant vision" Paul has ever seen, wearing a dress of "pale green gauze" that "seemed to cling in misty folds round her exquisite shape" (183), a garment that sounds more like one of Lucy Duff Gordon's Greek creations than Egyptian dress.

Further, the shift away from Egyptian imagery in the novel is seen when, after the Lady flees in order to protect Paul from her husband's wrath, Paul waits at sea for a sign that he can meet the Lady again, characterizing himself as a "tormented Tantalus" (252), the son of Zeus who was always just short of reaching the fruit that "tantalizes" him. When he finally receives the message that he should join the Lady, it is at a villa somewhere near Constantinople, an Eastern setting where one might expect to find Orientalist architecture. But, when Paul arrives at the villa, only to discover the Lady is not there, "No semi-Oriental architecture met his view, but a beautiful marble structure in the graceful Ionic style, seeming a suitable habitation for his Queen" (253). Another time, while he waits for word from her off the coast of Italy, he can see the temple to Poseidon (now known to be a temple to Hera) at Paestum, and he thinks, "How marvelously beautiful it all was, and how his Queen would have loved it! How she would have told him its history and woven round it the spirit of the past, until his living eyes could almost have seen the priests and the people, and heard their worshipping prayers!" (203–04).[11] Hera, the Greek goddess who oversees the consummation of marriage but does not necessarily serve as a model for motherhood herself (Rose, *Handbook* 84, 86), is similar to the Egyptian goddess Hathor in that she is often pictured as a cow. By characterizing the Lady as someone who would enjoy Hera's temple, Paul begins the process of revising the Lady's character, to make her more palatable to a Western audience. While Paul receives a letter from the Lady after she leaves him at Venice that includes her sphinx insignia, Paul believes the sphinx on the stationery "mocks" him (195), suggesting he cannot access Eastern culture now that he is separated from the Lady. A milder form of ancient culture, Greek culture, has replaced Egyptian culture as the lens through which he sees their relationship.

In shifting the emphasis from Egyptian to Greek culture, Glyn is perhaps following Charles Kingsley's idea, articulated in the preface to *The Heroes*, that the ancient Greeks were more advanced than people from other ancient cultures and that returning to ancient Greek culture was the way to improve contemporary British culture. Explaining to his own children (to whom *The Heroes* was dedicated) and to the children of Britain (who bought the book) why it was important to learn from the Greeks, Kingsley writes, "Some of you have heard already of the old Greeks; and all of you, as you grow up, will hear more and more of them. Those of you who are boys will, perhaps, spend a great deal of time in reading Greek books; and the girls, though they may not learn Greek, will be sure to come across a great many stories taken from Greek history" (vii). Kingsley acknowledges that the Greeks learned from other cultures: shipbuilding and lettering from the Phoenicians, painting and carving from the Assyrians, and astronomy "and many things which you would not understand" from the Egyptians (xi). But, he believes Greek culture was more advanced than the cultures that came before it, for "God rewarded these Greeks, as He rewarded our forefathers, and made them wiser than the people who taught them, in everything they learnt" (xi–xii). While some might argue God could not reward the Greeks because they became "heathens" (xii), Kingsley assures the children who read his book that God rewarded the Greeks before they became pagans, when they "still believed in the last six of the ten commandments, and knew well what was right and what was wrong" (xv).

In recharacterizing Paul and the Lady as more Greek than Egyptian, Glyn appears to draw on Kingsley's ideas about the importance of ancient Greece in contemporary British culture, but by the end of *Three Weeks*, even the Greek ideal Kingsley and Glyn found so inspirational is left behind for a thoroughly British ideal. When Paul finally meets his son, whom he has been unable to see because of his overwhelming grief over the Lady's death, the five-year-old boy is a "fair, rosy-cheeked, golden-haired English child" (272), who has all the features of Paul had when he was the same age. Referring to a miniature of Paul painted on his mother's writing table, the narrator tells us that Paul's son is "the living reality of that miniature painted on ivory and framed in fine pearls, which made the holy of holies on the Lady Henrietta's writing-table" (272). Not only is the child entirely British in his features, but the last image of Paul and his son together provide a Christianized ending to the novel, much as Kingsley's preface to *The Heroes* ends on a Christian note. Paul meets his son, who is now King of Russia, at a "special ceremony in the great church" in honor of his son's birthday. As Paul looks at his son, the rituals of the church take over: "while the organ pealed out a Te Deum and the sweet choir sang, a great rush of tenderness filled Paul's heart, and melted for ever the icebergs of grief and pain" (272). While this representation of Paul may be an example of racial hybridity between Western and Eastern Europe, as Horak has argued, it is important to note that the Egyptian and Greek qualities possessed by the Lady early in the novel, another sign of racial hybridity, are entirely forgotten by the end of the novel. Instead of representing racial hybridity, the Lady now functions strictly as the dead mother of Paul's British-looking son, exemplifying the British attitude that women's procreative abilities were primarily for advancing family status within the nation. As Paul describes the crowning of his son as King of Russia, he recalls the Lady and says, "it seemed as if his darling stood beside him, telling him that he must look up and thank God . . . for in her spirit's constant love, and this glory of their son, he would one day find rest and consolation" (272). The Lady has lost all the Eastern qualities that established her spiritual communion with Paul early in the novel, and while it might be argued only a spiritual communion can remain now that the Lady has died, Paul's reduction of the Lady to the role of deceased mother suggests that the physical aspect of the relationship—the ability to procreate—is what has been most important. Ultimately, a more Western view of womanhood emerges at the end of the novel, and while Paul may be emancipated by this kind of romance, it is difficult to see how the Lady is.

Though Glyn suggests in *Three Weeks* that real romance involves understanding your partner's national differences and reaching spiritual communion with this person—possible when a Western man accepts the guidance of a nonthreatening, imaginary Eastern goddess—she stops short of full acknowledgment of the influence of Eastern culture on the West, since that would be threatening to Western men. She instead reverts to a Greek notion of romance, in which the goddess Hera ensures physical consummation of the spiritual union, and ultimately reverts to a British notion of romance, in which women are reduced to the role of procreative mother rather than acknowledged as creators of the entire world, as ancient Egyptians recognized. This disruption of the West-to-East movement can be attributed in part to Glyn's commodified knowledge of the East. Unlike George Eliot, who had read deeply about the East origins of Western culture, Glyn's education was not exceptional in the way Eliot's was but was similar to that of most upper-class British women, especially those who had benefited from the British Empire's wealth. Still, Glyn seems to have been able to engage Egypt more fully than Michael Field had, in part by drawing on her own experience seeing Egypt and also by considering how previous writers, such as Shakespeare and Story, had represented the most commonly depicted Egyptian woman, Cleopatra. Yet, like Field, Glyn still had a romanticized view of Cleopatra, due in part to her own inclinations toward the romance genre but also to her position as an upper-class British subject. As I have argued throughout this book, Glyn, Field, Eliot, and Nightingale were all, to some degree, "bound by an English eye," and only once Egyptian women themselves had the same opportunities to publish literary work and represent themselves would this romanticized view of Cleopatra, as well as Egyptian goddesses such as Isis, be further complicated and questioned.

CHAPTER 6

"My ancestor, my sister": Ancient Heritage Imagery and Modern Egyptian Women Writers

The romanticization of Egyptian women is alive and well in the twenty-first century. At the time of her death in August 2013, the popular author Elizabeth Peters was working on a new Amelia Peabody novel (Mertz, "Notes" n. pag.), part of a mystery series that features an Amelia Edwards–like Englishwoman who solves crimes while traveling in Egypt. Though Peters's focus on an independent woman detective may be compelling to readers invested in women's emancipation, her descriptions of Egyptian women—"native women swathed to the eyebrows in dusky black" and "wailing" women at the tomb of Thutmose III (Peters, *Crocodile* 23; Peters, *Serpent* 32)—rely on the same imperialist attitudes toward women of color found in Nightingale's, Eliot's, Field's, and Glyn's writing. In addition to the stereotypes perpetuated by Peters's novels, popular representations of Cleopatra contribute to a superficial understanding of Egyptian women. "Sexy Cleopatra" outfits are more popular than ever at Halloween; fashion model Heidi Klum had an especially elaborate one, complete with face crystals, constructed for her 2012 Halloween party (Anonymous, "Heidi Klum" n. pag.). Also in 2012, *National Geographic* promoted its exhibit about underwater discovery of artifacts from Cleopatra's time with a sultry Cleopatra, who slinks through gauzy white curtains to seduce Julius Caesar and Mark Antony in the opening video that accompanied the exhibit in Los Angeles (Anonymous, "Cleopatra" n. pag.). Though the prevalence of distorted representations of Egyptian women is counteracted by the actions of real Egyptian women who, in 2011, were more involved in demonstrations aimed at changing the Egyptian government than they had been since the 1919 demonstrations (Coleman n. pag.) and who, in 2014, joined the

Egyptian Feminist Union's fundraising drive to support women candidates in the Egyptian parliamentary election (El Ghoul n. pag.), it remains imperative to highlight how Egyptian women have represented themselves rather than relying on others' representations of them.

By examining Egyptian women's representations of themselves, we can more fully recognize the limitations of the imperialist visions for emancipation constructed by Nightingale, Eliot, Field, and Glyn. Although Egyptian women did not have widespread access to publishing venues in the nineteenth and early twentieth centuries, they did respond to and revise imperialist representations in writing from the mid-nineteenth century on, and as the Egyptian nationalist movement grew over the course of the twentieth century, their responses envisioned new roles for women, especially in shaping Egyptian culture and establishing Egypt's independence from Britain. Once Egypt was fully independent from Britain in the latter part of the twentieth century, Egyptians remained cognizant of the ways in which British imperialism had shaped what Egypt had become, and Egyptian women writers today continue to respond to distorted representations of themselves and their country, using the same literary genres employed by the British women writers whose work has been analyzed in this book but with a different understanding of what it means to represent nations and the individuals who populate them. Whereas the British women writers discussed in this book were tied to the realist tradition, even as they often infused their works with romanticized visions of the East, late twentieth-century Egyptian women writers were no longer wedded to this tradition, instead using postmodern narrative strategies that assume a more fluid notion of identity.

This chapter traces the development of a tradition of Egyptian women writers who, especially after Egypt gained independence from Britain, articulated their own visions for emancipation. While some of these writers do not use images of ancient Egyptian women, using images of contemporary women to express their visions instead, many of these writers have drawn on images of ancient Egyptian women, using what Marilyn Booth calls "heritage imagery" to examine the social position of women in Egypt ("Introduction," *Open Door* xxvii). More important than the latest installment of the Amelia Peabody series are the works of women writers such as Latifa Al-Zayyat, Sahar Tawfiq, Alifa Rifaat, Ahdaf Soueif, Nawal El Saadawi, Radwa Ashour, and Iman Mersal, all of whom have made significant contributions to the representation of Egyptian women by drawing on images of ancient Egyptian women in their work. Next to their writings, the works of Nightingale, Eliot, Field, and Glyn become artifacts in the history of British imperialism, representative of a time before Egyptian women writers were able to shape representations of themselves and their role in Egyptian culture.

*   *   *

Although Egyptian women writers would not have widespread access to the publishing world until the mid-twentieth century, they had begun to think, talk, and write about their own representation well before that. As Margot Badran and Miriam Cooke point out in the introduction to *Opening the Gates: An Anthology of Arab Feminist Writing* (2004), there was a strong oral tradition of storytelling by Egyptian women before the mid-nineteenth century (xxxvii). Oral texts passed from one generation of Egyptian women to another, establishing the "foremothers" who would influence Egyptian women writers from the mid-nineteenth century onward (xxxvii). From the 1860s to the 1920s, Egyptian women began producing what Badran and Cooke call "invisible" feminist work, "books produced by middle and upper class women which were circulated in the harems" but not in the public sphere (xxix), and from the 1890s on, the concerns of Egyptian women were featured in woman-focused Arab journals, which were circulated to the public (xxxix). Although these journals often were founded and edited by Arab women who had not been born in Egypt—for example, two Syrians living in Egypt, Hind Nawfal and Labiba Hashim, founded *Al-Fatah* (*The Young Woman*) and *Fata Al-Shark* (*The Girl of the East*) in 1892 and 1906, respectively—these journals helped to establish the foundation for a feminist movement in Egypt. Although Hashim was sometimes critical of educated Egyptian women as she urged them to become more active in determining the conditions of their own lives, chastising them for not putting their education to good use in her 1898 article "The Eastern Woman," she clearly believed that Egyptian women could shape their own futures: "I believe it is the duty of every woman who has been favored by fate and has been given the tools to attain knowledge to follow the path of education, so that her knowledge may become a source of pride for her. She will realize that, just as she was capable of imitating foreign customs and the fashions, she is also capable of learning and putting her knowledge to work" (115).

Marilyn Booth, in *May Her Likes Be Multiplied: Biography and Gender Politics in Egypt* (2001), has shown how *The Young Woman, The Girl of the East*, and other journals from the same time period often featured biographies of "exemplary" women, including ancient Egyptian women, in order to encourage Egyptian women to meet their full potential. For example, the fifteenth-century BCE female pharaoh Hatshepsut was used in the journal *Fatat Misr* (*Young Woman of Egypt*) as an example of "those females who emerged as excellent in various eras . . . by administering, leading armies, or emerging as a people's leader" (67). While Hatshepsut was sometimes presented as "dependent on her partisans' strength more than her own actions," she possessed the "virtue" needed in role models for Egyptian women, and she sometimes was used as a contrast to the "sly and debauched" Cleopatra, who rarely was represented as "exemplary" (68, 80, 93–94). Still, Booth also makes the point that Egyptian women needed models for emancipation that were relevant to their current concerns, so when ancient Egyptian women's biographies were featured in these journals, they often were framed in an nationalist context: Hatshepsut, for example, was "particularly useful," since members of the nationalist movement "who deployed pharaonic Egypt as a symbol of modern Egypt's potential greatness saw the New Kingdom as the glory period. Hatshepsut could thus represent both national glory and female prominence" (52).

At the time these journals were providing a venue for discussion of the role of women in Egyptian culture, much about Egypt's relationship to Britain was changing, with Lord Cromer resigning from his position as administrator of imperialist policies in 1907 and the founding of Mustafa Kamil's Nationalist Party in the same year (Booth 38). Along with Kamil's party, Sa'd Zaghlul's Wafd Party—which came into existence in 1918 when Zaghlul headed the Egyptian delegation that requested and was denied independence by the British government, leading to the 1919 demonstrations—provided new avenues for upper- and middle-class Egyptians to voice their desire for independence from Britain. As Booth and Beth Baron, author of *Egypt as a Woman: Nationalists, Gender, and Politics* (2005), point out, women participated in the nationalist movement, even if they did not hold the prominent positions that men had within the movement, and these women, such as Zaghlul's wife Safiyya and her friend (and sometimes rival) Hudā Shaʻrāwī, referred to ancient Egyptian women when articulating their desire for women's independence and Egypt's independence. Of Shaʻrāwī's references to ancient Egyptian women, Booth writes: "Defining the legitimacy of her movement, Hudā Shaʻrāwī invoked the same double heritage proposed by biographers in the women's press. . . . [E]arly Muslim as well as ancient Egyptian women had full rights that had later eroded; and today's *fallāha* (peasant woman)—even if she was stereotyped . . . by urban upper- and middle-class women . . . —embodied the honorable continuation of that tradition" (40–41). In other words, nationalist women activists recognized the "liberation" of ancient Egyptian women (something I have shown Nightingale and Eliot also recognized) and saw a connection between their liberation and the liberation of modern Egyptian women (something Nightingale and Eliot could not see as clearly).

Beth Baron details the connection between ancient and modern Egyptian women's emancipation by examining visual images used by nationalists in the 1920s, which often combined images of ancient Egypt with images of the modern peasant woman, who became more relevant to the movement in the early twentieth century. For example, when Egyptian sculptor Mahmud Mukhtar created *Nahdat Miser* (*The Awakening of Egypt*), which "shows a peasant woman lifting her veil from her face with her left arm and placing her right arm on the back of a sphinx as it rises up on its forelegs," this sculpture was reconstructed on a "monumental" scale in front of a rail station in 1928 and also was used on the cover of the women's journal *al-Nahda al-Nisa'iyya* (*The Women's Awakening*) (Baron 1, 67). Though Baron argues it was primarily male nationalists who created these images, she also asserts that women nationalists did not resist these images, accepting them as legitimate representations of themselves and indicative of the centrality of women in articulating Egypt's identity—"Egypt as a woman," as Baron puts it in the title of her book. Furthermore, women nationalists accepted what today might be seen as "traditional" roles for women—motherhood, especially—and used these roles to establish themselves in the nationalist movement. Zaghlul's wife, Safiyya, who was an active participant in the "ladies' demonstrations" of 1919, established herself as the "mother of all Egyptians" (Baron 111, 139). Though not biologically a mother, she cared for her deceased sister's children and also for young nationalist men mortally injured in fighting the British, whose own mothers could not be with them as they were dying (160, 141). Though Baron does not specify whether Safiyya or her supporters ever directly tied her representation as a "mother to all Egyptians" to an ancient predecessor such as Isis, the connection is implied. Just as Isis had suckled Horus and contributed to the creation of Egyptian culture, nationalist women such as Safiyya were suckling the youth who would ensure Egypt's future, free from dependence on the British government.

The representations used by nationalist women established the role of Egyptian women in shaping their own identities and the identity of Egypt as an independent nation. These representations may have been influenced by the specific circumstances of Egyptian culture in the early twentieth century, including men's dominance in the nationalist movement, but it is clear that women were beginning to articulate visions for their emancipation that responded to and revised representations by the nineteenth-century British women writers discussed in this book. By 1923, Hudā Sha'rāwī (whose act of "unveiling" after returning to Egypt from a meeting of women in Rome established her as a leader in the Egyptian feminist movement) had founded the Egyptian Feminist Union (EFU), which published the journal *l'Egyptienne* and also ran a press that published books by women writers. The EFU's publications marked the production of "unambiguously feminist" work in Egypt, according to Badran and Cooke (xxxix, xl, xxv), and this work continued, albeit in new forms and under new women leaders, in the mid-twentieth century. The older generation of leaders had faded—Safiyya Zaghlul died in 1946 and Sha'rāwī in 1947—but a new generation, including Nawal El Saadawi and Latifa Al-Zayyat, both of whom were involved in the mid-1940s' demonstrations leading to the 1952 revolution, emerged. Al-Zayyat was secretary of the National Committee of Workers and Students at the time of the 1946 demonstrations, during which Egyptian students registered their frustration over Britain's continued presence in Egypt via the 1936 Anglo-Egyptian Treaty (Booth, "Introduction," *Open Door* xx–xxi), while El Saadawi was a high school student who marched in the demonstrations (El Saadawi, *Walking* 189).

Still, as Richard Jacquemond points out in *Conscience of a Nation: Writers, State, and Society* (2008), feminist expression for these women, especially during the years of Gamal Abd al-Nasser's presidency (1956–1970), was sometimes muted, since under Nasser, feminism had "subsidiary status" (187). Feminists were expected to downplay their gender and instead emphasize their national loyalty, something Al-Zayyat did more effectively than El Saadawi (187). It was not until 1960, with the publication of Al-Zayyat's novel *The Open Door*, that Egyptian women's literary writing about their own emancipation was taken seriously. The story of Layla, a young woman who is a generation younger than Al-Zayyat but observes the 1946 demonstrations and then participates in political resistance to British control of the Suez Canal in the 1950s, Al-Zayyat's novel reflected the "realist approach to social critique" that was typical of Egyptian writing at the time and, thus, established the idea that women's writing should be taken on the same terms applied to Egyptian men's writing (Booth, "Introduction," *Open Door* xviii). Further, *The Open Door* garnered attention because it broke stylistic ground, using colloquial Arabic in a way other Egyptian novels had not, and it brought to the forefront the unique perspective of Egyptian women, since Layla's interior thoughts about the political climate in Egypt drive the plot of the story (xviii). Al-Zayyat's contribution to Egyptian writing and the Arab feminist tradition is unparalleled, but because she wrote in a social realist style, in which the everyday events of the characters lives are emphasized over metaphors that draw on Egypt's past, her novel does not draw on the images of ancient Egyptian women. In fact, on the basis of Al-Zayyat's work, it might be argued that twentieth-century Egyptian women writers rejected the romanticized images of Egypt used by the British women writers discussed in this book. By focusing on the everyday events of twentieth-century Egypt, writers such as Al-Zayyat wrote against the notion that Egyptian women should be seen in relationship to ancient goddesses such as Isis and Hathor.

Nevertheless, late twentieth-century Egyptian women writers, who have benefited from the growth of international feminism from the 1970s on, have returned to imagery of ancient Egypt to express the place of women in contemporary Egyptian culture. As Booth explains in her introduction to the 2000 edition of *The Open Door*, more recent women writers have turned away from Al-Zayyat's "social realism" and toward "literary expression that focuse[s] more on inner formulations of identity and the fragmentary, self-contradictory subjectivity of characters" (xxvii). This postmodern form of literary expression is characterized by "a more impressionistic and fragmented kind of narrative," which includes "forms, images, and themes drawn from 'the heritage,'" especially "medieval Islamic, pharaonic, [and] Coptic" references (xxvii). Writers such as Sahar Tawfiq, Alifa Rifaat, Ahdaf Soueif, and Nawal El Saadawi have all worked in this manner. Tawfiq, a teacher who began publishing her work in the early 1970s, draws on the creation roles of ancient Egyptian goddesses, especially goddess of the sky, Nut, in her story "Points of the Compass," in which a young bride becomes Nut in order to restore the flooding of the Nile, which was impeded from making Egypt a productive land after the building of the Aswan Dam in the 1960s. As Booth, translator of Tawfiq's story, explains, "Tawfiq beautifully brings together Nut and the Bride of the Nile, the whole cycle of growth and renewal . . . in a female figure who makes her own choices, narrates her own story, and is transformed from sacrifice into goddess" ("Introduction," *Points* 9). Rifaat, whose story "My World of the Unknown" (1983) made her reputation in the Western world after her husband's death gave her the freedom to publish her work, compares the central woman character of her story to Cleopatra to suggest that this woman need not be confined by her traditional marriage. Like Cleopatra, "the very legend of love," the central character anticipates abandoning intimacy with men after developing an obsession for a serpent that haunts her home (71). Though the woman's husband ends up killing the animal, taking away the opportunity for same-sex intimacy represented by the serpent (76), the theme of potential agency for the central woman character resonates strongly in the story.

Tawfiq's and Rifaat's use of ancient Egyptian imagery in the late 1970s and early 1980s has been disseminated among the international feminist community through English translations by women academics interested in woman-centered texts, and this use of ancient imagery to address issues relevant to modern Egyptian women continues in more recent publications by Egyptian women writers. In an article originally written for the *Guardian*, "The Language of the Veil" (2001), novelist and political commentator Ahdaf Soueif, whose novels I will discuss in more detail later in this chapter, uses Cleopatra and Nefertiti to explore the opportunities for women to resist the control men have over their lives, arguing that contemporary Egyptian women, who struggle with whether to "veil" or not, do not yet have a form of dress that accurately represents their identity. Soueif urges Egyptian women to look to their ancient foremothers, who understood the power of dress by fashioning themselves after the goddess Isis, to find a form of dress that will "embody our Egyptian notion of ourselves" (274). El Saadawi, in her memoir *A Daughter of Isis* (1999), also uses Isis to show the ways in which Egyptian women might be empowered, especially when faced with challenges establishing their professional identities in a world that does not always support women in these endeavors. Presenting herself as a goddess-figure from a very early age, when she played Isis "sobbing over the death of Osiris" in a school play, El Saadawi emphasizes how the creativity she was allowed to express as a child sustained her as an adult, after she chose to become a doctor but was not always accorded professional respect. "I never saw myself as a doctor holding a syringe and plunging the needle into people's arms," El Saadawi writes about herself as a child. "In my dreams I saw myself seated at a piano playing music, or singing, or dancing, my feet beating on the ground, my head crowned with the disc of the sun, lifting it up like the goddess Isis" (100). For El Saadawi, the reality of life for an Egyptian woman doctor, who sometimes came under fire for her work on women's health issues, is made tolerable by the memories of her childhood and her ability to express herself creatively. The dreams of ancient Egypt she was able to indulge in as a child remind her that women were once respected for their powers, even if that respect is not accorded to contemporary Egyptian women, and El Saadawi survives the difficulties of professional life by turning to writing, the creative work that began with her childhood identification with Isis.

It is tempting to analyze the turn toward postmodern literary expression seen in the work of Tawfiq, Rifaat, Soueif, and El Saadawi as a complete rejection of Al-Zayyat's social realism, but even Al-Zayyat herself seems to have recognized the connection between contemporary and ancient Egypt in her later work. In the essay "In Her Own Mirror" (1993), Al-Zayyat writes of her experience of becoming involved in political activism during her university years by focusing on its connection to ancient Egyptian history. She writes,

> I entered the university as enthusiastic patriot. My hair used to stand on end, literally, when I remembered the history of Pharaonic Egypt and compared it with the presence at that time of English soldiers on the streets. Egyptian reactionary forces stood hand in hand with the king in opposition to the people. At university, two options were open to those wishing to dissent . . . the Muslim Brothers . . . and the communists. . . . Being a woman with a special temperament, it was inevitable that I chose the communists. (282)

With a return to heritage imagery accepted as a legitimate form of representing Egyptian women's emancipation by a writer as rooted in social realism as

Al-Zayyat, it is worth focusing on two novelists who especially have embraced heritage imagery in the postmodern age, when a more fluid understanding of identity has emerged. Ahdaf Soueif and Radwa Ashour both use a more non-linear form of literary expression than Al-Zayyat does, yet they also build off al-Zayyat's focus on women's emancipation, with Soueif claiming Al-Zayyat as an important influence (Soueif and Massad 89) and Ashour directly referencing *The Open Door* in her work and earning the title of Al-Zayyat's "spiritual daughter" from some critics (Seymour-Jorn 108).

Soueif's novels *In the Eye of the Sun* (1992) and *The Map of Love* (1999) pay homage to Al-Zayyat's *The Open Door* by focusing on the development of women's identities within the context of contemporary Egyptian politics, but they also make use of a postmodern narrative style by flashing back and forth between times and locations and by incorporating multiple genres, especially letters, diary entries, and newspapers excerpts. Further, both novels make use of intertextuality, a key postmodern literary technique, engaging the British literary tradition by referencing nineteenth-century writers such as George Eliot, another important influence on Soueif (Soueif and Massad 88). In *In the Eye of the Sun*, the main character Asya Al-'Ulama—whose first name "integrates Pharaonic Egypt with Judaism and Islam," since "in the Muslim tradition," it is "the name of the Pharaoh's childless wife who adopted and loved the baby prophet Musa (Moses)" (Malak 146)—negotiates romantic relationships with men of various nationalities as Egypt confronts its relationship to the Middle East during and after the 1967 Arab-Israeli War. *The Map of Love* returns to late-nineteenth- and early-twentieth-century Egypt and its relationship with Britain with the story of Anna Winterbourne, an English widow who travels to Egypt, marries an Egyptian Muslim, and embraces all aspects of Egyptian nationalist life, including harem life. This novel, which offers an important alternative to the more popular Elizabeth Peters's Amelia Peabody series because it more fully demonstrates the effects of British imperialism on Egyptian life, shows how nationalist resistance to British imperialism still lingers in late-twentieth-century Egypt, since Anna's story is uncovered and retold by two late-twentieth-century women, Amal and Isabel, Anna's great-grandchildren, who themselves are struggling with the effect of contemporary politics on personal relationships.

In the Eye of the Sun has been considered seriously by literary critics, who read Soueif's novel in diverse ways. Nadine Sinno, in "The Power of Place and Space: (Re)constructing Identity and Selfhood in Ahdaf Soueif's *Eye of the Sun*" (2006), reads the novel as an "Anglophone" work that captures the effect of "physical and cultural environment" on the main character Asya's complex journey to "construct the self of her own choice," a journey that is "not bound by place of origin" but "draw[s] on the various resources she benefits from as a result of her encounters with other places and cultures" (195). Further, Sinno sees Asya's "romantic and sexual experience—in various places" as key to the development of "her overall sense of selfhood and identity" (195). Like Sinno, Lindsey Moore, in "Voyages Out and In: Two (British) Arab Muslim Women's Bildungsroman" (2012), sees the novel as focused on individual identity via the experience of travel, especially how leaving home (or the "voyage out") provides a mechanism through which "female protagonists define themselves in relation to national and supranational communities" (68). Yet, Moore sees Asya's "voyage out," which results in "heightened feminist awareness," as "delimited by 'second wave' definitions of spatial and sexual emancipation" (75). Asya's return to Egypt and adoption of "Nasserite" principles does not satisfy current readers, in Moore's opinion, though her return home points to "the ongoing challenges of defining feminism in the historically, politically and culturally complex field that is contemporary Egypt" (75). Mrinalini Chakravorty, however, complicates this reading of the novel as focused on individual identity by arguing, in "To Undo What the North Has Done: Fragments of a Nation and Arab Collectivism in the Fiction of Ahdaf Soueif" (2007), that the novel is rooted in the Arab rather than the British tradition and is an expression of the benefits of Pan-Arabism in developing a *collective* identity for Egyptians, even as Pan-Arabism must confront and resolve issues surrounding women's autonomy, especially economic autonomy (131, 135). Writes Chakravorty,

> Asya represents herself in English but also . . . presents herself as different from both the English . . . and the [Middle Eastern] subalterns [in the novel]. . . . Her narrative practice is to illuminate precisely the ways in which these others remain outside of the means of self-articulation that is her privilege. The mode of self-articulation as inauthentic, unoriginal self-inscription . . . substantiates the grounds for the larger historical platform of Pan-Arabism as a means for negotiating individual and collective struggles against imperialism in the Arab world. (136)

In other words, Chakravorty sees the novel as doing more than just focusing on individual identity, and she challenges the notion that self-articulation of identity can be an "authentic" process, especially if readers are to recognize the issues surrounding collective identity in the novel.

While all of these critics offer important points about the novel, and while Chakravorty's view of it is particularly helpful in analyzing the relationship between the text and historical/cultural context, only Moore offers any discussion of the ancient Egyptian imagery used by Soueif, and this discussion does not trace how Soueif's use of this imagery parallels Asya's development as an Egyptian woman who engages various national traditions in her construction of the self within the collective identity Chakravorty lays out. I would agree with Moore's claim that Soueif presents a narrative that follows many of the assumptions of second-wave feminism about women's agency (particularly the notion that women's consciousness is raised by thinking about their oppression, speaking out about the situation to their oppressors, and taking action to change their situation to end oppression), but like Chakravorty, I believe Soueif uses multiple national traditions to present this narrative in a manner that moves beyond the concepts of second-wave feminism, by emphasizing third-wave feminist understandings of identity as more fluid, especially in a global context. As already indicated, Chakravorty focuses on Pan-Arabism as part of the global context with which Soueif is concerned, and this is helpful in understanding how Soueif addresses agency issues for Egyptian women, who are immersed in a complex political and social situation. Yet, as also mentioned, Chakravorty does not discuss any of the ancient Egyptian imagery used by Soueif in the novel, which is a key element in presenting the global context for Asya's construction of the self.

As Soueif draws on a variety of national traditions in the novel, she incorporates a variety of representations of women from these traditions to chart Asya's understanding. Many of these representations of women are drawn from literary traditions, both British and Arabic; Soueif regularly refers to women characters in George Eliot's novels, especially Maggie Tulliver in *The Mill on the Floss* (1860) and Dorothea Brooke in *Middlemarch* (1871), but she also refers to "the beautiful long-haired ladies languishing on tasselled cushions" in *One Thousand and One Nights* (or *Arabian Nights* as it is more commonly called in the Western tradition) and to Chedja el-Temimia, the woman protagonist in the fifteenth-century erotic Arabic text, *The Perfumed Garden* (303, 450, 457). These literary references—along with references to historical and mythological women, such as Cleopatra, unnamed Greek "demi-goddesses," and ancient Egyptian princesses preserved as mummies (538, 569, 429)—enable Soueif to comment on both the universal and culturally specific struggles that women face. At one point in the novel, as Asya reflects on her decision to cheat on her Egyptian husband Saif, who has been indifferent toward Asya for much of their marriage, and have an affair with an attentive but obsessive Englishman named Gerald, Asya feels guilty about her decision but also believes that if she carries this guilt, she is "still in her glass case" (586), an image that already has been used to describe statues of Greek demi-goddesses who must be "protected" from "pollution" (567) and a mummified Egyptian princess, whom Asya thinks of as "My ancestor, my sister" when she sees her "in [a] glass case" at the British Museum (429). Asya's realization that she is like both ancient Greek demi-goddesses and mummified

Egyptian princesses, restricted in her life as though she is under glass, points to the assumption of second-wave feminism that all women experience similar forms of oppression, yet Soueif combines such commentary with the social realist description of specific cultural conditions brought to the novel tradition by Al-Zayyat, in order to highlight the importance of cultural conditions in assessing women's agency. Asya realizes her similarity to the Greek demi-goddesses and Egyptian princesses only after Soueif has provided over four hundred pages of details about the problems in her relationship with Saif, as well as detailed descriptions of the relationships of her women friends, whose unique situations are shaped by specific cultural conditions within Egyptian culture. Soueif does not generalize even within cultures, allowing for different results within each culture.

Though Soueif clearly uses representations from a variety of national traditions, there is a movement toward more ancient Egyptian imagery as the novel progresses, and this trend suggests Soueif is not merely relying on second-wave feminism in her development of Asya's character. Marta Cariello, in "Bodies Across: Ahdaf Soueif, Fadia Faqir, Diana Abu Jaber" (2009), has discussed briefly Asya's comments about the mummified Egyptian princesses she encounters (320–21), but no critic I am aware of has discussed Asya's identification with Cleopatra, which comes at a key point in the novel, when Asya decides she will pursue the Englishman Gerald. "He would be nice to make love to," Asya thinks, as she looks at Gerald when he come to her house to hang out on a Sunday afternoon while Asya works on her PhD thesis (538). Initially, she checks herself, mocking herself for her own inexperience with men: "Is that *right?* She snaps, 'You're the great expert, are you . . . sitting behind your table surveying him as though you were Colette or Piaf or Cleopatra or even Kushuk Hanim—a vast experience you have, have you? Such a variety of men you've tasted, you've ensnared and bedded'" (538). While the references to Cleopatra, the French courtesans Colette and Piaf, and the Egyptian courtesan Kushuk Hamim are based on negative stereotypes about women, particularly their seductive qualities, ultimately these images are empowering to Asya, who seduces Gerald that afternoon and takes the first step in ending her unhappy marriage with Saif. Of course, Asya's relationship with Gerald is far from perfect (and sections of the novel describing it—such as the episode when Gerald steals one of Asya's shoes, so she doesn't leave him (658)—are painful to read), but Soueif's use of the Cleopatra image to signal Asya's first step toward emancipation begins a broader shift in the novel away from British women as models for Asya and toward Egyptian women as models. Shortly after her "bedding" of Gerald, which is the first pleasurable sexual experience Asya has had in her life (540), she finds herself not feeling guilty and, instead, thinks about herself as a different kind of woman, who no longer identifies with her earlier ideals, Eliot's Maggie and Dorothea, whom Asya has admired for their "renunciation" when they find themselves in unhappy relationships (Dorothea) or when family expectations prevent them from pursuing their romantic desires (Maggie). "You've committed adultery," thinks Asya after she sleeps with Gerald, "you've done it, you've joined Anna and Emma and parted company forever with Dorothea and Maggie" (540). Though the company Asya now keeps—Anna (Karenina) and Emma (Bovary)—are still European models, Asya has begun to release self-sacrificing models, though she thinks "Dorothea would have understood" her decision to sleep with Gerald, since Dorothea herself seems to desire Will Ladislaw while still married to her husband (540). Still, Asya notes, Dorothea "would not have approved" of Asya's actions (540).

Once Asya releases the ideal of renunciation, she does not immediately turn to Egyptian models for behavior, but she does resist models that seem to restrict her. When she and Gerald begin to experience problems in their relationship because of Gerald's obsessive behavior, Asya continues to be "polite" to him in her home because of the Egyptian cultural expectation that one will be "hospitable" (558), but she also asks Gerald whether what he wants is an "odalisque," a term she must explain to him because he doesn't understand what it means (563). Although it takes Asya considerable time to extricate herself from her relationships with Gerald and Saif, with her mother's support she does, leaving behind a difficult period she refers to via Cleopatra's speech in act 5, scene 2 of *Antony and Cleopatra* about her captivity: "Rather a ditch in Egypt / Be gentle grave unto me" (qtd. in Soueif, *Eye* 690). Once through this difficult period, Asya returns to Egypt to teach at Cairo University, where she realizes she is a "porno-spread" to her more conservative women students, who have "screened themselves off entirely" by wearing the full veil and refusing to speak in class, since "the voice of a woman is an 'awra' [can't be heard in public]" (754). It should be noted that Soueif articulates diverse views about women veiling across her work. As I already have mentioned, she seems to reject veiling in her essay "The Language of the Veil" (2001), as Asya does at this moment in the novel, but she also complicates the issue in the scene that follows the one in which she refers to herself as pornographic to her students. Feeling frustrated about her conservative students, who encourage Asya to change her views and follow theirs, Asya discusses veiling with her radical leftist sister Deena, who interestingly does not believe the conservatism Asya's students profess will envelop Egypt entirely (755). In this conversation, Asya clarifies that she believes there is a difference between the way city women veil, which seems to reflect a rigid Islamic perspective, and the way rural women veil, which is done "naturally, without a fuss. They do it because that's what their mothers and grandmothers have always done" (755).

Asya meets these rural women after she leaves Cairo University, moves in with her family in Zamalek (where the family still has pictures of Nasser on the wall), and goes to work as a government translator and family planning educator (756). Here, she finds her niche after leaving behind her relationships with Gerald and Saif, since as she talks to rural women about family planning, she also works to empower these women to take action on local issues that are important to them, such as the unlawful imprisonment of men in their community (757–59). As the novel ends, Asya finds inspiration for her new life both in the rural women she works with and in the figure of another mummified woman, who is shown to Asya by some local children. While there is disagreement among members of the community about whether this woman was an ancient queen, Ramesses II's sister, a court dancer, or some combination of the three, Asya doubts she was a court dancer "elevated into a sister-wife," since "[t]he composure, the serenity, of her smile tells of someone who had always known who she was" (785). In reflecting on the smile of this mummified woman, Asya notes that she had come to see ancient Egyptian monuments in a diminished light after viewing Ramesses II's "paltry" mummified body in London, but she now feels connected to her ancient Egyptian heritage (785). She assesses the mummy of this woman, "who in some way belonged to [Ramesses II]" as having "found a gentle grave," the same kind of grave Asya referenced when she considered Cleopatra's captivity and her own captivity in her relationships with Gerald and Saif. Finally, it seems at the end of the novel, Asya will be able to bury her past and move forward with confidence, having built an identity that draws on various national traditions and recognizes both the shared struggles of women and the specific cultural contexts for their struggles.

Soueif's second novel, *The Map of Love*, also takes up issues of individual and collective identity for Egyptian women but with a stronger emphasis on the ways in which late-nineteenth- and early-twentieth-century British imperialism shaped identity, since the main character in the novel, Anna Winterbourne, is an Englishwoman who, after her husband returns from fighting for the British in the Sudan and dies from psychological trauma related to his war experience, travels to Egypt, where she falls in love with an Egyptian Muslim man and embraces all aspects of Egyptian life, including harem life. Critics who discuss the novel typically contrast it to *In the Eye of the Sun*, asserting that it is more historical than Soueif's earlier novel. Amin Malak, in *Muslim Narratives and the Discourse of English* (2004), writes that the novel is "a revisionist metahistory," which "articulate[s Soueif's] nationalist version of Egypt's modern history" (137), while Joseph Massad, in "The Politics of Desire in the Writings of Ahdaf Soueif" (1999), states: "Whereas history and politics were almost *hors de texte* [outside the text] in *In the Eye of the Sun*, they are *au fond du texte* [at the bottom of the text] in *The Map of Love*" (Soueif and Massad 81). Soueif confirms that the role of history in each novel is different:

> *In the Eye of the Sun* really started out as the story of Asya al-'Ulama and then the story of the family and friends surrounding her. It was not possible to do that with the history and the politics, but the impulse that generated the novel was interest in this character. . . . History and politics come into it only insofar as they affect our protagonist and those around her. . . . The impulse behind *The Map of Love* was different. It was more overtly historical and political, to do with crosscultural relationships, with history, with the relationship of the Western world to Egypt and to our area. . . . Part of what *The Map of Love* is about is how much room personal relationships have in a context of politics and history. (Soueif and Massad 83)

More so than *In the Eye of the Sun*, too, *The Map of Love* draws on multiple genres: whereas in *In the Eye of the Sun*, Soueif uses letters and diary entries to chart Asya's relationships with other people, in *The Map of Love*, she uses not only letters and diaries entries but also newspaper accounts to illustrate how the political situation in Egypt affects personal relationships. Further, as Malak points out, Soueif presents real turn-of-the-century Islamic texts, such as Qasim Amin's *Tahrir al Mara'a* [*The Liberation of Women*] (1899) as "nourishing sources" (144), something readers do not necessarily receive from *In the Eye of the Sun*.

Malak also points out that one of the ancient Egyptian images in the book, a tapestry depicting the ancient Egyptian family of Osiris, Isis, and Horus, includes "Islamic imprints" (146). As we learn at the end of the novel, these imprints are the Arabic words "From the dead come the living" and "the branch is cut but the tree remains" (Soueif, *Map* 516), and Malak uses the tapestry and other images in the novel that draw on multiple national and religious traditions to argue that *The Map of Love* is "a site for foregrounding, gently but assertively, a potently positive image about Arab-Muslim culture that is seldom witnessed in such an appealing humane and cogent context" (147). Further, Malak believes Soueif's novel advocates a "progressive" form of Islam, which can contribute to women's "liberation" (148–49). "Arab and Muslim women writers [such as Soueif] recognize that religion and nationalism are actives forces to engage with: for them, the discourse of liberation passes not through ridiculing or rejecting their Islamic heritage, but through appealing to its most enlightened and progressive tradition" (149). Still, Malak does not fully analyze the ancient Egyptian imagery in relationship to women's agency in the novel, which should be discussed in relation to Soueif's treatment of it in *In the Eye of the Sun*, where the progression of heritage imagery mirrors Asya's construction of an individual and a collective self.

Tara McDonald, in "Resurrecting Isis in Ahdaf Soueif's *The Map of Love*" (2004), does bring attention to the ways in which the tapestry reflects issues of women's agency in the novel, arguing that Anna's weaving of the tapestry, which Anna characterizes as her "contribution to the Egyptian renaissance," shows how Anna strives to emulate Isis, who serves as an important model for women seeking agency, since she "invented weaving" and, through it, was able to "control . . . Destiny" (164–65). Still, McDonald argues that Anna's narrative of marrying an Egyptian set the precedent for women in the family to "marry foreign men and live far from home," as Isabel, one of the younger women in the novel, states (165). As a result, McDonald takes the view that later generations of women in the family do not emulate Isis as fully as Anna did, for they leave Egypt for the West and do not pursue the roles of "weaver, a great mother, or a determiner of fate" (166). Ultimately, McDonald sees Soueif's novel as pointing to the "emptiness" late-twentieth-century Egyptians experience "due to the loss of Isis" as a model (170). McDonald's argument brings attention to the importance of the tapestry in exploring issues surrounding women's agency in the novel, but my own understanding of how women's agency is presented in the novel has a more favorable view of the identities constructed by women in both the older generation (via Anna and Layla, Anna's Egyptian sister-in-law) and the younger generation (via Isabel and Amal).

In *The Map of Love*, Soueif uses some of the same European literary references used in *In the Eye of the Sun* to track the development of women characters' construction of identity, including their shift away from identification with European women and toward identification with Egyptian women. For example, like Asya in *In the Eye of the Sun*, Anna is compared to Anna Karenina, as well as Colette's heroines, yet the narrator also comments that even as Anna wears the peignoir hairstyle of these women, she "seems worlds away from Coline and Rezi," Colette's heroines, since she is living in Egypt and learning to embrace its culture (65). Anna also is likened to Eliot's Dorothea, when Amal, one of the younger women who is recovering and telling Anna's story, thinks: "I am obsessed with Anna['s . . .] journal. She has become as real to me as Dorothea Brooke" (26). However, this is before Amal knows the details of Anna's story, and it quickly becomes clear that Anna is different from Dorothea as well, since she engages Egyptian culture more fully than any ideal British woman living in England can.

For Anna herself, the key representations through which she processes her own identity as she becomes part of Egyptian society and (in her mind) becomes more similar to Egyptian women are visual rather than literary representations. Specifically, Anna processes her own identity through a John Frederick Lewis painting, possibly *The Siesta* (1873), which she sees in the South Kensington Museum before she travels to Egypt, as well as through the aforementioned tapestry of Isis and Osiris, which she weaves after her marriage to the Egyptian nationalist Sharif Basha al-Baroudi. Soueif herself has written about the influence of Lewis's paintings on her writing in a review of the 2008 exhibit "The Lure of the East," which was held at the Tate Britain and included a number of paintings by Lewis. Though Soueif finds many of nineteenth-century British paintings of Egypt, especially those of William Holman Hunt and Thomas Seddon, to uphold British imperialist attitudes toward the East, she sees Lewis's work differently, as capturing the "spirit" of Egypt more fully than that of other painters (Soueif, "Visions" n. pag.). Writes Soueif:

> I find Lewis's work so attractive that it became a source of sustenance for the heroine, Lady Anna Winterbourne, of my novel *The Map of Love*: recently widowed, Anna visits the South Kensington museum and takes pleasure in "the wonderous colors, the tranquility, the contentment with which [Lewis's paintings] are infused." Of all the "oriental" paintings I had come across, only those of Lewis beckoned me in. At the simplest level, the world he shows is a happy one, filled with sunlight, people, animals, flowers, food. But something else is transmitted from his surfaces: empathy. (n. pag.)

The empathy Soueif sees in Lewis's work is what Anna learns in Egypt, especially after she is "abducted" by "young Radicals" who want to "retaliate" for the imprisonment of one of its members, Husni al-Ghamrawi, after a "peaceful demonstration" (Soueif, *Map* 138). Anna ends up at the home of al-Ghamrawi, where she meets his wife, Layla, and later his brother-in-law Sharif. Upon meeting Layla, the Lewis painting provides a reference point for Anna's first interaction with Layla, for as Anna wakes up to find herself in an unfamiliar domestic space, she compares Layla to the woman in the Lewis painting: "[A]s I sat up, my altered perspective brought me once again into the world of those beloved paintings, for there, across the room, and on a divan similar to mine, a woman lay sleeping" (134). Although Anna first thinks Layla is a "princess" from "the Oriental tales" she has read, in which "a Houri or princess has ordered the abduction of a young man to whom she has a fancy," since Anna was abducted while dressed as a man (134), it quickly becomes clear that, just as Anna is not a typical Englishwoman, Layla is not a stereotypical Egyptian woman. In their first conversation, conducted in their only shared language of French, Anna learns that Layla has kept her own name in marriage and finds her to be an intelligent woman, qualities that take Anna by surprise (138). The women immediately have a bond with each other, and as I will show later in this section, become active participants in the Egyptian women's rights movement after Anna marries Sharif.

Although the Lewis painting that inspires and guides Anna in her initial interaction with Layla does not include references to ancient Egypt, Soueif uses references to ancient Egypt early in the novel to establish the importance of heritage in the lives of Egyptian women. Soueif does this mainly through one of the two women from the younger generation of the family, Isabel, who has been raised in the United States but comes to Egypt to see her cousin Amal with a trunk full of Anna's journals, which Isabel wants Amal to translate. Isabel's name alone connects the family to ancient Egyptian culture, since Isa Bella means "Isis the Beautiful"; further, she has been raised to believe she is like Isis, since her father has told her, "You have the name of the first goddess, the mother of Diana, of all goddesses, the mother of the world" (22). Importantly, along with Anna's journals, Isabel possesses one-third of the tapestry Anna wove during her marriage to Sharif. Isabel has the portion that features "Osiris, seated," with his "hands crossed over his chest carrying the sceptre and the flail" (392), and Omar, Isabel's cousin and love interest, has the portion that features "Isis, mother of every king, queenly in poise, on her head the Cow-horned crown and the Sun-disc of Ra" (488). The third portion, which features "the infant Horus, small and naked and still with his human head on which rests the hand of Isis his mother" (495), cannot be found until late in the novel, when Isabel finds this portion in her bag and believes a woman she met while visiting Sharif's house put it there (500).

In my reading of the importance of the tapestry, the tapestry functions as a metaphor for the familial relationships between both the older generation (where Anna is Isis, Sharif is Osiris, and their baby Nur is Horus) and the younger generation (where Isabel is Isis, Omar is Osiris, and their child Sharif is Horus). The tapestry's role in linking the two generations is particularly evident at the end of the novel, when Amal, concerned that Omar will not survive a trip to Sarajevo because of threats on his life due to his involvement in Palestinian politics, recognizes that she may have to help Isabel care for baby Sharif. Amal envisions herself placing Sharif in front of the now-complete tapestry, just as Anna used to place her baby Nur in front of it (315). Although Anna does not foresee this use of the tapestry when she weaves it, she certainly sees her weaving as an important contribution to linking past and present, for she says she "shall use nothing but what the Ancients themselves might have used in the way of flax or silk or dye, and it shall be my contribution to the Egyptian renaissance" (403).

As already stated, Malak notes that the tapestry includes both ancient Egyptian and Islamic elements, and Soueif's presentation of the tapestry in this light seems to revise significantly nineteenth-century British women

writers' assumptions that ancient Egypt and modern Egypt could not be connected because of the influence of Arab/Muslim culture. Early in the story,
Anna and her British friends discuss whether any groups in contemporary
Egypt can claim ancient heritage; while one person, Mr. S., thinks only
the Christian Copts can, "and they are few and without influence," Anna's
friend Mrs. Butcher rejects this notion and believes the "definite" and "vivid"
qualities of the ancient Egyptians can be found in the various contemporary
groups in Egypt, including Arabs/Muslims (98). Mr. S.'s perspective reflects
the typical British view about the religious and political situation in Egypt at
the turn of the century, yet Anna, who remains friends with the more liberal
Mrs. Butcher even after she separates herself from other Britons in Egypt,
comes to a different understanding, in part through the weaving of the tapestry, of the relationship between past and present in Egypt, in which Christian
Copts are not the only group that can claim ancient heritage. Muslims have
a legitimate and important claim as well.

Ultimately, Anna's construction of self complicates constructs we have
seen in the writings of nineteenth-century British women writers, and
Soueif's novel provides an alternative interpretation of this relationship than
that present in popular, late-twentieth-century fiction, such as the Elizabeth
Peters's Amelia Peabody novels. Interestingly, much criticism has been leveled
at *The Map of Love* for its emphasis on the "love story" of Anna and Sharif,
with Catherine Wynne arguing that it is "an escapist fantasy that creates a
benign vision of intercultural exchange" (64) and Noha Hamdy asserting that
the novel works with two "synchronous yet opposing narrative paradigms:
the orientalist tale and its postcolonial counterpart" and contains "problematic politico-aesthetic junctures at which the novel seems to pull in opposite
directions" (185). Wynne also objects to Soueif's emphasis on domesticity in
the novel; while she acknowledges that Soueif portrays "the harem as desirable domestic space" to present "a positive vision of nineteenth-century Arab-
Muslim domesticity and culture" (56) and, at the end of the novel, "creates
a female-centred, hybrid family in which the child promises regeneration
at least within a familial context" (64), Wynne believes that the "return to
domesticity and family" at the end of the novel "provides only a transient
respite from the relentless political exclusivity of East and West" (65).

I would agree with Wynne's argument that the harem is presented in a
positive light and the end of the novel emphasizes a community of women,
but I would challenge her reading of the ending as simply a return to domesticity, since the model Anna provides is not simply domestic. Both Wynne
and Hamdy put strong emphasis on Soueif's use of Lewis's painting in the
novel, but as I have shown, there is a shift away from this emphasis as the
novel progresses, and the tapestry replaces the Lewis painting as Anna's

primary reference point for her engagement with Egyptian culture. Further, reading against McDonald's argument that the tapestry illustrates the lack of engagement with Egyptian culture because Anna sets up a model for the younger generation that involves turning away from Egyptian culture, I would argue that Anna provides a model of social engagement with Egyptian culture for the younger generation. At the same time Anna is weaving the tapestry, she (and Layla) become significant contributors to the Egyptian women's rights movement. Anna writes articles for periodicals that address women's issues (355, 395), teaches Friday-night art classes for women at the university (435), and works with Sharif to convince non-Egyptian visitors who come to their home that the current political situation (which involved the reinstatement of British occupation laws from the 1880s) is not good for the country (447). In my reading of the end of the novel, both the older Osiris (Sharif) and the younger one (Omar) are gone, but the younger Isis figures (Isabel and Amal) remain, and neither is a woman who will only play domestic roles. Both have significant creative projects they want to finish, just as Anna (the older Isis figure) finished her weaving of the tapestry, which, along with her activities aimed at social reform, made up her creative work. Amal plans to finish translating Anna's journals, and Isabel plans to make a film about Anna, which may very well include her efforts at anti-imperialist social reform. Ultimately, Anna presents a much more sophisticated model for the younger generation of women than McDonald and Wynne suggest, and the younger generation of women lives up to this model.

Like Soueif's work, Radwa Ashour's *Specters* (2011), the story of two women (one fictional and one real) who live parallel lives in contemporary Egypt, uses a nonlinear, postmodernist form of literary expression to address the construction of self as Egyptian women seek emancipation in modern Egypt. Ashour, who has been called Al-Zayyat's "spiritual daughter" because of her use of the historical novel to discuss women's issues within specific Egyptian political contexts (Seymour-Jorn 108), uses images of Isis and other ancient Egyptian creation goddesses to inspire the central woman character, Radwa, as she confronts the "specters" of British imperialism. Early in novel, Radwa, who is writing a novel about another intellectual woman named Shagar, ponders how to develop Shagar's character by thinking about other novels she has read, including Al-Zayyat's *The Open Door* (50). Recalling that *The Open Door* begins with a scene from the 1946 demonstrations, Radwa recalls her own involvement in the 1972 demonstrations by Cairo University students (51–52), and this prompts Radwa to send her fictional character Shagar to the university, where Shagar decides to study *modern* rather than ancient Egyptian history (53, 58). In a pivotal scene after deciding to study modern history, Shagar packs up all but one of the ancient Egyptian items that populate her bedroom, leaving only a picture of Thoth, the god of writing and knowledge, to guide her study of modern Egypt (61–62). Among the items she packs up are pictures of the ancient Egyptian goddesses Maat, Isis, Hathor, and Nut. Referring to Nut, the sky-goddess who is interchangeable with the cow-goddess Hathor, the narrator states: "Above the desk was a picture of Nut, the sky-woman. She touched the earth with the tips of her toes on one side and her fingertips on the other. With her legs and arms and her star-studded torso she formed an arch that was encircled by the body of her brother and husband. Geb rested in her embrace, and on this back his burgeoning vegetation grew" (61).

Having established the richness of the images of ancient goddesses in Shagar's room, the narrator goes on to characterize Shagar's removal of these pictures as a stripping away of the past that is necessary for Shagar to concentrate on the present and her research about modern Egypt:

> She took them down from the wall, wrapped them in a sheet, and tied it. She fetched Ani's papyrus *Book of the Dead*—the copy she always placed on her desk—and tossed it into the box. She asked her mother to help her move the boxes, then got a ladder and carried them one by one to the storage loft. Her mother asked her why she was doing this; Shagar muttered something incoherent. She returned to her room, and looked around. Nothing now, except shelves on which were some dictionaries, a small empty library, and the desk, the bed, and the vanity. The room looked naked—desolate and cold. A colored card the size of her palm rested under the glass top of her desk: the high scales with their two pans. Thoth stood supervising the balance, his papyrus in his left hand and his pen in the right. Shagar had forgotten to remove the picture. The following day she noticed that it was still in its place. She contemplated it, then decided to keep it there. (61–62)

Even as Shagar strips the images that connect her to Egypt's past, she accidentally leaves one behind and allows it to remain, anticipating the inspiration she finds through ancient Egypt that occurs later in the novel.

Early in the novel, though, it appears that both the fictional character Shagar and the narrator Radwa (whom we inevitably read as the author Radwa Ashour) are set to reject ancient Egyptian imagery, especially that of ancient Egyptian women, in order to tell the story of contemporary Egyptian women's struggles. But, heritage imagery resurfaces throughout the book, suggesting that contemporary Egypt cannot be separated from its past. After Shagar finishes her studies and becomes a history professor, she articulates her struggles with the university administration, which does little to support faculty, and her struggles with her students, whom she loves but discovers are susceptible to the "corruption" of contemporary Egyptian culture (147–48).

When she learns that more than a quarter of her class has cheated on one of the exams and she decides to confront her students, the students detail the ways in which contemporary culture encourages dishonesty, telling Shagar how the exam proctors themselves help the students cheat (146). One student, revealing that he suspects he will continue to cheat because it is so hard to "swim against the current," nevertheless emphasizes how much he respects Shagar, saying, "You said that you thought about leaving the university, and I say to you that if you do that you wrong all of us . . . because your presence here preserves something of value for us, a light that assures us the darkness is no longer total, and chaos, wickedness, ignorance, injustice, and corruption, even if we can't get away from them entirely, aren't the law of the land" (147). This student goes on to characterize Shagar as similar to the ancient goddess Maat, saying, "People naturally need a star in their sky. You said that you hung a picture of Maat over your desk when you were a young student. The picture inspired you and you moved forward on your path. Don't cut off that power source, Dr. Shagar. I might look to you and move forward as you did, or even if I can't do it one of my classmates might be able to" (147).

Shagar is not entirely inspired by this student's speech, but when she calls on the dean of the college to nullify the exam, he refuses and denies that there was any cheating among the students (149). Still, despite disappointment in the dean, Shagar recognizes that she can be a "source of enlightenment" for her students, just as the ancient goddesses have been a source of enlightenment for her (154), but she also insists that one must be in touch with reality, the "land mine" that her students live in, and not remain stuck in the past (154). Shagar's—and Radwa's—struggle to reconcile the past and the present becomes the dominant theme of *Specters*, with Ashour emphasizing the numerous ghosts, or specters, contemporary Egyptian women must come to terms with in order to find their place in contemporary society. At one point, the narrator presents an extended discourse about the ancient Egyptian concept of "ba," the bird with a human head that follows a deceased person to the tomb but "[does] not remain confined with him; rather it migrate[s] freely between the grave and the world of the living, visiting the family of the dead person or the places he had frequented . . . in the daytime, and returning at night to its master's grave" (192). The "ba" seems to function as one specter that haunts contemporary Egyptian, and the narrator continues on, to discuss the ancient Egyptian concept of "ka" and the Arabic word "qarin," both of which loosely mean "double" (193), to suggest another specter that influences contemporary Egyptian culture. All of these concepts dovetail into a section of the novel in which Radwa writes about Shagar's research about a contemporary event, the Deir Yassin massacre (the 1948 killing of 107 Palestinians by Zionist paramilitaries), in relationship to these ancient concepts. Shagar initially titles her book *Deir Yassin: Investiga-tion Concerning a Massacre*, but at the last minute, right before she goes to an appointment with her publisher, she changes the title to *Al-Atyaaf: The Story of Deir Yassin*, a title that emphasizes the return of ghosts from the past, since the word "al-atyaaf" means "the specter" (197–98). Ashour's own book takes nearly the same title, *Atyaaf*, "specters," and the point here is that contemporary women can only understand themselves in relationship to specters from the past.

While the specters of Deir Yassin are not those of ancient Egypt but con-temporary Palestine, Ashour (who died in 2014 and whose husband, the Palestinian poet Mourid Barghouti, was prevented from living in Egypt for nearly 20 years) recognizes the multiple specters that still haunt Egyptian culture, and at the end of the novel, this multiplicity is highlighted by return-ing to Egypt's imperialist past. Shagar, angered by oversimplified attitudes toward Egyptian history, leaves an annual festival held at her university, in which students wear costumes that reinforce stereotypes about ancient Egypt. She drives into the countryside, where she is reminded of the connections between different periods of history: ancient, Arab, British, and contem-porary Egyptian. At the Suez Canal, a location that brings together vividly many of the imperialist influences on contemporary Egyptian culture, she sees an image of Nut, the "woman-cow" who, "with her body, formed a roof over the horizon" (275). The narrator tells us that something has "come over" Shagar, that she is "mesmerized by images that are nothing anymore except engravings on tombs" (276), yet it is clear that these images from the past, these specters, are important to Shagar. In fact, they are what allow her to feel some sense of resolution about the life she has led. The last lines of the novel show Shagar leaving the Suez Canal and returning to Cairo, where she will eventually die. "She wasn't sleeping, her mind wasn't wandering," the narra-tor says of Shagar as she prepares to return to Cairo. "Shagar was putting her house in order, setting her mind to rest. She got into the car and set out, back to Cairo" (277). Ultimately, Shagar has come to terms with the contradic-tions of her life—and the lives of other contemporary Egyptian women—and this reconciliation comes about through Shagar's encounter with the specters of ancient Egyptian culture. Though the novel ends with Shagar's death, an event that might appear to work against the concept of emancipation, it is clear that Shagar has lived the life of an emancipated woman, an intellectu-ally and financially independent woman who has been able to negotiate the demands of professional life, marriage, and motherhood, without succumb-ing to the demands of masculine authority. "Her cousins hated her indepen-dence . . . hated her capability in managing her own affairs," readers are told early in the novel (5). Unlike women of previous generations, constrained by gender expectations, Shagar has lived a relatively free life, even if she dies at the end of the novel.

Ashour's novel, then, illustrates well how contemporary Egyptian women writers' work significantly revises the work of the British women whom I have discussed in this book, and Ashour herself publicly discussed the difficulties Egyptian women face, as the history of imperialism continues to shape the place of Egypt (and Egyptian women) in the world. "I love writing," Ashour said in a 1992 interview with Caroline Seymour-Jorn, "because I love books and also because I fear . . . being buried alive . . . because I am a woman and a citizen of the third world, and the heritage of both is like that of the baby girl who is buried alive" (Seymour-Jorn 109). This heritage is further threatened, Ashour suggested in a 2007 interview with Seymour-Jorn, by the way imperialist powers have used Egypt in their wars with Eastern countries. "In 1991, when America bombed Iraq, Egypt was part of the Alliance. It was shown on TV, and we were supposed to be happy. But I was very depressed. Any intellectual or educated Egyptian person feels that Baghdad is part of our heritage" (109). It is evident from Ashour's remarks that Western influence still shapes Egyptian politics, yet, by placing the images of ancient Egyptian women in a contemporary context, in which Egyptian women are represented as active agents in the political landscape of Egypt, writers such as Ashour move beyond the stereotypes of Egyptian women that British women writers could not avoid, since they did not fully understand the position of Egyptian woman in their own time.

Ashour and Soueif, then, provide the strongest examples of modern Egyptian women writers' use of heritage imagery to address issues surrounding women's emancipation. Still, while Ashour's work does much to revise the visions for emancipation presented by British women writers, it might be argued that Ashour still relies on romanticized views of ancient Egypt to some degree: for example, by presenting Shagar as similar to the creation goddess Maat. Another important step for contemporary Egyptian women's writing is more thorough exposure of the stereotypes about Egyptian women perpetuated through a revival of heritage imagery, a gesture perhaps suggested but not fully pursued by Ashour when Shagar flees the university festival at which students wear costumes based on figures from ancient Egypt. Further, it might be argued that one weakness in Soueif's work is the upholding of domestic roles for women through these representations. While I believe I have shown that Soueif's novels do more than uphold domestic roles for women, it is important to recognize other Egyptian women writers who more overtly question stereotypes associated with ancient Egyptian women, even as they use this heritage imagery in their work. Poet Iman Mersal—who is associated with the 1990s group of poets *al-Garad* (*The Locusts*), was coeditor of the late-1980s feminist journal *Bint al-Ard* (*Daughter of the Earth*), and now teaches at the University of Alberta—perhaps more thoroughly suggests the importance of exposing stereotypes regarding ancient Egyptian women in her poems. While Mersal's translator, Khaled Mattawa, claims that Mersal's work is "not feminist in any traditional sense," he does believe it is "informed and emboldened by feminism," since it focuses on the "failure of ideologies" that result in the "oppression . . . of women within the context of overwhelming and intractable economic inequity and political corruption in Egypt" (ix). Further, Mersal herself has discussed the central dilemma for diasporic women in "Eliminating Diasporic Identities" (2008), a reflection on the ways in which diasporic individuals are pushed into fixed identities based on their migration experiences. Describing Milan Kundera's character Sabina in *The Unbearable Lightness of Being* as "a painter in diaspora . . . facing the imposition of a ready-made identity" (1581), Mersal writes: "I take Sabina's dilemma . . . as my point of entry in interrogating the possibilities and limitations of diasporic identities" (1581).

Although the diasporic experience often requires adaptation, adjustment, and fluidity, Mersal argues that it has come to assume a "search for identity," in which "the diasporic artist or writer is burdened with the imposition of a great number of ready-made identities circulating through the cultural and institutional discourses" (1581). For Mersal, it has been the pressure to speaker as a "representative voice" for certain groups that has frustrated her most: "What does it mean to be a writer who writes in Arabic, who grew up in an Arabic-speaking Islamic environment, who came to live in North America, but who sees herself not as an Arab American writer, not as a writer of color, not as a Muslim writer?" (1581). These questions indicate that refusal is one solution to the problem of imposition of fixed identities, yet Mersal makes it clear that she does not want to fall into the trap of an unthinking "refusenik" position, which she attributes to Irshad Manji, author of *The Trouble with Islam: A Muslim's Call for Reform of Her Faith* (2004), a book that has been the subject of much discussion since its publication. Describing Manji's 2006 visit to the University of Alberta, Mersal relays how the "self-proclaimed Muslim refusenik" gave a "historically and intellectually thin" speech, which had such a strong effect on faculty and students that Mersal found herself "forced" to "defend" Islam, something she had never been inclined to do (1585). This experience is just one in which Mersal realizes that even as she tries to avoid the fixed identities imposed on her as a diasporic person, she continually is pressured into such identities. Still, she continues to try to express "the hidden life or subjectivity that remains unseen in diaspora" (1586), and it is by exposing "failed ideologies," the aspect of her work Mattawa admires, that one can most effectively express this hidden life.

The exposure of failed ideologies, especially those that shape diasporic women's experiences, certainly is evident in "Reading the Past," one of several poems in *These Are Not Oranges, My Love* that features a woman professor of Egyptian heritage who has emigrated to North America. In this poem, readers can see how movement between East and West by a woman with a feminist perspective exposes the stereotypes about Eastern women perpetuated by Westerners. The poem begins with the provocative statement, "By the way, how do you free yourself from being dominated by a dead body?" (1). Taking up this question, which Eastern women face as they move West, Mersal focuses on the woman speaker's relationship with a student, who seems to be romantically pursuing her through intellectual conversation. "He touched the head of a Cleopatra strung up on a chain around her neck" (9), writes Mersal of the student, who has touched the pendant on a necklace worn by the professor (37–38). The professor interprets this act of touching the pendant of Cleopatra's head as an attempt on the part of the student to "understand her" (36), as they talk about the "difference between history and memory" (70). Still, to the professor, the head of Cleopatra does not seem particularly significant: although it was given to her by a former lover, a "young novelist" who "snared around her neck / . . . a symbol of her future life" (37–38), it is a symbol that can easily be replaced by another "corpse," that of the student, who will "hang himself," so she can "dangle him where Cleopatra's head used to be" (74).

In exposing the stereotypes that Western men use to "understand" Eastern women, the professor also rejects the idea that "history depends on antiquities" (4), a rejection similar to that made by Shagar in Ashour's *Specters* when she leaves the university festival at which students wear stereotypical Egyptian costumes. Though the speaker in Mersal's poem does not offer a clear vision of what history is, she suggests that memory plays an important role in it, since those who leave one place for another, as she has, do not "leave their scents behind when they go through airport gates" (5). In other words, immigrants remain tied to their old culture in some way, but their pasts are more than just symbols, such as the Cleopatra pendant, that emerge when history depends only on antiquities. Egypt's history, Mersal suggests, is made up of the memories of individual Egyptians who have dispersed over the globe and who possess the "post-dislocational sensibility" to which Mattawa refers in his introduction to Mersal's collection.

A similar theme of memory influencing history emerges in another of Mersal's poems, "Why Did She Come?," in which the speaker, again a woman emigrant of Egyptian descent, comes to the "New World" as a "mummy," a "subject of spectacle / sleeping in her full ornament of gray gauze, / an imaginary life in a museum display case" (1–3). Although there is no direct reference to Cleopatra here, the link to Cleopatra's head in "Reading the Past" is suggested, since the speaker also feels herself to be a "corpse," who "did not choose migration" and, like other immigrants, still "dream of returning when they become corpses" (5–7). History based on antiquities is again presented as an incomplete understanding of how history actually works, since Mersal contrasts this mummy-woman who emigrated from Egypt to the immigrant woman she is now—living in the New World, buying "organic food" and residing on a street where access is only by "remote control" (31, 34). Still, the woman immigrant does feel a connection to her past and must negotiate this past by writing letters home that meet the expectations of family members still in the Old World (41–51). Again, history is more complex than the stereotypes of antiquities can encompass, and by revealing such stereotypes Mersal's poetry suggests that, when contemporary Egyptian women writers use ancient references, they may be relying on a romanticized view of Egypt, if only to a lesser degree than British women did.

Ultimately, modern Egyptian women writers such as Soueif and Ashour, who use heritage imagery to express women's struggles to construct their identities in a postcolonial world, make important contributions to a developing literary tradition that works against imperialist perspectives about Eastern women, but the contributions of writers such as Mersal, who work to expose stereotypes about Egyptian women, are equally important, since their contributions remind us of the continuing need to think critically about the imagery we use, especially in relation to the pressing issue of women's emancipation.

Afterword

Mersal's exposure of some of the problems associated with a return to heritage imagery begs the questions with which this book must conclude: Is every vision of women's emancipation, especially one that can include women of diverse ethnic backgrounds, reliant on romantic ideals? Is it the illusion of emancipation that drives the women's movement? And, is there a way to drive the movement when the illusion of emancipation is exposed, as it is in Mersal's work? Mattawa's argument that Mersal's work is "informed and emboldened by feminism" but "not feminist in any traditional sense" (ix) suggests that feminism *needs the exposure of illusion* present in Mersal's work, yet Badran and Cooke, in the introduction to the second edition of *Opening the Gates* (2004), argue that the women's movement also *needs the illusion of emancipation*, since it distinguishes literature devoted to addressing women's advancement from literature that might be more broadly interested in women but not necessarily interested in their advancement (and even, perhaps, interested in regression to a time when women were less valued) (xviii). Third-wave theorists, Badran and Cooke argue, initially rejected the notion that feminism, "niswiyya" in Arabic, was necessary in the postmodern world, but many theorists now recognize that they "*acted* as feminists who [enjoyed] the gains for which their feminist foremothers had fought" (xviii). The notion of acting as a feminist, even as some women decide not to declare themselves feminists when asked, provides a way to acknowledge the role of feminism in the postmodern world, where one can expose the illusion of emancipation yet still use that illusion as a strategy to be employed in order to advance women's cultural status.

In this context, then, the sometimes romanticized representations of Egyptian women by both of the groups of women writers discussed in this book—nineteenth-century British women and twentieth- and twenty-first-century Egyptian women—are necessary to understand the development of a fully feminist representation of Egyptian women (and a fully feminist representation of all women). The nineteenth-century British women writers whose work occupies the bulk of this book could only provide a limited, nationalist vision of women's emancipation, but a more fully internationalist feminist vision comes to fruition in the twentieth and twenty-first centuries through the work of Egyptian women writers, even as these writers themselves sometimes rely on romanticized representations. It is only by revising the representations of ancient Egyptian culture seen in the work of writers such as Florence Nightingale, George Eliot, Michael Field, and Elinor Glyn that recent Egyptian women writers have established their own visions of emancipation, which include women of color, and thus fill in the gaps left by nineteenth-century British women writers' visions. The literary-historical background laid out in this book, which traces the development of nationalist to internationalist feminism, can (and should) be used to advocate a more internationalist approach to women's issues, an important gesture in a period of world history where nationalism still contributes to gender inequality. Yet, even as this book provides this literary-historical background as a tool for future generations, it is evident that there is still more work to be done as feminism continues to evolve in the twenty-first century. Ultimately, the more fully feminist representation of Egyptian women (and all women) must recognize that there is an illusory aspect of women's emancipation—as Mersal's work suggests—and yet still deploy this illusion in order to advance the status of women.

Notes

Introduction

1. This project is concerned with *white* British women writers' encounters with ancient Egyptian women. Although there were a few British women of color writing during this time period, most notably Mary Seacole, the overwhelming majority of women writers were white. For ease of reading, when I refer to white British women writers, I will simply identify them as British women writers, with the understanding that I am referring to white women.

2. I define "emancipation" according to key elements of woman's agency—the ability to think, speak, and act for oneself—which I discuss in my first book, *Feminist Realism at the Fin de Siècle: The Influence of the Woman's Press on the Development of the Novel* (2007). These elements came to define late-twentieth-century feminism, especially second-wave feminism of the 1970s, but they can be traced back through the nineteenth and eighteenth centuries, via writers such as John Stuart Mill and Mary Wollstonecraft. Although these writers did not use the term "feminism," which according to the *Oxford English Dictionary* came into use in 1895, they articulated principles that advocated the improvement of women's cultural status and built the foundation for what came to be known as "feminism."

    In this study, I use the term "emancipation" to signify a commitment to the principles of *liberal* feminism. While this form of feminism has rightly been critiqued by third-wave feminists, liberal feminism is relevant to an historical study of nineteenth-century British women writers, since advocates for the improvement of women's cultural status used liberal feminist principles to articulate their goals. Still, this study recognizes that not all the women writers included in this study embraced liberal feminism fully: Glyn, for example, had a distinctly different definition of emancipation, which focused on a "spiritual union" between man and woman. Each woman writer's perspective on emancipation is discussed more fully in the chapter about her work.

3. In this study, I define "Eastern" primarily through examples from Egyptian culture, but a variety of other cultures are relevant as well. As we will see in my chapter on Nightingale, India especially was a key site for British women writers to negotiate their encounters with Eastern women. Much critical work has been done on these encounters: for example, the aforementioned work by Antoinette

Burton and the work by Gayatri Spivak and Sara Suleri discussed in Chapter 1. Except in the case of Nightingale, whose writing about Indian women is central to understanding her encounters with Egyptian women, I do not discuss other Eastern cultures in detail, but of course, Britain's relationships with these cultures informed writers' assumptions about Eastern women, and the "color" of Eastern women was a factor in how British women writers defined "Eastern." See note 4 for more detail about this issue, especially as it pertains to Egyptian women.

4. Although some scholars have argued that ancient Egyptians did not see themselves as "people of color," viewing themselves as "white" rather than "black," I follow Jan Marsh's lead in *Black Victorians: Black People in British Art, 1800–1900* (2003), where she includes nineteenth-century Egyptian women in the broad identity category of "women of color," a category that has provided women of African, Asian, and other non-European descent political power in the twentieth and twenty-first centuries. Marsh's book includes discussion of "[i]ndividuals from North Africa . . . except where an Arab or Turkish identity is plainly intended" (14) as people of color and devotes an entire chapter, "Observations and Interpretation: Travelling Artists in Egypt," to representations of Egyptians of color by European artists. While the focus of this chapter is Nubian Egyptians, who are thought to have been closest to black Africans in terms of physical characteristics, the author of this chapter, Briony Llewellyn, stresses that Egypt was "racially and socially diverse" (40), suggesting that Egyptians of non-Nubian descent might also be considered people of color.

Still, I recognize that debate over the ethnic origins of ancient Egyptians has been and continues to be complicated. In the nineteenth century, white British men such as George Gliddon and Samuel Morton argued that ancient Egyptians were "white." Gliddon, in *Ancient Egypt: Her Monuments, Hieroglyphics, History, and Archaeology* (1844), wrote that Egyptians were "of no darker hue than a pure Arab, a Jew, or a Phoenician" (46), and Morton, who obtained human skulls from Gliddon for his own studies, made a similar argument in *Crania Aetgyptiaca, or Observations on Egyptian Ethnography* (1844). Nevertheless, as some of the sources discussed in Chapter 1 show, other nineteenth-century figures, such as Frederick Douglass, believed that contemporary Egyptians had ethnic ties to Africa and might be considered "black."

Most recently, debate over the ethnic origins of ancient Egyptians has focused on Martin Bernal's claim, in *Black Athena: The Afroasiatic Roots of Classical Civilization* (1987), that ancient Egyptians have Asian and African roots and that this knowledge should change not just our understanding of ancient Egyptian but also ancient Greek culture. Mary Lefkowitz's response to Bernal's claim in *Not Out of Africa: How Afrocentricism Became an Excuse to Teach Myth as History* (1996) is well known. Lefkowitz argues that Bernal's claim is based on myth rather than history and that evidence suggesting Egyptian culture had influenced Greek culture can be traced to other sources. Bernal and Lefkowitz have continued to debate this topic in books such as Bernal's *Black Athena Writes Back: Martin Bernal Responds to His Critics* (2001) and Lefkowitz's *History Lesson:*

A Race Odyssey (2008), and other scholars have elaborated on this debate in books such as Jacques Berlinerblau's *Heresy in the University: The Black Athena Controversy and the Responsibilities of American Intellectualism* (1999) and Molefi Kele Asante and Ama Mazama's *Egypt vs. Greece and the American Academy: The Debate Over the Birth of Civilization* (2002).

5. The conflation of Arab and Muslim cultures in British imperialist discourse is problematic, of course. Where I use the term "Arab/Muslim" in this study, it is only to signify the conflation of these cultures during the nineteenth century, not to suggest that the two cultures should be conflated.

Chapter 1

1. Like Nightingale, whose judgments about such images I discuss in Chapter 2 of this book, Edwards had distinct preferences about the images she saw. She was "fascinate[ed]" with "mother figures" such as Isis and Hathor but was "repulse[d]" by the "femme fatale" image of Cleopatra at Dendera (142). Although I certainly could have included additional analysis of Edwards's work in this book, since Edwards was concerned with women's emancipation and sometimes uses fictional elements while writing about Egypt, I have chosen to focus on Nightingale instead, since Edwards's work on Egypt has already been well discussed.

   For more about Edwards's writing about Egypt, see Patricia O'Neill's introduction to "The Social and Political Position of Woman in Ancient Egypt," which details how Edwards used ancient Egyptian marriage contracts to argue that nineteenth-century Englishwomen were oppressed (844–45), and O'Neill's "Destination as Destiny: Amelia B. Edwards's Travel Writing" (2009), which discusses how Edwards, in *A Thousand Miles Up the Nile*, moved away from "literary" views of the East, such as those found in the "personal accounts of gentleman travelers such as William Thackeray and Alexander Kinglake" (59), but still incorporated the more "personal" aspects of travel accounts that were appealing to readers (67).

   Joan Rees highlights Edwards's ability to combine fictional and nonfictional forms in *Amelia Edwards: Traveller, Novelist and Egyptologist* (1998), by comparing Edwards's essay, "The Story of Tanis" (1886), to her 1864 novel *Barbara's History*. In "The Story of Tanis," which details Flinders Petrie's excavation of the ancient Greek city located on the Nile delta, Edwards uses a fictional "stranger" who visits Tanis and "witnesses a procession in honour of . . . Rameses II" (58) to write about Tanis in a manner that makes readers feel as though they are in the city during ancient times. This technique of placing a character in the position of seeing an event that happened centuries ago also appears in *Barbara's History*, when Barbara travels to Tivoli, where "she astonishes her companion by a dazzling description of a scene in Hadrian's Villa as vivid and intimate as though she were personally present in the past of eighteen hundred years ago" (58).

2. The most commonly cited critiques of Said's theory are Dennis Porter's "*Orientalism* and Its Problems" (1983), Aijaz Ahmad's "*Orientalism* and After" (1992), and

John Mackenzie's *Orientalism: History, Theory, and the Arts* (1995). While these critiques should be acknowledged, more helpful to this project are those works that expand and complicate Said's theory in substantial ways. Spivak's "Can the Subaltern Speak?" expands Said's theory to examine the fragmented nature of the colonized subject, especially the colonized woman, since Spivak shows how discourse about the Indian practice of *suttee* serves as an example of how "There is no space from which the sexed subaltern can speak" (103). In reading about the outlawing of *suttee* by the British, justified as the "protection" of Indian women from Indian men, Spivak asserts: "One never encounters the testimony of the women's voice-consciousness. . . . As one goes down the grotesquely mistranscribed names of these women, the sacrificed widows[,] . . . one cannot put together a 'voice'" (93).

Like Spivak, Suleri expands and complicates Said's theory using India as an example, but with more emphasis on the role allegory plays in Western depictions of the East. Arguing that Western allegories that "other" colonial subjects, both in nineteenth-century literature and in twentieth-century theoretical works, prevent readers from seeing a full representation of the colonized subject, Suleri writes: "Much like the category of the exotic in the colonial narratives of the prior century, contemporary critical theory names the other in order that it need not be further known; more crucially, alteritism [the process of othering] represses the detail of cultural factivity by citing otherness as a universal trope, thereby suggesting that the discursive site of alterity is nothing other than the familiar and unresolved confrontation between the historical and allegorical" (16).

Spivak and Suleri are especially helpful to this project, since they take up the problem of women colonial subjects and consider the nonrepresentation and allegorizing of such subjects in literature. Equally helpful is Homi Bhabha's *The Location of Culture*, although Bhabha takes a very different approach to Orientalism. Bhabha argues that there is room for colonial subjects to resist Western nonrepresentation and allegorization, particularly through the concept of "mimicry," in which the colonized is empowered by returning or refusing to return the colonizer's gaze. "The menace of *mimicry*," writes Bhabha, "is its *double* vision which in disclosing the ambivalence of colonial discourse also disrupts its authority" (88). Bhabha's emphasis on more complex relations between colonizer and colonized suggests that although it may be very difficult for the subaltern to speak, there are moments in which resistance is possible, and this possibility allows for greater flexibility in interpreting literary texts.

Marilyn Butler confirms that flexibility in interpretation is important in "Orientalism" (1994), in which she argues that Western fictional narratives about the East are "rich in metaphor, allegory and myth" (398). Butler acknowledges the problem Suleri points out, that allegorization results in romanticized visions of the East, but she also shows how allegorizing narratives nevertheless expose the complexity of romanticized visions. Since the texts discussed in this book contain romanticized visions, Butler's point is a helpful reminder that my own literary analysis should not be reductive and can draw on Bhabha's understanding of how Orientalism works, even as my overarching point may be closer to that of Said, Spivak, and Suleri.

3. It is worth noting the attention given to Aphrodite, or Venus as I will refer to her most of the time in this book, by these writers. It also is worth noting other Greek goddesses associated with love, marriage, and childbirth. As I discuss in more detail in my chapter about Field, the oldest known artistic representation of Venus is Praxiteles's fourth century BCE statue *Aphrodite of Knidos*, which is believed to have been destroyed in a fire in the fifth century CE but is remembered through a number of variants, including the *Venus de Milo*, the *Venus de Medici*, and the *Venus Capitoline* (Havelock 9, 1). The earliest literary representations of Venus are found in second century BCE poetry, which expresses appreciation for Praxiteles's statue (3). Through these artistic and literary representations, and the many representations from later centuries, Venus came to be known as the goddess of love, beauty, and sexuality, someone whose beauty was "divine" and who could assist others facing difficult love situations (8).

   The prominence of references to Venus by British women writers is not surprising, given that Venus was central to nineteenth- and twentieth-century discussions about women's agency, the power over one's relationship to other people and cultural institutions. Whether Venus should be seen as a powerful woman because of her ability to control love situations or whether she is a more submissive figure because of her supposedly "modest" pose, her hands covering her genitals in some artistic representations of her, has been well debated by critics. Christine Havelock's discussion of this debate, in *The Aphrodite of Knidos and Her Successors: A Historical Review of the Female Nude in Greek Art* (1995), is most helpful in recognizing that Venus's "shame" is a nineteenth-century construct, advanced by the Swiss archaeologist J. J. Bernoulli and followed by many nineteenth-century artists who represented her (22–27). Yet, as we will see in my chapter about Field, many British women writers saw Venus as possessing great power, rejecting Bernoulli's notion that she should feel guilty about her sexuality.

   In addition to Venus, British women writers found other ancient Greek goddesses relevant to their concerns, including Diana (goddess of hunting but also the moon and childbirth), Hebe (goddess of youth who also assists brides), and Hera (goddess who oversees consummation of marriage). All of these women are associated to some degree with the roles women play in love and marriage, so it makes sense that they would appeal to nineteenth-century women writers, who were living in a culture that strongly emphasized women's roles as wives and mothers, even as these writers worked to transform roles for women.

4. With chapters about how Brontë, Anna Jameson, Nightingale, and Eliot "amalgamated" women figures from multiple religious traditions to show Victorian women writers' desire for a "feminine divine" (68, 18), Houston's book is also relevant to some of the other points I make in this book. My argument differs from Houston's by placing emphasis on the disruption of this amalgamation, caused by the prevalence of imperialist attitudes in the Victorian period. While Houston shows the many instances of merging diverse women figures, I show the limits of such amalgamation, which is illustrated in British women writers' reluctance to incorporate their knowledge of Egyptian goddesses directly into their writing about emancipation.

Chapter 2

1. She also consulted Samuel Sharpe's *History of Egypt* series (1838, 1842, 1846), Christian Carl Josias von Bunsen's *Egypt's Place in Universal History* (1848), and George Gliddon's works, which included *An Appeal to the Antiquaries of Europe on the Destruction of the Monuments of Egypt* (1841), *Ancient Egypt* (1843), and *The Nile: Its Ancient Monuments, Its Modern Scenery* (1849) (Vallée, *Florence Nightingale on Mysticism* 124).

2. In Suggestions for Thought *by Florence Nightingale: Selections and Commentaries* (1994), Calabria and Macrae argue that Nightingale's understanding of Egyptian notions about "good" and "evil" influenced her discussion of "sin and evil" in *Suggestions for Thought* (79), and her comments about the Holy Trinity were shaped by her recognition of a similar triad in ancient Egyptian thought (129).

3. As they traveled, Selina created images that complement the written descriptions of specific places in Nightingale's letters. Her watercolors are reprinted in Calabria's *Florence Nightingale in Egypt and Greece: Her Diary and "Visions"* (1997).

4. This clearly is a rationalization, since Raphael completed the Dresden Madonna nearly five years before he finished *La Fornarina*.

5. For example, when describing the busts of ancient Greeks and Romans at the Capitoline Museum in Rome, Nightingale categorizes these busts according to nationality and seems to privilege Greek and English phrenological profiles over Roman ones (167). She also applies physiognomical hierarchies to real-life women when she and Liz Herbert, wife of the English statesman Sidney Herbert, visit Adelaid Kemble Sartoris, stating that one woman's head is "the perfection of the feminine type," another's "the angelic type," and yet another's "the expressive type" (224). While all the women Nightingale assesses during her visit to Sartoris are English, she also assesses women of other nationalities, whom she meets at one of the hospitals she visits. The French nuns of Saint-Vincent-de-Paul at the Conservatorio are "so different from the grubby nuns I have seen at the other places or from anything Roman—nice clean merry active clear-complexioned, clear-starched, clear-minded women. . . . The Romans evidently not fit for the task" (224).

6. Rarely does Nightingale comment on peasant women, choosing instead to focus on women in harems, which attracted the interest of upper-class British women travelers. One exception occurs when she explores the tombs at Lycopolis and comments that government control of agricultural prices "leaves the wretched fellah nothing but taxes to live upon" (205). The female equivalent of the fellah, she adds, is "dirty beyond description" and uses her "one veil as a basket," but still is part of "a noble-looking race" (205).

7. Sara Salih, in her introduction to Seacole's *The Wonderful Adventures of Mrs Seacole in Many Lands* (1857), details how women of color such as Seacole were denied the opportunity to travel to the Crimea with the government-supported group led by Nightingale (xxviii). Although Seacole presents her interactions with Nightingale in positive terms in her narrative, an 1870 letter from Nightingale to her brother-in-law Sir Harry Verney, marked *Burn*, reveals that

Nightingale did not think positively about Seacole (180). The letter also indicates Nightingale thought a "shameful or ignorant imposture" had been made on Queen Victoria, who contributed to a fund set up to support Seacole after the war (180). Still, Mark Bostridge's recent biography indicates that Nightingale herself may have contributed to the fund she criticizes in the letter, and she purportedly told Alexis Soyer, the French chef who helped improve the kitchens at Scutari, that she wanted to meet Seacole before she left the Crimea because Seacole had "done a great deal of good for the poor soldiers" (274).

8. Poovey explains that Nightingale was typical of her class in that she saw nurses as incapable of caring for people properly, and she made it her goal to train women of all classes in the ideal qualities for a nurse (174, 180). According to Poovey, Nightingale advocated accepting a number of upper-class ladies into nurse training programs to ensure that working-class women would be "respectable" (180), but Lynn McDonald, in *The Collected Works of Florence Nightingale: Florence Nightingale on Women, Medicine, Midwifery and Prostitution* (2005), provides evidence from Nightingale's letters she firmly rejected the idea that upper-class "ladies" were better suited for nursing (91).

9. Showalter claims that Nightingale cut the details in 1858 at the suggestion of Benjamin Jowett, who likely did not accept Nightingale's "angry feminist message" (*Female Malady* 66), but McDonald indicates that Jowett did not read the text until after it had been printed in 1860 (*Florence Nightingale's* Suggestions for Thought 32). Though Jowett did suggest revisions, they mostly regarded style and the theological issues presented in the text (37–40).

Chapter 3

1. See my article "'Narrative readings of the images she sees': Principles of Nineteenth-Century Narrative Painting in George Eliot's Fiction" (2015), which lays out how Eliot developed a narrative way of seeing while analyzing visual art during her travels and then translated this way of seeing into her fiction via narrative-oriented character portraits.

2. Zimmerman, in "Gwendolen Harleth and 'The Girl of the Period'" (1980), argues that Gwendolen is a "Girl of the Period," the independent woman satirized by Eliza Lynn Linton in her 1868 articles in the *Saturday Review*. In using this type as a model, Eliot "created her most rebellious and egoistic heroine, her most dreadful punishment, and her most rigorous renunciation to illustrate how serious had become the problem of women's needs and duties" (197). Rose, in "The Englishness of a Gentleman: Illegitimacy and Race in *Daniel Deronda*" (2007), argues that Gwendolen is fashioned in the tradition of Guinevere, who might be seen as a "queen with resistant subjectivity," as she was interpreted by William Morris in his 1858 poem "The Defence of Guenevere" (126).

3. Felicia Bonaparte, Shanyn Fiske, Isobel Hurst, and Hilary Mackie all have discussed Eliot's understanding of the influence of Eastern culture on the West in relation to Eliot's use of classical Greek in her works. Barbara Hardy, in *George*

Eliot: A Critic's Biography (2006), and Brenda McKay, in *George Eliot and Victorian Attitudes to Racial Diversity, Colonialism, Darwinism, Class, Gender, and Jewish Culture and Prophecy* (2003), have discussed the development of Eliot's thinking about Eastern origins of Western culture primarily with an eye to her understanding of race and ethnicity, and John Clark Pratt and Victor A. Neufeldt have focused on Eliot's appreciation of Eastern culture in relation to her engagement with history and philosophy.

4. Acknowledging Eliot's understanding of the influence of Greek mythology on Victorian values, critics such as Felicia Bonaparte and Hilary Mackie, in "Ancient Paradigms, Modern Texts: Classical Keys to George Eliot's Mythologies" (2002) and "The Key to Epic Life?: Classical Study in George Eliot's *Middlemarch*" (2009), respectively, have shown how Eliot used Antigone and other Greek women in her portrayals of Maggie Tulliver and Dorothea Brooke.

5. In an 1840 letter to her teacher and friend Maria Lewis, Eliot reports reading Sarah Lewis's anonymously published *Woman's Mission*, which attempted to translate the ideas found in the French writer Louis Aimé-Martin's *De l'education des meres de famille, ou las civilisation du genre humain par les femmes* (1834). Though only a month later Eliot was reading Aimé-Martin's book and pronounced that it was "the real Greece" whereas *Woman's Mission* had "only imported to us a few marbles" (1:72), she initially recommended *Woman's Mission* to Lewis and "all [her] married friends," since it was "the most philosophical and masterly" discussion of the subject she had seen (1:66).

Eliot's letters also provide evidence of her reading of Mill's *The Subjection of Women*. In 1867, when Mill was in the midst of pushing for a women's suffrage amendment to the Second Reform Act, Eliot wrote to John Morley, editor of the *Fortnightly Review*, about the articles he was running in favor of Mill's amendment, affirming that she "would not oppose any plan which held out any reasonable promise of tending to establish as far as possible an equivalent of advantages for two sexes" (4:364). In the same month, she wrote to her friend Clementia Taylor that she "sympathise[d]" with her "desire to see women socially elevated" and hoped "for much good from a serious presentation of women's claims before Parliament," especially after Mill's "sober and judicious" speech in Parliament (4:366). Finally, in July 1869, she told her friend and feminist Barbara Bodichon that she had read *The Subjection of Women*. Though she thought Chapters 3 and 4 could be strengthened, she believed Chapter 2 "excellent" (8:458).

It is not clear precisely when Eliot read Wollstonecraft's *A Vindication of the Rights of Woman*, but her copy, part of the George Henry Lewes library trusted to Dr Williams, is "heavily marked" (Wiesenfarth, *A Writer's Notebook* 145). Likely, Eliot read it in 1855, when she reviewed it, as well as Margaret Fuller's *Woman in the Nineteenth Century* (1845), for the *Leader*. Fuller mentions Wollstonecraft in her book (62), and it is possible that this mention by Fuller prompted Eliot to read Wollstonecraft and include it in the review.

6. Recent Catholic encyclopedias, such as *The HarperCollins Encyclopedia of Catholicism* (1995), doubt Barbara's existence entirely (McBrien 139).

7. Alicia Carroll's reading of the novel in *Dark Smiles: Race and Desire in George Eliot* (2003) suggests this manner of understanding Gwendolen's character, since Carroll argues that Eliot uses Eastern references, especially from *A Thousand and One Nights*, to explore the desire felt by Daniel, Gwendolen, and Mirah. Still, Carroll focuses on Daniel and Mirah, so Gwendolen's identification with the East is less thoroughly discussed in Carroll's reading.

   Patrick Brantlinger also suggests Gwendolen is drawing on a romanticized form of Orientalism. Though Brantlinger focuses solely on Daniel, arguing that Daniel's "discovery" of his Jewish identity is an example of a "romantic nationalism" based on the "liberation from provincial confinement" that relies on "'oriental' mystery" (268–69), the notion of romantic nationalism might also be applied to Gwendolen's view of herself as a queen of the East.

8. A. S. Byatt, in her conversation with the psychoanalyst Ignês Sodré in *Imagining Characters: Six Conversations about Women Writers* (1997), points out that the serpent image can also refer to Lilith, the Jewish equivalent of Eve (86). Certainly, Eliot was aware of Lilith's place in the Jewish tradition, since she copied passages about Lilith from Johann Eisenmenger's *Entdecktes Judenthum* (1711) into her *Daniel Deronda* notebooks and wrote, "Lilith, Adam's first wife, came to him against his will, & they were always wretched together. . . . Of her in 130 years Adam begat the giants, devils, genii, witches. She was called the crooked snake. Was chased away (or dissolved herself?) into the air by the Shem-hamphorasch" (59).

9. Stanhope, the niece of Prime Minister William Pitt the Younger, ran her unmarried uncle's household until his death in 1806. After his death, she traveled extensively and, in the 1820s and 1830s, lived in Djoun, a village in modern-day Lebanon where she provided refuge for people fleeing tyrannical rulers. Known as "Queen of the East," she had enough power over the area around Djoun that Ibrahim Pasha sought her assistance when his father, Muhammad Ali Pasha, Ottoman ruler of Egypt beginning in 1811, sent him to invade Syria in 1832 (Childs 192–93).

10. This characterization by Hennell echoes John Morley's comment in the *Saturday Review* that Romola was a "goddess"—in fact, "too much of a goddess to make it fair play for such a weak mortal as Tito to have to love her" (211).

11. Meyrick pushes Daniel to tell Gwendolen about his proposal to Mirah, saying, "You monster! . . . do you want [Gwendolen] to wear weeds for *you* all her life—burn herself in perpetual suttee while you are alive and merry?" (685–86). While Meyrick's comment may be a reenactment of the typical imperialist discourse about *suttee*, which Spivak exposes in "Can the Subaltern Speak?," his comment prompts Daniel to come clean and allows Gwendolen to realize she cannot depend on Daniel anymore.

12. Among those critics who have brought attention to Daniel's role as Christian priest are Bonaparte, in *"Daniel Deronda*: Theology in a Secular Age" (1993), and Kirstie Blair, in "Priest and Nun?: Daniel Deronda, Anti-Catholicism and the Confessional" (2001). Other critics have referred to Daniel in less overtly

Christian terms, calling him a "moral guide" but still seeing him perform a role similar to that of Christian priest, as in Timothy Pace's "Who Killed Gwendolen Harleth?: *Daniel Deronda* and Keats's 'Lamia'" (1988). Still others have referred to him as anticipating Freud's psychoanalytic therapist, as in Eugene Hollahan's "Therapist or the Rapist?: George Eliot's *Daniel Deronda* as a Pre-Freudian Example of Psychoanalysis in Literature" (1984).

Still, the problems with reading Daniel as a guide, of whatever form, for Gwendolen have been pointed out by Jeanette Shumaker, who, in "The Alcharisi and Gwendolen: Confessing Rebellion" (1991), argues that Gwendolen's and Daniel's mother's confessions point to the Victorian notion that women's "rebelliousness" was "a sin" (55). More recently, Rachel Hollander, in "*Daniel Deronda* and the Ethics of Alterity" (2009), shows that Daniel's role as Gwendolen's guide might be problematic by arguing that Eliot uses Daniel's relationship with Gwendolen to show the limits of the realist novel's ability to "represent and account fully for Gwendolen's identity in the narrative" (270), a comment suggesting that Gwendolen's identity is restrained by the restrictions Daniel places on her.

Chapter 4

1. Bradley and Cooper further complicate how Alexandrine culture might be defined when they write, at the end of the 1895 volume of their journal, notes about Friedrich Nietzsche's *The Birth of Tragedy* (1872). Here, in Cooper's hand, are notes about the three forms of culture that Nietzsche defines in this work, with Alexandrine, or Socratic, culture as one of the three forms. In this sense, Alexandrine culture is defined in relation to the Classical period, and its approach survives in the modern world, which has as its "model" the "Theoretic Man (Socrates)" and as its "product . . . poetry founded in learning" (Ms. 46784).

2. Use of pronouns when discussing Field's work is complicated, but it is a widely accepted practice to refer to Field as "they," since both Bradley and Cooper are represented by Field.

   Further, whether to refer to Bradley and Cooper by their given names or as Field is complicated. When discussing the creative work produced by Bradley and Cooper, I will refer to them as Field, since most critics think of Field as an authorial persona constructed by Bradley and Cooper. When quoting the collaborative journals, I will refer to them as Bradley and Cooper, even though it could be argued that, since they intended that the journals be published, they were developing a persona here as well. When their views on a particular topic differ in the journals, I indicate this distinction by attributing the ideas either to Bradley or to Cooper, to make their differences of opinion clear.

3. Ana Parejo Vadillo, in "*Sight and Song*: Transparent Translations and a Manifesto for the Observer" (2000), argues that, with *Sight and Song*, Field resisted Berenson's instruction by revising Walter Pater's "sensorial epistemology," in which the subjective view of the art observer creates meaning to the aesthetic experience: Field's new epistemology accounts for a wider range of observers,

particularly the lesbian observer, and through their "transparent translation" of works of art into poetry in *Sight and Song*, they create a "sexualized observer," who is better able to identify with the women figures in the paintings (15–16).

Jill Ehnenn builds upon Vadillo's argument in "Looking Strategically: Feminist and Queer Aesthetics in Michael Field's *Sight and Song*" (2004), explaining the specific ways in which the sexualized, lesbian observer identifies with the objects in the paintings featured in *Sight and Song*. Ehnenn shows that this observer identifies with the women figures through homoerotic and autoerotic imagery but also with the feminized men in the paintings, such as St. Sebastian and the young male dancer in Antoine Watteau's *L'Indifferent*. Bradley and Cooper thereby critique Victorian gender ideology more fully than they might otherwise, since identifying with figures of both sexes creates stronger gender subversion (214).

Finally, Hilary Fraser, in "A Visual Field: Michael Field and the Gaze" (2006), more thoroughly accounts for Bradley and Cooper's collaboration under their male pseudonym, asserting that it is a "binocular" gaze Field uses to revise the more "monocular," masculine gaze that Berenson employed, even as he attempted collaborative aesthetic viewing with women such as Bradley, Cooper, and Costelloe (554). Because Bradley and Cooper were more successful in achieving a binocular gaze, their poetry expresses emotion toward the women objects they observe, an activity influenced by female aesthetes Vernon Lee and Kit Anthruser-Thomson's experiments with physiological aesthetics, in which the observer experiences a physical reaction to the painting (557).

4. We know Cooper and Bradley were familiar with Berenson's concept of tactile imagination, since Cooper assessed Robert Browning's son Pen's artistic ability according to this concept (Ms. 46783).

5. In "The Artist as Critic," Wilde argues that it is the artist who is best equipped to provide a critical view, since he is the one who can reinterpret art with "personality," rather than simply "repeat[ing] in another form a message that has been put into his lips to say" (336). Wilde acknowledges that the "literary critic" has a certain status in the critical world, since he has "the wider range and larger vision, and nobler material," but he also suggests that many other people can play the role of critic. "The actor is a critic of the drama. He shows the poet's work under new conditions, and by a method special to himself. . . . The singer or the player on lute and viol is the critic of music. . . . Sculpture, too, has its critic, who may be either the carver of a gem, as he was in Greek days, or some painter like Mantegna. . . . And in the case of all these creative critics of art it is evident that personality is an absolute essential for any real interpretation" (337).

6. Here, I assume Cooper is referring to portraits from the Morgue at Notre Dame, which she and Bradley would see in person in June 1892 while in Paris with Berenson. Regarding their visit to the Morgue, Berenson commented, "It is not Greek, it is morbid and shocking," but Cooper defended their decision to go, saying that "death is one of the facts of life, modernity reaches to all facts and includes them" (Ms. 46780).

7. In particular, critics have focused on how the poem based on Giorgione's *Sleeping Venus* has been characterized as offering the alternative of autoeroticism. Jill

Ehnenn and Krista Lysack, whose articles have already been mentioned in this chapter, as well as Julia F. Saville, author of "The Poetic Imaging of Michael Field" (2005), all point out the "autoeroticism" of the poem, which is especially evident in the description of Venus's left hand in lines 62–70: "Her hand the thigh's tense surface leaves, / Falling inward. Not even sleep / Dare invalidate the deep, / Universal pleasure sex / Must unto itself annex— / Even the stillest sleep; at peace, / More profound with rest's increase, / She enjoys the good / Of delicious womanhood."

Ehnenn argues that this stanza is "perhaps the only positive contemporary description of female masturbation" and results in a Venus that is "free from shame" (228). Lysack places the passage in a larger argument about "an economy of expenditures in which excess is valued over the utility of procreative sex," where Venus's autoeroticism allows her to avoid the "collecting and commodifying enterprise of masculine aestheticism" (952). Saville explains how this stanza is the last of three describing certain parts of Venus's body as "natural" because of their "harmony with the landscape," making the gesture of the left hand an affirmation for "the body's pleasure in itself," or "unapologetic onanism" (197).

8. Bradley's comments about Venus's eyes also are interesting in light of recent discoveries by art historians about Correggio's revisions to the painting. X-rays reveal Correggio changed the expression on Venus's face, beginning first with a look of affection toward Cupid but ultimately transferring that look to Mercury and giving Venus a more serious look (Ekserdjian 270). Art historians have seen Venus's serious look in the context of the male gaze and argue that Venus attempts to engage the viewer, bringing attention to her sexuality (270). Bradley's comments seem to anticipate this interpretation of the painting, while putting less emphasis on Venus as seducer and more on Venus as object of the male gaze.

9. Joanne Snow-Smith, in *The* Primavera *of Sandro Botticelli: A Neoplatonic Interpretation* (1993), details the ways in which Venus in *Spring* looks like a "medieval statue of the Madonna" and follows "Marian dress": "The white of her gown is regarded as the first of the liturgical colors, emblematic of virginity. . . . The golden 'virgin's girdle' encircling her breasts, an attribute of Mary in Christian art, perhaps had its literary provenance in Ovid's *Fasti*. . . . Draped over the right shoulder of the figure of Venus/Mary and held up by the left hand is a red mantle with a checkered pattern while the blue lining is decorated with a gold embroidery of a star or quatrefoil design. Red, the second of the Christian liturgical colors . . . designates her love for her Divine Son. Blue . . . is not one of the five liturgical colors . . . ; however, in Christian art, the Virgin is traditionally shown in a blue mantle . . . alluding to her role as Queen of Heaven" (228–29).

10. Fraser is one of the few critics who mentions it, discussing it as the poem in which Field identifies with "heterosexual lovers" and contrasting this identification with their affinity to the "homoerotic Sebastian," seen in their poems about Correggio's *Madonna of Saint Sebastian* and Antonello da Messina's *Saint Sebastian* (567).

11. Bradley and Cooper would later purchase a photograph of Giorgione's painting for Cooper's birthday in January 1892, and Cooper proudly states in the journal that it was the largest photograph in the house (Ms. 46780).

12. Before this, they had only published a volume of poetry and the verse drama *Bellephron* under the names Arran and Isla Leigh.

13. For more recent criticism than Sturgeon, see Vickie Taft's "*The Tragic Mary*: A Case Study in Michael Field's Understanding of Sexual Politics" (2001), Sharon Bickle's "Kick[ing] Against the Pricks: Michael Field's *Brutus Ultor* as Manifesto for the 'New Woman'" (2006), Wendy Bashant's "Aesthetes and Queens: Michael Field, John Ruskin, and *Bellerophôn*" (2006), Jennifer Krisuk's "Moving Beyond 'Michael Field': Identity Through Anonymity in *Borgia*" (2010), and Bickle's "Victorian Mænads: On Michael Field's *Callirrhoë* and Being Driven Mad" (2010).

Chapter 5

1. Vincent L. Barnett's "The Novelist as Hollywood Star: Author Royalties and Studio Income in the 1920s" (2008), for example, examines how Glyn's reputation as an author and member of British high society allowed her to negotiate for net royalties that resulted in percentages significantly higher than the 5 percent most screenwriters received (289). Barnett's "Picturization Partners: Elinor Glyn and the Thalberg Contract Affair" (2007) supplements this argument with details about why Glyn's literature, which is probably best described as middle brow, was so appealing to studio executives, especially Irving Thalberg (321). Glyn and Thalberg made a natural team, since both had enough experience with high art to raise the level of writing in Hollywood, while still having the commercial interests to ensure that the films they wrote and produced appealed to a wide audience.

    Other articles about Glyn and the film industry include Anne Morey's "Elinor Glyn as Hollywood Labourer" (2006), Annette Kuhn's "The Trouble with Elinor Glyn: Hollywood, *Three Weeks* and the British Board of Censors" (2008), and Laura Horak's "'Would you like to sin with Elinor Glyn?': Film as a Vehicle of Sensual Education" (2010). Morey focuses on the position of scriptwriters in early Hollywood and argues that the "male" model of scriptwriter as "the poor relation of the studio system" does not apply in the case of women scriptwriters (110). Women scriptwriters such as Glyn strategically gave up some of their writing and directorial power and developed their influence in other areas, such as "story conception," in order to become successful in the industry (110). Kuhn indicates how Glyn's success in the American film industry was possible in part because she allowed the film version to incorporate more action into the story than the novel had and focused her energy on making sure the scenes were as "sumptuous" as possible (26–28).

    Horak, who discovered a copy of the film version of *Three Weeks*, which was thought to have been lost, uses the film version to argue that Glyn employs film as a "vehicle of sensual education" to promote her sexual ideology of "spiritual communion," which was co-opted by a distorted version of Glyn's concept of animal magnetism. Following Morey's argument that Glyn had a "compliant conception of authorship," in which she exerted control over the execution of the scenes rather than the writing of them (77), Horak shows how Glyn educated actors (and therefore the audience) to understand a form of love that emphasized spiritual communion rather than physical sex (91–94). All of these articles make important points about Glyn's understanding of authorship as she made the transition from literature to film, but none provide detailed textual analysis of the novel *Three Weeks*, which is the focus of this chapter.

2. Glyn's memoir makes it clear she was middlebrow, since she did not aspire to literary greatness and did not perceive herself as part of the highbrow literary community. She had little interest in making sure her work was remembered for its literary qualities, a common motive for authors writing memoirs in the early twentieth century, who tried to ensure their work still would be read beyond their lifetimes. As I have written elsewhere, George Moore epitomizes the early twentieth-century author who sought to establish his literary reputation beyond his own lifetime. For more on this, see my article, "George Moore's Quest for Canonization and Esther Waters as Female Helpmate" (2003). In Glyn's memoir, there is little mention of the writing and publication process, and no mention of her literary contemporaries, except brief references to those who came to Hollywood at the same time she did but left quickly, after they realized commercial interests would dominate and they would not be able to retain authorial control over their work (292).

    Anthony Glyn, Elinor's grandson and first biographer, reinforces the idea that Glyn did not aspire to literary reputation and even played down her own literary accomplishments: for example, during her very short speech to PEN International in 1931, she characterized herself as "a mere amateur," who happened to "scribble for fun" and was lucky enough that "a foolish publisher printed it" (329). Assessing her relationship to her contemporaries, Anthony Glyn writes, "Elinor was at no time a member of a literary set. . . . The number of her fellow authors with whom she had had even a slight acquaintance can be numbered on the fingers of the hands. . . . This cutting herself off from the society of others who earned their living in the same way was largely Elinor's own doing. She had not much in common with her own contemporaries; she had not read their books or the books in which they were interested. It is doubtful, indeed, if she knew many of them even by name" (328).

3. Robins is known for her pro-suffrage play *Votes for Women*, and Peter Keating includes Robins with Glyn in his list of early twentieth-century sex novelists in *The Haunted Study: A Social History of the English Novel 1875–1974* (209).

4. Glyn attributes to the more moderate suffra*gists* what the more radical suffrag*ettes* were doing. The distinction between suffragists, who petitioned the Parliament to achieve the right to vote, and suffragettes, who staged more radical demonstrations, is an important one, examined thoroughly in Gertrude Colmore's novel, *Suffragette Sally* (1911).

5. Duff Gordon's translation of Gamela's name as "Black Beauty" is a racialized translation. Gamela, or Jamila as it is also spelled, simply means "beautiful" or "lovely."

6. I have not successfully identified this palace, but it may be the palace belonging to Princess Semiha Husayn, wife of Prince Ismail Daoud, since Glyn recounts

how the Princess supposedly "flashed" her eyes at European men and sent notes inviting them to the palace through her slaves, until the British government told Prince Ismail that the Princess had to stop her "pranks" (106).

7. Elinor and Clayton's marriage never seems to have been as romantic as Elinor wanted, primarily because the two had distinctly different personalities and expectations about what marriage would be. Anthony Glyn recounts how Clayton, a "country gentleman" who served as a village squire, expected Elinor to fit into his already established life in Essex, which she found "provincial and dull" (63). Though both of them enjoyed traveling, Clayton primarily wanted to spend his time in hotels and restaurants, while Elinor wanted to venture out and see historical sights (93). Still, Elinor and Clayton managed to tolerate their differences; Elinor pursued romantic relationships with other men but stayed with Clayton after she learned he had financially "ruined" the family with his extravagant spending (163). In 1913, their marriage finally ended, when Clayton moved out of the family house, unable to bear the "humiliation of his position" any longer (210).

8. I suspect Michael Field also knew these productions, since Katherine Bradley and Edith Cooper regularly attended the theatre at the time Sardou and Tree were staging their productions. In addition, their play *A Question of Memory* was unfavorably compared to Sardou's work in the *Speaker* in November 1893 (Anonymous, "The Drama" 494), and Cooper records in the journal a story about Tree told by Charles Ricketts at a New Year's dinner in 1901 (Thain and Vadillo, *Michael Field, the Poet* 271).

9. There is also a picture from Sardou's *Theodora*, in which Theodora and her lover, Andreas, die on a tiger skin draped over a couch (Salmon 153). Even if Glyn was not familiar with the tiger-skin rug from Tree's production of *Cleopatra*, she would have been familiar with it from this production.

10. Story's companion poem opens with Cleopatra waking from a dream about Antony. Although Cleopatra tries to enjoy the morning by listening to Charmian play the lute, she cannot get Antony out of her mind (21–22) and calls for her cockatoo to "shriek for Antony" to "come home!" (53–56). Though this Cleopatra is aggressive, threatening to break the neck of a gazelle because she is so anxious about being separated from Antony, she soon falls back into her dream world, where she becomes a "smooth and velvety tiger, / Ribbed with yellow and black, / Supple and cushion-footed" (81–83). Hearing Antony, in the form of a tiger, approach, she watches his tail, which is characterized as a serpent in line 111, and then meets him "as two clouds in heaven / When the thunders before them fly" (115–16). As tigers, Antony and Cleopatra make love so wildly that Antony sinks his teeth into her neck and draws blood (117–20). Finally, in the last stanza of the poem, Cleopatra comes out of her dream state and calls for Antony to come back to her, calling him her "hero," whom she hopes will "Take me with triumph and power, / As a warrior storms a fortress!" (141, 146–47). Though this Cleopatra may be a bit "barbaric" when making love, she is not barbaric in the sense Shakespeare and some Graeco-Roman historians saw

her—because she possessed political power. She waits for Antony to return and "take" her, rather than plotting about how she will seduce him.

11. Like Glyn's visit to the Sphinx in 1902, her trip to Paestum on the way home from Egypt had a profound impact on her. At the temple to Poseidon, she had what she refers to as a "vision" in *Romantic Adventure*: "I saw quite plainly a number of draped figures around me. They were dancing a strange dance, and I longed to join them. . . . The extraordinary, pagan, emotions which I remembered feeling when I saw Sarah Bernhardt act the part of Theodora overcame me once more" (111).

Works Cited

Ahmad, Aijaz. "*Orientalism* and After." *In Theory: Classes, Nations, Literature.* By Ahmad. London: Verso, 1992. 159–220.

Al-Zayyat, Latifa. "In Her Own Mirror." 1993. Sadiqi et al. 280–85.

Anonymous. "About What the Old Egyptians Knew." *Blackwood's Magazine* (Aug. 1870): 220–36.

———. "Art. V. *Monuments de l'Egypte et de la Nubie.*" *The Foreign Quarterly Review* 18 (1836): 110–20.

———. "Cleopatra: The Exhibition." *California Science Center.* 27 Dec. 2012.

———. "The Drama." *The Speaker* 4 Nov. 1893: 494–95.

———. "Elinor Glyn Talks About Her American Critics." *New York Times* 6 Oct. 1907: n. pag.

———. "Heidi Klum Wears Cleopatra Costume, 100s of Face Crystals at Haunted Holiday Party." *Us Weekly.* Web. 26 Dec. 2012. <http://www.usmagazine.com /celebrity-news/news/heidi-klum-wears-cleopatra-costume-100s-of-face-crystals -at-haunted-holiday-party-2012212>.

———. "On the Character of Cleopatra." *The Cornhill Magazine* 24 (1871): 344–59.

———. Rev. of *Daniel Deronda. Academy* 5 Feb. 1876: 120. Rpt. in *George Eliot: The Critical Heritage.* Ed. David Carroll. New York: Barnes and Noble, 1971. 360–62.

———. Rev. of *Daniel Deronda. Saturday Review* 16 Sept. 1876: 356–58. Rpt. in *George Eliot: The Critical Heritage.* Ed. David Carroll. New York: Barnes and Noble, 1971. 376–81.

———. Rev. of *Romola. Westminster Review* October 1863: 344–52. Rpt. in *George Eliot: The Critical Heritage.* Ed. David Carroll. New York: Barnes and Noble, 1971. 213–20.

Asante, Molefi Kele, and Ama Mazama, eds. *Egypt vs. Greece and the American Academy: The Debate Over the Birth of Civilization.* Chicago, IL: African American Images, 2002.

Ashcroft, Bill, Gareth Griffiths, and Helen Tiffin. *The Empire Writes Back: Theory and Practice in Post-Colonial Literatures.* 2nd ed. New York: Routledge, 2002.

Ashour, Radwa. *Specters.* Trans. Barbara Romaine. Northampton, MA: Interlink Books, 2011.

Avery, Simon, and Rebecca Stott. *Elizabeth Barrett Browning.* London: Longman, 2003.

Badran, Margot, and Miriam Cooke. Introduction. Badran and Cooke xxv–xlvii.

———. Introduction to the Second Edition. Badran and Cooke xv–xxi.

———, eds. *Opening the Gates: An Anthology of Arab Feminist Writing*. Bloomington: Indiana UP, 2004.

Baker, William. *George Eliot and Judaism*. Salzburg, Austria: Institut für Anglistik und Amerikanistik, 1975.

———. *The George Eliot-George Henry Lewes Library: An Annotated Catalogue of Their Books at Dr. Williams's Library, London*. New York: Garland Publishing, 1977.

Barnett, Vincent L. "The Novelist as Hollywood Star: Author Royalties and Studio Income in the 1920s." *Film History* 20 (2008): 281–93.

———. "Picturization Partners: Elinor Glyn and the Thalberg Contract Affair." *Film History* 19 (2007): 319–29.

Baron, Beth. *Egypt as a Woman: Nationalism, Gender, and Politics*. Berkeley: U of California P, 2005.

Barrett, Clive. *The Egyptian Gods and Goddesses: The Mythology and Beliefs of Ancient Egypt*. London: HarperCollins/Aquarian Press, 1992.

Bashant, Wendy. "Aesthetes and Queens: Michael Field, John Ruskin, and Bellerophôn." *The Journal of Pre-Raphaelite Studies* 15 (Spring 2006): 74–94.

Bate, Jonathan, and Eric Rasmussen, eds. *Antony and Cleopatra/William Shakespeare*. New York: Modern Library, 2009.

Berenson, Bernhard. *The Florentine Painters of the Renaissance with an Index to Their Works*. London: G. P. Putnam's Sons, 1896.

Berlinerblau, Jacques. *Heresy in the University: The Black Athena Controversy and the Responsibilities of American Intellectualism*. New Brunswick, NJ: Rutgers UP, 1999.

Bernal, Martin. *Black Athena: The Afroasiatic Roots of Classical Civilization*. New Brunswick, NJ: Rutgers UP, 1987.

———. *Black Athena Writes Back: Martin Bernal Responds to His Critics*. Durham, NC: Duke UP, 2001.

Bhabha, Homi. *The Location of Culture*. London: Routledge, 1994.

Bickle. Sharon. "Kick[ing] Against the Pricks: Michael Field's *Brutus Ultor* as Manifesto for the 'New Woman.'" *Nineteenth Century Theatre and Films* 33.2 (2006): 12–29.

———. "Victorian Mænads: On Michael Field's *Callirrhoë* and Being Driven Mad." *The Michaelian* (Dec. 2010): n. pag.

Bingham, Madeleine. *"The Great Lover": The Life and Art of Herbert Beerbohm Tree*. London: Hamish Hamilton, 1978.

Blair, Kirstie. "Priest and Nun? Daniel Deronda, Anti-Catholicism and the Confessional." *George Eliot Review: Journal of the George Eliot Fellowship* 32 (2001): 45–50.

Blind, Mathilde. *Birds of Passage: Songs of the Orient and Occident*. 1895. London: Chatto and Windus, 1896.

Bonaparte, Felicia. "Ancient Paradigms, Modern Texts: Classical Keys to George Eliot's Mythologies." *International Journal of the Classic Tradition* 8.4 (2002): 585–603.

———. "*Daniel Deronda*: Theology in a Secular Age." *Religion and Literature* 25.3 (1993): 17–44.

———. *The Triptych and the Cross: The Central Myths of George Eliot's Poetic Imagination*. New York: New York UP, 1979.

Bonomi, Joseph. *Nineveh and Its Palaces*. London: H. G. Bohn, 1857.

Booth, Marilyn. Introduction. *The Open Door*. By Latifa al-Zayyat. Trans. Booth. Cairo, Egypt: The American U in Cairo P, 2000. ix–xxxi.

———. Introduction. *Points of the Compass: Stories by Sahar Tawfiq*. Trans. Booth. Fayetteville: U of Arkansas P, 1995.

———. *May Her Likes Be Multiplied: Biography and Gender Politics in Egypt*. Berkeley: U of California P, 2001.

Bostridge, Mark. *Florence Nightingale: The Making of an Icon*. New York: Farrar, Straus and Giroux, 2008.

Brantlinger, Patrick. "Nations and Novels: Disraeli, George Eliot, and Orientalism." *Victorian Studies* 35 (1992): 255–75.

Brendel, Otto J. *Etruscan Art*. New Haven, CT: Yale UP, 1995.

Brontë, Charlotte. *Villette*. Ed. Mark Lilly. Intro. Tony Tanner. New York: Penguin, 1985.

Brown, John Russell. *Shakespeare/Antony and Cleopatra: A Case Book*. Rev. ed. London: Macmillan, 1991.

Browning, Elizabeth Barrett. *Aurora Leigh and Other Poems*. Eds. John Robert Glorney Bolton and Julia Bolton Holloway. New York: Penguin, 1995.

Browning, Robert, and Elizabeth Barrett Browning. *The Letters of Robert Browning and Elizabeth Barrett Browning 1845–46 with Portraits and Facsimiles*. Vol. 2. New York: Harper and Brothers, 1899.

Bulfin, Ailise. "The Fiction of Gothic Egypt and British Imperial Paranoia: The Curse of the Suez Canal." *English Literature in Transition, 1880–1920* 54.4 (2011): 411–43.

Burton, Antoinette. *Burdens of History: British Feminists, Indian Women, and Imperial Culture, 1865–1915*. Chapel Hill: U of North Carolina P, 1994.

Butler, Judith. *Gender Trouble*. New York: Routledge, 1990.

Butler, Marilyn. "Orientalism." *The Penguin History of Literature: The Romantic Period*. Ed. David B. Pirie. London: Penguin, 1994. 395–447.

Byatt, A. S., and Ignês Sodré. *Imagining Characters: Six Conversations About Women Writers*. Ed. Rebecca Swift. New York: Random House/Vintage, 1997.

Calabria, Michael D. *Florence Nightingale in Egypt and Greece: Her Diary and "Visions."* Albany: State U of New York P, 1997.

Calabria, Michael D., and Janet A. Macrae. Suggestions for Thought *by Florence Nightingale: Selections and Commentaries*. Philadelphia: U of Pennsylvania P, 1994.

Cariello, Marta. "Bodies Across: Ahdaf Soueif, Fadia Faqir, Diana Abu Jaber." *Arab Voices in Diaspora: Critical Perspectives on Anglophone Arab Literature*. Ed. Layla Al Maleh. New York: Rodopi, 2009. 313–38.

Carroll, Alicia. *Dark Smiles: Race and Desire in George Eliot*. Athens, OH: Ohio UP, 2003.

Caves, Terence. Introduction. *Daniel Deronda*. New York: Penguin, 1995. ix–xxxv.

Chakravorty, Mrinalini. "To Undo What the North Has Done: Fragments of a Nation and Arab Collectivism in the Fiction of Ahdaf Soueif." *Arab Women's Lives Retold: Exploring Identity Through Writing*. Ed. Nawar al-Hassan Golley. Syracuse, NY: Syracuse UP, 2007. 129–54.

Chapman, Alison, and Jane Stabler, eds. *Unfolding the South: Nineteenth-Century British Women Writers and Artists in Italy*. Manchester, England: Manchester UP, 2003.

Childs, Virginia. *Lady Hester Stanhope: Queen of the Desert*. London: Weidenfeld and Nicolson, 1990.

Chowdharay-Best, Elspeth. Letter to Molly Youngkin. 12 June 2011.

Cixous, Hélène. "Laugh of the Medusa." 1975. *Feminisms Redux: An Anthology of Literary Theory and Criticism*. Eds. Robyn Warhol-Down and Diane Price Herndl. New Brunswick, NJ: Rutgers UP, 2009. 416–31.

Coleman, Isobel. "'Blue Bra Girl' Rallies Egypt's Women vs. Oppression." 22 Dec. 2011. *CNN*. Web. 27 Dec. 2012. <http://www.cnn.com/2011/12/22/opinion /coleman-women-egypt-protest/index.html?iref=allsearch>.

Colmore, Gertrude. *Suffragette Sally*. 1911. Ed. Alison Lee. Peterborough, ON: Broadview P, 2008.

Corelli, Marie. *Ziska: The Problem of a Wicked Soul*. Kansas City, KS: Valancourt Books, 2009.

Curl, James Stevens. *The Egyptian Revival: Ancient Egypt as the Inspiration for Design Motifs in the West*. New York: Routledge, 2005.

David, Deidre. *Rule Britannia: Women, Empire, and Victorian Writing*. Ithaca, NY: Cornell UP, 1995.

Deane, Bradley. "Mummy Fiction and the Occupation of Egypt: Imperialist Striptease." *English Literature in Transition* 51 (2008): 381–410.

Dekel, Mikhal. "'Who Taught This Foreign Woman About the Ways and Live of the Jews?': George Eliot and the Hebrew Renaissance." *ELH* 74.4 (2007): 783–98.

Delyfer, Catherine. "New Woman Fiction, Gender and Empire: Egyptian Encounters and Subversions in Marie Corelli's *Ziska* (1896) and Victoria Cross's *Six Chapters of a Man's Life* (1903)." *Cross-Cultural Encounters between the Mediterranean and the English-Speaking Worlds*. Ed. Christine Reynier. New York: Peter Lang, 2011. 149–61.

Dick, Dr. H. A. "Cleopatra: A Biographical Sketch." *The Dublin University Magazine* (Feb. 1872): 229–40.

Donoghue, Emma. *We Are Michael Field*. Bath, England: Absolute P, 1998.

Dowling, Linda. *Hellenism and Homosexuality in Victorian Oxford*. Ithaca, NY: Cornell UP, 1994.

Duff Gordon, Lucy. *Discretions and Indiscretions*. New York: Frederick A. Stokes Co., 1932.

Duruy, Victor. *History of Greece and of the Greek People*. Boston, MA: Estes and Lauriat, 1892.

Ebers, George. *An Egyptian Princess*. 1864. Trans. Eleanor Grove. New York: Bigelow, Brown, and Co., Inc., 1880.

Edwards, Amelia B. *A Thousand Miles Up the Nile*. London: Longmans, Green, 1876.

Ehnenn, Jill. "Looking Strategically: Feminist and Queer Aesthetics in Michael Field's *Sight and Song*." *Victorian Poetry* 42 (2004): 213–43.

Ekserdjian, David. *Correggio*. New Haven, CT: Yale UP, 1997.

El Ghoul, Marwa. "Feminist Union Launches Campaign to Support 100 Women in Parliamentary Elections." 30 Jan. 2014. *The Cairo Post*. Web. 4 June 2014. <http://thecairopost.com/news/82491/news/feminist-union-launches-campaign-to-support-100-women-in-parliamentary-elections>.

El Saadawi, Nawal. *A Daughter of Isis: The Autobiography of Nawal El Saadawi*. Trans. Sherif Hetata. London: Zed Books, 1999.

———. *Walking Through Fire: A Life of Nawal El Saadawi*. Trans. Sherif Hetata. New York: Palgrave, 2002.

Eliot, George. "The *Antigone* and Its Moral." *Leader* 29 Mar. 1856. Rpt. in *Selected Essays, Poems, and Other Writings*. Eds. A. S. Byatt and Nicholas Warren. New York: Penguin, 1990. 363–66.

———. "The Art of the Ancients." *Leader* 17 Mar. 1855: 257–58. Rpt. in Wiesenfarth, *Writer's Notebook* 244–48.

———. *Daniel Deronda*. 1876. Ed. Graham Handley. Oxford, England: Oxford UP, 2009.

———. *The George Eliot Letters*. Ed. Gordon S. Haight. 9 vols. New Haven, CT: Yale UP, 1954.

———. *George Eliot's* Daniel Deronda *Notebooks*. Ed. Jane Irwin. Cambridge, England: Cambridge UP, 1996.

———. *George Eliot's* Middlemarch *Notebooks: A Transcription*. Eds. John Clark Pratt and Victor A. Neufeldt. Berkeley: U of California P, 1979.

———. *Middlemarch*. 1871. Ed. W. J. Harvey. New York: Penguin, 1985.

———. *Romola*. 1862. Ed. Andrew Brown. Oxford, England: Oxford UP, 1993.

Etherington-Smith, Meredith, and Jeremy Pilcher. *The "It" Girls: Lucy, Lady Duff Gordon, the Couturière "Lucile," and Elinor Glyn, Romantic Novelist*. New York: Harcourt Brace Jovanovich, 1986.

Evangelista, Stefano. *British Aestheticism and Ancient Greece: Hellenism, Reception, Gods in Exile*. New York: Palgrave Macmillan, 2009.

Felski, Rita. *The Gender of Modernity*. Cambridge, MA: Harvard UP, 1995.

Field, Michael [Katharine Bradley and Edith Cooper]. "The Beauty of Gratitude." *Wild Honey from Various Thyme*. London: T. Fisher Unwin, 1908.

———. *The Fowl and the Pussycat: Love Letters of Michael Field, 1876–1909*. Ed. Sharon Bickle. Charlottesville: U of Virginia P, 2008.

———. '*Michael Field' Correspondence*. British Library, Add Ms. 45853.

———. '*Michael Field' Journals*. British Library, Add Mss. 46777–46784, 46799.

———. *Queen Mariamne*. London: Sidgwick and Jackson, 1908.

———. *Sight and Song*. London: Elkin Mathews and John Lane, 1892.

———. *Stephania*. London: Elkin Mathews and John Lane, 1892.

———. "Tafnûit." *Wild Honey from Various Thyme*. London: T. Fisher Unwin, 1908.

———. *The Tragic Mary*. London: George Bell and Sons, 1890.

————. *Works and Days: From the Journal of Michael Field*. Eds. T. and D. C. Sturge Moore. London: John Murray, 1933.

Fisher, Devon. *Roman Catholic Saints and Early Victorian Literature: Conservatism, Liberalism, and the Emergence of Secular Culture*. Burlington, VT: Ashgate, 2012.

Fiske, Shanyn. *Heretical Hellenism: Women Writers, Ancient Greece, and the Victorian Popular Imagination*. Athens OH: Ohio UP, 2008.

Fletcher, Robert P. "'Heir of All the Universe': Evolutionary Epistemology in Mathilde Blind's *Birds of Passage: Songs of the Orient and Occident*." *Victorian Poetry* 43 (2005): 435–53.

Flower, Benjamin Orange. *Gerald Massey: Poet, Prophet and Mystic*. Boston, MA: Arena Publishing Co., 1895.

Francillon, Robert Edward. "Earl's Dene.—Part X." *Blackwood's Magazine* (Aug. 1870): 189–219.

Frank, Katherine. *Lucie Duff-Gordon: A Passage to Egypt*. London: Tauris Parke, 2007.

Fraser, Hilary. "A Visual Field: Michael Field and the Gaze." *Victorian Literature and Culture* 34 (2006): 553–71.

Frawley, Maria H. *A Wider Range: Travel Writing by Women in Victorian England*. Rutherford, NJ: Fairleigh Dickinson UP, 1994.

Freeman, Charles. *Egypt, Greece, and Rome: Civilizations of the Ancient Mediterranean*. 2nd ed. Oxford, England: Oxford UP, 2004.

Friedman, Susan Stanford. "Gender and Genre Anxiety: Elizabeth Barrett Browning and H. D. as Epic Poets." *Tulsa Studies in Women's Literature* 5 (1986): 203–28.

Fuller, S. Margaret. *Woman in the Nineteenth Century*. New York: Greeley and McElrath, 1845.

Gilmour, David. *Curzon: Imperial Statesman*. New York: Farrar, Straus and Giroux, 1994.

Gliddon, George. *Ancient Egypt: A Series of Chapters on Early Egyptian History, Archaeology and Other Subjects Connected with Hieroglyphical Literature*. 1843. New York: J. Winchester, 1844.

Glyn, Anthony. *Elinor Glyn: A Biography*. 1955. Rev. ed. London: Hutchinson, 1968.

Glyn, Elinor. *Halcyone*. [Published under the title *Love Itself* in the U.S.] New York: The Macaulay Co., 1912.

————. *His Hour*. Auburn, NY: The Authors' Press, 1910.

————. "The Old Order Changeth." *Three Things*. London: Duckworth and Co., 1915.

————. *Romantic Adventure*. New York: E. P. Dutton, 1937.

————. *Three Weeks*. Leipzig, Germany: Bernhard Tauchnitz, 1907.

Goldhill, Simon. *Victorian Culture and Classical Antiquity: Art, Opera, Fiction, and the Proclamation of Modernity*. Princeton, NJ: Princeton UP, 2011.

Grewal, Inderpal. *Home and Harem: Nation, Gender, Empire, and the Cultures of Travel*. Durham, NC: Duke UP, 1996.

Griffiths, Siân B. "Dissolving Pearls: Charlotte Brontë's Textual Hieroglyphics." *Women's Writing* 14.1 (2007): 49–69.

Guadalupi, Gianni, ed. *Treasure in Gold: Masterpieces of Jewelry from Antiquity to Modern Times*. Vercelli, Italy: White Star, 2008.

Haggard, H. Rider. *Cleopatra, Being an Account of the Fall and Vengeance of Harmachis, the Royal Egyptian, as Set Forth by His Own Hand*. Leipzig, Germany: Bernhard Tauchnitz, 1889.

———. *The Days of My Life*. Vol. 1. Ed. C. J. Longman. London: Longmans, Green, 1926.

Haight, Gordon S. *George Eliot: A Biography*. New York: Oxford UP, 1968.

Hamdy, Noha. "Remapping Territories of Fiction in Ahdaf Soueif's *The Map of Love*." *Locating Postcolonial Narrative Genres*. Eds. Walter Goebel and Saskia Schabio. New York: Routledge, 2012. 184–94.

Hardy, Barbara. *George Eliot: A Critic's Biography*. London: Continuum, 2006.

Hart, George. *A Dictionary of Egyptian Gods and Goddesses*. London: Routledge, 1986.

Hashim, Labiba. "The Eastern Woman: How She Is and How She Should Be." 1898. Sadiqi et al. 113–15.

Hatchuel, Sarah. *Shakespeare and the Cleopatra/Caesar Intertext: Sequel, Conflation, Remake*. Madison, NJ: Fairleigh Dickinson UP, 2011.

Havelock, Christine Mitchell. *The Aphrodite of Knidos and Her Successors: A Historical Review of the Female Nude in Greek Art*. Ann Arbor: U of Michigan P, 1995.

Himmelfarb, Gertrude. *The Jewish Odyssey of George Eliot*. New York: Encounter Books, 2009.

Hollahan, Eugene. "Therapist or the Rapist? George Eliot's *Daniel Deronda* as a Pre-Freudian Example of Psychoanalysis in Literature." *Journal of Evolutionary Psychology* 5.1–2 (1984): 55–68.

Hollander, Rachel. "*Daniel Deronda* and the Ethics of Alterity." *Levinas and Nineteenth-Century Literature: Ethics and Otherness from Romanticism Through Realism*. Eds. Donald R. Wehrs and David P. Haney. Newark: U of Delaware P, 2009. 264–87.

Holloway, Julia Bolton. "The Egyptian Book of the Dead and Elizabeth Barrett Browning." Web. 9 Jan. 2015. <http://www.florin.ms/egyptbkdead.html>.

Horak, Laura. "'Would you like to sin with Elinor Glyn?': Film as a Vehicle of Sensual Education." *Camera Obscura* 25.2 (2010): 75–117.

Horville, Robert. "The Stage Techniques of Sarah Bernhardt." *Bernhardt and the Theatre of Her Time*. Ed. Eric Salmon. Westport, CT: Greenwood P, 1984. 35–65.

Houston, Gail Turley. *Victorian Women Writers, Radical Grandmothers, and the Gendering of God*. Columbus: Ohio State UP, 2013.

Humfrey, Peter, and Mauro Lucco. *Dosso Dossi: Court Painter in Renaissance Ferrara*. New York: Metropolitan Museum of Art/Harry N. Abrams, 1998.

Hurst, Isobel. *Victorian Women Writers and the Classics*. Oxford, England: Oxford UP, 2006.

Jacquemond, Richard. *Conscience of a Nation: Writers, State, and Society*. Cairo, Egypt: American U in Cairo P, 2008.

Jameson, Anna. *Sacred and Legendary Art*. Vol. 2. 1848. New York: Longmans, Green, 1900.

Jeal, Tim. *Explorers of the Nile: The Triumph and Tragedy of a Great Victorian Adventure*. New Haven, CT: Yale UP, 2011.

Jenkins, Ruth Y. "Rewriting Female Subjection: Florence Nightingale's Revisionist Myth of 'Cassandra.'" *Weber Studies* 11.1 (1994): 16–26.

Jenkyns, Richard. *The Victorians and Ancient Greece*. Cambridge, MA: Harvard UP, 1980.

Kahane, Claire. "The Aesthetic Politics of Rage." *States of Rage: Emotional Eruption, Violence, and Social Change*. Eds. Renée R. Curry and Terry L. Allison. New York: New York UP, 1996. 126–45.

Keating, Peter. *The Haunted Study: A Social History of the English Novel 1875–1974*. London: Secker and Warburg, 1989.

Keightly, Thomas. *The Mythology of Ancient Greece and Italy*. 1831. 2nd ed. London: Whitaker and Co., 1838.

Kingsley, Charles. *The Heroes; or, Greek Fairy Tales for My Children*. Cambridge, MA: Macmillan, 1856.

Klaver, J. M. I. *Apostle of the Flesh: A Critical Life of Charles Kingsley*. Boston, MA: Brill, 2006.

Krisuk, Jennifer. "Moving Beyond 'Michael Field': Identity Through Anonymity in Borgia." *The Michaelian* (Dec. 2010): n. pag.

Kuhn, Annette. "The Trouble with Elinor Glyn: Hollywood, *Three Weeks* and the British Board of Censors." *Historical Journal of Film, Radio and Television* 28.1 (2008): 23–35.

Kyle, Richard. "Out of Time's Abyss: The Martian Stories of Edgar Rice Burroughs, A Speculation." *Riverside Quarterly* 4.2 (1970): 110–22.

Lane, Edward. *An Account of the Manners and Customs of Modern Egyptians*. 1836. Vol. 1. London: Charles Knight, 1837.

Lefkowitz, Mary. *History Lesson: A Race Odyssey*. New Haven, CT: Yale UP, 2008.

———. *Not Out of Africa: How Afrocentrism Became an Excuse to Teach Myth as History*. New York: BasicBooks, 1996.

Lesko, Barbara S. *The Great Goddesses of Egypt*. Norman: U of Oklahoma P, 1999.

Levine, Robert S. "Road to Africa: Frederick Douglass's Rome." Martin and Person 226–45.

Lewes, George Henry. *The Letters of George Henry Lewes*. Vol. 3. Ed. William Baker. Victoria, BC: U of Victoria, 1999.

Lewis, Sarah. *Woman's Mission*. London: John W. Parker, 1839.

Linett, Maren Tova, ed. *Cambridge Companion to Modernist Women Writers*. Cambridge, England: Cambridge UP, 2010.

Logan, Deborah. *Harriet Martineau, Victorian Imperialism, and the Civilizing Mission*. Farham, England: Ashgate, 2010.

Loos, Anita. *A Girl Like I*. New York: Viking, 1966.

Lysack, Krista. "Aesthetic Consumption and the Cultural Production of Michael Field's *Sight and Song*." *SEL* 45 (2005): 935–60.

Mack, Charles R. *Looking at the Renaissance: Essays Toward a Contextual Appreciation*. Ann Arbor: U of Michigan P, 2005.

Mackenzie, John. *Orientalism: History, Theory, and the Arts.* Manchester, England: Manchester UP, 1995.

Mackie, Hilary. "The Key to Epic Life?: Classical Study in George Eliot's *Middlemarch.*" *Classical World* 103.1 (2009): 53–67.

MacLeod, Kirsten, ed. *Wormwood: A Drama of Paris.* By Marie Corelli. Peterborough, ON: Broadview P, 2004.

Mahn, Churnjeet. *British Women's Travel to Greece 1840–1914: Travels in the Palimpsest.* Burlington, VT: Ashgate, 2012.

Malak, Amin. *Muslim Narratives and the Discourse of English.* Albany: State U of New York P, 2004.

Marsh, Jan. *Black Victorians: Black People in British Art, 1800–1900.* Aldershot, England: Lund Humphries, 2005.

Martin, Robert K., and Leland S. Person. *Roman Holidays: American Writers and Artists in Nineteenth-Century Italy.* Iowa City: U of Iowa P, 2002.

Martineau, Harriet. *Eastern Life: Present and Past.* Philadelphia: Lea and Blanchard, 1848.

Massey, Gerald. *Ancient Egypt: The Light of the World.* Vol. 1. London: T. Fisher Unwin, 1907.

———. "The Aryan Mother." *Tale of Eternity and Other Poems.* Boston: Fields, Osgood, and Co., 1870.

———. "The Coming Religion." 1887. *Gerald Massey.* Web. 27 Dec. 2012. <http://gerald-massey.org.uk/massey/dpr_10_coming_religion.htm>.

Mattawa, Khaled. Introduction. *These Are Not Oranges, My Love: Selected Poems.* By Iman Mersal. Riverdale-on-Hudson, NY: The Sheep Meadow P, 2008. vii–xv.

Matus, Jill. "The 'Eastern-Woman Question': Martineau and Nightingale Visit the Harem." *Nineteenth-Century Contexts* 21 (1999): 63–87.

———. "Looking at Cleopatra: The Expression and Exhibition of Desire in *Villette.*" *Victorian Literature and Culture* 21 (1994): 345–67.

McBrien, Richard P., ed. *The HarperCollins Encyclopedia of Catholicism.* San Francisco, CA: HarperCollins San Francisco, 1995.

McCormack, Kathleen. *George Eliot in Society: Travels Abroad and Sundays in the Priory.* Columbus: Ohio State UP, 2013.

McDonald, Lynn, ed. *Florence Nightingale on Women, Medicine, Midwifery and Prostitution.* Vol. 8. *The Collected Works of Florence Nightingale.* Waterloo, ON: Wilfrid Laurier UP, 2005.

———. *Florence Nightingale's European Travels.* Vol. 7. *The Collected Works of Florence Nightingale.* Waterloo, ON: Wilfrid Laurier UP, 2004.

———. *Florence Nightingale's Suggestions for Thought.* Vol. 11. *The Collected Works of Florence Nightingale.* Waterloo, ON: Wilfrid Laurier UP, 2008.

———. *Florence Nightingale's Theology: Essays, Letters, and Journal Notes.* Vol. 3. *The Collected Works of Florence Nightingale.* Waterloo, ON: Wilfrid Laurier UP, 2002.

McDonald, Tara. "Resurrecting Isis in Ahdaf Soueif's *The Map of Love.*" *Hermes and Aphrodite Encounters.* Ed. Metka Zupančič. Birmingham, AL: Summa Publications, 2004. 163–70.

McKay, Brenda. *George Eliot and Victorian Attitudes to Racial Diversity, Colonialism, Darwinism, Class, Gender, and Jewish Culture and Prophecy.* Studies in British Literature Ser. Vol. 78. Lewiston, NY: The Edwin Mellen P, 2003.

Melman, Billie. *Women's Orients: English Women and the Middle East, 1718–1918.* Ann Arbor: U of Michigan P, 1992.

Menefee, David W. *Sarah Bernhardt in the Theatre of Films and Sound Recordings.* Jefferson, NC: McFarland, 2003.

Menpes, Mortimer. "The Actualists. Some Impressions of Shilito Jessop, Artist." *The National Review* 23 (1894): 544–65.

Mersal, Iman. "Eliminating Diasporic Identities." *PMLA* 123.5 (2008): 1581–89.

———. "Reading the Past." Mersal, *These Are Not Oranges* 64–66.

———. *These Are Not Oranges, My Love: Selected Poems.* Trans. Khaled Mattawa. Riverdale-on-Hudson, NY: The Sheep Meadow P, 2008.

———. "Why Did She Come?" Mersal, *These Are Not Oranges* 59–62.

Mertz, Barbara [Elizabeth Peters]. "Notes from MPM." Feb. 2012. Web. 4 June 2014. <http://www.mpmbooks.com/notes/february2012.pdf>.

Meyer, Susan. "'Safely to Their Own Borders': Proto-Zionism, Feminism, and Nationalism in *Daniel Deronda.*" *ELH* 60.3 (1993): 733–58.

Milder, Robert. "'The Connecting Link of Centuries': Melville, Rome, and the Mediterranean, 1856–57." Martin and Person 206–25.

Mill, John Stuart. *The Subjection of Women.* London: Longmans, Green, Reader, and Dyer, 1869.

Moore, Lindsey. "Voyages Out and In: Two (British) Arab Muslim Women's Bildungsroman." *Culture, Diaspora, and Modernity in Muslim Writing.* Eds. Rehana Ahmed, Peter Morey, and Amina Yaqin. New York: Routledge, 2012. 68–84.

Morey, Anne. "Elinor Glyn as Hollywood Labourer." *Film History* 18 (2006): 110–18.

Moriarty, David J. "'Michael Field' (Edith Cooper and Katherine Bradley) and Their Male Critics." *Nineteenth-Century Women Writers of the English-Speaking World.* Ed. Rhoda B. Nathan. New York: Greenwood P, 1986. 121–42.

Morley, John. Rev. of *Romola. Saturday Review* 25 July 1863: 124–25. Rpt. in *George Eliot: The Critical Heritage.* Ed. David Carroll. New York: Barnes and Noble, 1971. 207–12.

Morton, Samuel. *Crania Aetgyptiaca, or Observations on Egyptian Ethnography.* London: Madden and Co., 1844.

Moscucci, Ornella. "Clitoridectomy, Circumcision, and the Politics of Sexual Pleasure in Mid-Victorian Britain." *Sexualities in Victorian Britain.* Eds. Andrew H. Miller and James Eli Adams. Bloomington: Indiana UP, 1996. 60–78.

Müller, F. Max. *Auld Lang Syne: Second Series: My Indian Friends.* London: Longmans, Green, 1899.

Murphy, Patricia. "The Gendering of History in *She.*" *Studies in English Literature, 1500–1900* 39.4 (1999): 747–72.

National Inventory of Continental European Paintings. "Saint Catherine of Alexandria Crowned with a Garland of Flowers." Web. 9 Sept. 2015. <http://www.vads.ac.uk/large.php?uid=88069&sos=0>

Nichols, Beverley. *The Sweet and Twenties*. London: Weidenfeld and Nicolson, 1958.

Nightingale, Florence. Introduction. *Behramji M. Malabari: A Biographical Sketch*. By Dayaram Gidumal. London: T. Fisher Unwin, 1892.

Ockman, Carol, and Kenneth E. Silver. *Sarah Bernhardt: The Art of High Drama*. New Haven, CT: Yale UP, 2005.

Olverson, T. D. *Women Writers and the Dark Side of Late-Victorian Hellenism*. New York: Palgrave Macmillan, 2010.

O'Neill, Patricia. "Destination as Destiny: Amelia B. Edwards's Travel Writing." *Frontiers* 30.2 (2009): 43–71.

——, ed. "The Social and Political Position of Woman in Ancient Egypt." By Amelia B. Edwards. *PMLA* 120.3 (2005): 843–57.

Pace, Timothy. "Who Killed Gwendolen Harleth?: *Daniel Deronda* and Keats's 'Lamia.'" *The Journal of English and Germanic Philology* 87.1 (1988): 35–48.

Parramore, Lynn. *Reading the Sphinx: Ancient Egypt in Nineteenth-Century Literary Culture*. New York: Palgrave Macmillan, 2008.

Pemble, John. *The Mediterranean Passion: Victorians and Edwardians in the South*. Oxford, England: Clarendon P, 1987.

Peters, Elizabeth. *Crocodile on the Sandbank*. New York: Time Warner, 1975.

——. *The Serpent on the Crown*. New York: HarperCollins, 2005.

Pinch, Geraldine. *Magic in Ancient Egypt*. Austin: U of Texas P, 1995.

Poovey, Mary. *Uneven Developments: The Ideological Work of Gender in Mid-Victorian England*. Chicago, IL: U of Chicago P, 1988.

Porter, Dennis. "*Orientalism* and Its Problems." *The Politics of Theory*. Ed. Francis Barker et al. Colchester, England: U of Essex, 1983. 179–93.

Powers, Elizabeth. "'Interrogation of the Past': Henry James and William Wetmore Story." *Arion: A Journal of the Humanities and the Classics* 16.2 (2008): 51–70.

Pratt, John Clark, and Victor A. Neufeldt. Introduction. *George Eliot's Middlemarch Notebooks*. By George Eliot. Berkeley: U of California P, 1979. xvii–lii.

Price, Cheryl Baker. "Poison, Sensation, and Secrets in *The Lifted Veil*." *Victorian Review* 36.1 (2010): 203–16.

Prins, Yopie. "Greek Maenads, Victorian Spinsters." *Victorian Sexual Dissidence*. Ed. Richard Dellamora. Chicago, IL: U of Chicago P, 1999. 43–81.

——. *Victorian Sappho*. Princeton, NJ: Princeton UP, 1999.

Ramabai, Pandita. *Letters and Correspondence of Pandita Ramabai*. Ed. A. B. Shah. Bombay: Maharashtra State Board for Literature and Culture, 1977.

——. *Pandita Ramabai's American Encounter: The Peoples of the United States (1889)*. Trans. and ed. Meera Kosambi. Bloomington: Indiana UP, 2003.

Ramli, Aimillia Mohd. "From *Pasha* to Cleopatra and Vashti: The Oriental Other in Charlotte Brontë's *Villette*." *Brontë Studies* 35.2 (2010): 118–27.

Rees, Joan. *Amelia Edwards: Traveller, Novelist & Egyptologist*. London: The Rubicon P, 1998.

Richards, Jeffrey. *The Ancient World on the Victorian and Edwardian Stage*. New York: Palgrave Macmillan, 2009.

Rifaat, Alifa. "My World of the Unknown." *Distant View of a Minaret and Other Stories*. Trans. Denys Johnson-Davis. London: Heinemann, 1983. 61–76.

Rose, H. J. *A Handbook of Greek Mythology*. New York: Routledge, 2005.

Rose, Natalie. "The Englishness of a Gentleman: Illegitimacy and Race in *Daniel Deronda*." *Troubled Legacies: Narrative and Inheritance*. Ed. Allan Hepburn. Toronto, ON: U of Toronto P, 2007. 109–36.

Royal Philatelic Society. "The Egypt Study Circle: 70th Anniversary, 1935–2005: February 24 2005: Members' Display to the Royal Philatelic Society London."

Sadiqi, Fatima, Amira Nowaira, Azza El Kholy, and Moha Ennaji, eds. *Women Writing Africa: The Northern Region*. New York: The Feminist P at CUNY, 2009.

Said, Edward. *Orientalism*. New York: Vintage, 1978.

Saintsbury, George. Rev. of *Daniel Deronda*. *Academy* 9 Sept. 1876: 253–54. Rpt. in *George Eliot: The Critical Heritage*. Ed. David Carroll. New York: Barnes and Noble, 1971. 371–76.

Salih, Sara, ed. *Wonderful Adventures of Mrs Seacole in Many Lands*. 1857. By Mary Seacole. New York: Penguin, 2005.

Salmon, Eric. *Bernhardt and the Theatre of Her Time*. Westport, CT: Greenwood P, 1984.

Saville, Julia F. "The Poetic Imaging of Michael Field." *Fin-de-Siècle Poem: English Literary Culture and the 1890s*. Athens, OH: Ohio UP, 2005. 178–206.

Sayce, A. H. "The Gods of Canaan." *The Contemporary Review* 44 (1883): 385–99.

Schaffer, Talia. *Literature and Culture at the* Fin de Siècle. New York: Pearson/Longman, 2007.

Semmel, Bernard. *George Eliot and the Politics of National Inheritance*. Oxford, England: Oxford UP, 1994.

Seymour-Jorn, Caroline. *Cultural Criticism in Egyptian Women's Writing*. Syracuse, NY: Syracuse UP, 2012.

Shaw, David. *Gerald Massey: Chartist, Poet, Radical and Freethinker*. London: Buckland, 2009. Web. 27 Dec. 2012. <http://gerald-massey.org.uk/massey/biog _contents.htm>.

Showalter, Elaine. *The Female Malady: Women, Madness, and English Culture, 1830–1980*. New York: Pantheon Books, 1985.

———. "Florence Nightingale's Feminist Complaint: Women, Religion, and 'Suggestions for Thought.'" *Signs* 6.3 (1981): 395–412.

Shumaker, Jeanette. "The Alcharisi and Gwendolen: Confessing Rebellion." *George Eliot-George Henry Lewes Newsletter* 18–19 (1991): 55–62.

Shumway, David R. "Romance in the Romance: Love and Marriage in Turn-of-the-Century Best Sellers." *Journal of Narrative Theory* 29.1 (1999): 110–34.

Silverman, David P., ed. *Searching for Ancient Egypt: Art, Architecture, and Artifacts from the University of Pennsylvania Museum of Archaeology and Anthropology*. Ithaca, NY: Cornell UP, 1997.

Sinno, Nadine. "The Power of Place and Space: (Re)constructing Identity and Selfhood in Ahdaf Soueif's *Eye of the Sun*." *Representing Minorities: Studies in Literature and Criticism*. Eds. Larbi Touaf and Soumia Boutkhil. Cambridge, England: Cambridge Scholars, 2006. 194–206.

Skinner, Cornelia Otis. *Madame Sarah*. Boston: Houghton Mifflin, 1967.

Smith, William. *Dictionary of Greek and Roman Biography and Mythology*. 3 vols. London: Taylor and Walton, 1844.

Snow-Smith, Joanne. *The Primavera of Sandro Botticelli: A Neoplatonic Interpretation*. New York: Peter Lang, 1993.

Snyder, Katherine V. "From Novel to Essay: Gender and Revision in Florence Nightingale's 'Cassandra.'" *The Politics of the Essay: Feminist Perspectives*. Eds. Ruth-Ellen Boetcher Joeres and Elizabeth Mittman. Bloomington: Indiana UP, 1993. 23–39.

Soueif, Ahdaf. *In the Eye of the Sun*. New York: Random House/Anchor, 1992.

———. "The Language of the Veil." 2001. *Mezzaterra: Fragments from the Common Ground*. New York: Anchor Books, 2005. 266–74.

———. *The Map of Love*. London: Bloomsbury, 1999.

———. "Visions of the Harem." *The Guardian*. 5 July 2008. Web. 3 Jan. 2015. <http://www.theguardian.com/books/2008/jul/05/art.exhibition>.

Soueif, Ahdaf , and Joseph Massad. "The Politics of Desire in the Writings of Ahdaf Soueif." *Journal of Palestine Studies* 28.4 (1999): 74–90.

Sova, Dawn B. *Literature Suppressed on Sexual Grounds*. New York: Facts on File, 2006.

Spivak, Gayatri Chakravorty. "Can the Subaltern Speak?" *Marxism and the Interpretation of Culture*. Eds. Cary Nelson and Lawrence Grossberg. Basingstoke, England: Macmillan, 1988. 271–313.

———. "Three Women's Texts and a Critique of Imperialism." *Critical Inquiry* 12.1 (1985): 243–61.

Stahr, Adolph. *Torso: Kunst, Künstler und Kunstwerk der Alten*. Brunswick, Germany: n.p., 1854.

Stauffer, Andrew. Introduction. *She*. By H. Rider Haggard. 1889. Petersborough, ON: Broadview P, 2006. 11–26.

Story, William Wetmore. "Cleopatra." *Graffiti D'Italia*. Edinburgh, Scotland: William Blackwood and Sons, 1868.

———. "Marcus Antonius." *Graffiti D'Italia*. Edinburgh, Scotland: William Blackwood and Sons, 1868.

Sturgeon, Mary. *Michael Field*. 1922. New York: Arno P, 1975.

Suleri, Sara. *The Rhetoric of English India*. Chicago, IL: U of Chicago P, 1992.

Taft, Vickie L. "*The Tragic Mary*: A Case Study in Michael Field's Understanding of Sexual Politics." *Nineteenth-Century Contexts* 23 (2001): 265–95.

Thain, Marion. *"Michael Field": Poetry, Aestheticism and the Fin de Siècle*. Cambridge, England: Cambridge UP, 2007.

Thain, Marion, and Ana Parejo Vadillo, eds. *Michael Field, the Poet: Published and Manuscript Materials*. Peterborough, ON: Broadview, 2009.

Thompson, Jason. *A History of Egypt: From Earliest Times to the Present*. Cairo, Egypt: American U in Cairo P, 2008.

Traill, H. D. "Our Cleopatra." *National Review* (March 1894): 118–27.

Tyldesley, Joyce. *Cleopatra: Last Queen of Egypt*. New York: Basic Books, 2008.

Vadillo, Ana Parejo. "*Sight and Song*: Transparent Translations and a Manifesto for the Observer." *Victorian Poetry* 38 (2000): 15–34.

Vallée, Gérard, ed. *Florence Nightingale on Mysticism and Eastern Religions*. Vol. 4. *The Collected Works of Florence Nightingale*. Waterloo, ON: Wilfrid Laurier UP, 2003.

———. *Florence Nightingale on Social Change in India*. Vol. 10. *The Collected Works of Florence Nightingale*. Waterloo, ON: Wilfrid Laurier UP, 2007.

Vance, Norman. *The Victorians and Ancient Rome*. Oxford, England: Blackwell, 1997.

Verneuil, Louis. *The Fabulous Life of Sarah Bernhardt*. 1942. Trans. Ernest Boyd. Westport, CT: Greenwood P, 1972.

Vicinus, Martha. "Faun Love: Michael Field and Bernard Berenson." *Women's History Review* 18 (2009): 753–64.

Wiesenfarth, Joseph, ed. *George Eliot: A Writer's Notebook, 1854–1879, and Uncollected Writings*. Charlottesville, VA: UP of Virginia, 1981.

Wilde, Oscar. "The Critic as Artist." 1890. *The Picture of Dorian Gray*. By Wilde. Ed. Michael Patrick Gillespie. 2nd ed. New York: W. W. Norton, 2007. 335–42.

Wilkinson, John Gardner. *Manners and Customs of the Ancient Egyptians*. 1837. Vol. 2. London: John Murray, 1841.

Wilt, Judith. "'He would come back': The Fathers of Daughters in *Daniel Deronda*." *Nineteenth-Century Literature* 42.3 (1987): 313–38.

Withey, Lynne. *Grand Tours and Cook's Tours: A History of Leisure Travel, 1750–1915*. New York: W. Morrow, 1997.

Witt, R. E. *Isis in the Ancient World*. Baltimore, MD: Johns Hopkins UP, 1997.

Wollheim, Richard. *F. H. Bradley*. Baltimore, MD: Penguin, 1959.

Wollstonecraft, Mary. *A Vindication of the Rights of Woman: With Strictures on Political and Moral Subjects*. 3rd ed. London: J. Johnson, 1796. New York: McGraw-Hill, 1951.

Woodham-Smith, Cecil. *Florence Nightingale, 1820–1910*. New York: McGraw-Hill, 1951.

Wyke, Maria. *The Roman Mistress: Ancient and Modern Representations*. Oxford, England: Oxford UP, 2002.

Wynne, Catherine. "Negotiating the Mezzaterra: Home, Harem and the Hybrid Family in Ahdaf Soueif's 'The Map of Love.'" *Critical Survey* 18.2 (2006): 56–66.

Youngkin, Molly. *Feminist Realism at the Fin de Siècle: The Influence of the Late-Victorian Woman's Press on the Development of the Novel*. Columbus, OH: Ohio State UP, 2007.

Youngkin, Molly. "George Moore's Quest for Canonization and *Esther Waters* as Female Helpmate." *English Literature in Transition* 46.2 (2003): 116–39.

———. "'Narrative readings of the images she sees': Principles of Nineteenth-Century Narrative Painting in George Eliot's Fiction." *George Eliot-George Henry Lewes Studies* 67.1 (2015): 1–29.

Zimmerman, Bonnie. "Gwendolen Harleth and 'The Girl of the Period.'" *George Eliot: Centenary Essays and an Unpublished Fragment*. Ed. Anne Smith. New York: Barnes and Noble, 1980. 196–217.

Zipes, Jack. *When Dreams Came True: Classical Fairy Tales and Their Tradition*. 2nd ed. New York: Routledge, 2007.

Zonana, Joyce. "The Embodied Muse: Elizabeth Barrett Browning's *Aurora Leigh* and Feminist Poetics." *Tulsa Studies in Women's Literature* 8.2 (1989): 240–62.

Index

CPSIA information can be obtained
at www.ICGtesting.com
Printed in the USA
LVOW12*1521020816

498763LV00019B/206/P